IN THE
WORDS
OF THE
WINNERS

ALA Editions purchases fund advocacy, awareness, and accreditation programs for library professionals worldwide.

IN THE WORDS OF THE WINNERS

THE NEWBERY AND CALDECOTT MEDALS 2001–2010

ASSOCIATION FOR LIBRARY
SERVICE TO CHILDREN

—

THE HORN BOOK

AMERICAN LIBRARY ASSOCIATION
CHICAGO   2011

Text, photo, and art credits appear on page 209.

Printed in the United States of America
15 14 13 12 11   5 4 3 2 1

While extensive effort has gone into ensuring the reliability of the information in this book, the publisher makes no warranty, express or implied, with respect to the material contained herein.

ISBN: 978-0-8389-3586-6

Library of Congress Cataloging-in-Publication Data
In the words of the winners : the Newbery and Caldecott medals, 2001-2010 / Association for Library Service to Children and the Horn Book.
    p. cm.
  Includes bibliographical references and index.
  ISBN 978-0-8389-3586-6 (alk. paper)
  1. Newbery Medal--Bio-bibliography. 2. Caldecott Medal--Bio-bibliography. 3. Children's literature, American--Bio-bibliography. 4. Picture books for children--United States--Bio-bibliography. 5. Children--Books and reading--United States. I. Association for Library Service to Children. II. Horn Book, Inc.
  Z1037.A2I52 2011
  011.62'079--dc22

                                                                    2010033258

Book design in Minion Pro and DIN by Casey Bayer.

∞ This paper meets the requirements of ANSI/NISO Z39.48-1992 (Permanence of Paper).

ALA Editions also publishes its books in a variety of electronic formats. For more information, visit the ALA Store at www.alastore.ala.org and select eEditions.

CONTENTS

PREFACE

I AM THRILLED to introduce *In the Words of the Winners: The Newbery and Caldecott Medals, 2001–2010,* compiled in collaboration with The Horn Book, Inc. This publication is a companion book to *The Newbery and Caldecott Medal Books, 1986–2000: A Comprehensive Guide to the Winners,* published by ALA Editions in 2001.

The Association for Library Service to Children (ALSC), which administers the prestigious Newbery and Caldecott awards, and The Horn Book, Inc., which publishes children's book reviews and biographical essays about award winners, are pleased to team up once again to provide this unparalleled resource that is sure to interest librarians, educators, parents, and bibliophiles.

Award acceptance speeches by and biographical essays about each award-winning author and illustrator provide valuable and useful insight into the creative process of each work and the individual behind the pen or brush. *The Horn Book Magazine* reviews provide a glimpse of the outstanding qualities and subtle nuances that make each title medal-worthy. Essays penned by recognized authorities in the field of children's literature reflect back on the decade of winning books—how they stand individually and how they compare and contrast with their counterparts—and on changes in children's book publishing, children's reading, and the ways we discuss literature and awards in this new century.

Nina Lindsay is the children's services coordinator for the Oakland Public Library, California. She served on the 1998 and 2004 Newbery and 2001 Sibert Award committees, and chaired the 2002 Sibert and 2008 Newbery committees. She coauthors *Heavy Medal: A Mock Newbery Blog* at the *School Library Journal* website, and has reviewed for *Kirkus, The Horn Book Magazine, School Library Journal,* and *Bayviews*. In her essay, Nina takes on the controversy and debate that are part of the Newbery standard and further evidence that the Newbery is the best-known and most discussed children's book award in this country.

Joanna Rudge Long, a regular contributor to *The Horn Book Magazine,* is a former editor and principal reviewer of young people's books for *Kirkus Reviews*. She has been a frequent core lecturer at Children's Literature New England and has taught children's literature at Rutgers and Trenton State universities. As a librarian, she served on numerous award committees, including the Newbery (1995) and Caldecott (1986) committees; in 2000 she chaired the Boston Globe–Horn Book Award committee. Her essay here skillfully explores the varied art techniques employed in each Caldecott Medal–winning book.

Roger Sutton has been the editor in chief of The Horn Book, Inc., since 1996. He began his career as a children's and young adult librarian in the public library setting. He has served on the Newbery and Caldecott committees and chaired the 2007 Wilder Award committee. With Martha V. Parravano, he is the author of *A Family of Readers: The Book Lover's Guide to Children's and Young Adult Literature* (Candlewick). Roger has written a contemplative piece that looks at publishing trends of the past decade and how they have affected the number of children's books eligible for award consideration.

ALSC would like to acknowledge and thank Roger Sutton and The Horn Book, Inc., for their willingness to continue this collaborative publication with us. We thank the essayists for their outstanding contributions. We also thank Laura Schulte-Cooper, ALSC communications program officer, for shepherding this project to publication, and Michael Jeffers, publisher of ALA Editions, and his staff, for continuing to recognize the value of this publication as a major contribution to the field of children's literature.

And thank you, reader, for your interest. We hope you will find this to be an exceptional volume. Ideas and suggestions for improving the work in future editions are always welcome.

Aimee Strittmatter
Executive Director, Association for Library Service to Children
American Library Association

THE CHANGING LANDSCAPE OF CHILDREN'S BOOK PUBLISHING

Roger Sutton

IN 2008, ANITA Silvey's *School Library Journal* article "Has the Newbery Lost Its Way?" caused much discussion among medal-watchers. Stemming from interviews with "more than one hundred" anonymous librarians, teachers, and booksellers, the article claimed that most Newbery winners since 1999 lacked the wide appeal of previous medalists such as *A Wrinkle in Time* or, more recently, *Holes*. While debate thrived over whether this was so, why this was so, and if it mattered, what was missing was much consideration of the fact that the landscape of children's book publishing—and children's reading—had changed in ways that would directly impact the pool of potential prizewinners for both of this country's most prestigious prizes for children's literature. Publishing, economic, and population trends of the first decade of the twenty-first century presented a challenge to the Newbery and Caldecott awards: what should be done when books eligible for these prizes become an increasingly smaller slice of what gets published?

While there has long been tension between the retail and school-and-library markets and between what is popular and what wins awards, the landscape of publishing in the period 2001–2010 is a very different place from what it was just ten years ago.

Let's talk about Harry Potter, whose first adventure, *Harry Potter and the Sorcerer's Stone,* was published in this country in the fall of 1998. Over the next decade, J. K. Rowling's series about the boy wizard firmly put to rest several myths about children and books, most notably the notions that children would not willingly read long books and that they and their parents would not buy hardcover fiction. Billions of dollars later, we now know that these received theories are not true. We also know that Harry Potter set off a spree of fantasy book publishing, much of it imported from the United Kingdom (and not always possessed of the same magic evinced by Harry and his wizard pals). Books from England acquired a cachet not seen here since the success of such fantasists as Joan Aiken, Penelope Lively, and Neil Garner during the 1960s and '70s, and then on a smaller scale. However good this trend may be for Anglophilic fantasy fans, it's not so good for the Newbery Medal, as these books born abroad are not eligible for consideration even while they take up space on American publishers' lists.

The Harry Potter books also reinforced a fact about readers we already knew—and one, in truth, that the Newbery Medal was in part established to battle: people love to read books in series. While sequels or books in a series are not necessarily ineligible for Newbery recognition (see Richard Peck's *A Year Down Yonder,* the 2001 winner, a sequel to *A Long Way from Chicago,* a Newbery Honor Book in 1999), any winner or Honor Book must be able to stand on its own, its sense or literary worth not dependent upon a book or books published in previous years. Although series books have always dominated the mass-market paperback wing of children's book publishing (Nancy Drew, Sweet Valley High, etc.), in the past ten years they have made up an increasingly large part of hardcover lists as well. In attempting to lure readers into reading a promised sequel, books such as Suzanne Collins's cliff-hanging *The Hunger Games* may simultaneously be recusing themselves from Newbery consideration.

Another factor in the shrinking number of Newbery and Caldecott contenders is the increased percentage of children's books being published for teenagers age fourteen and up, right through to a "crossover" readership of adults. This happened because the number of teenagers increased and because Harry Potter taught publishers that the right book with the right marketing could be sold to a dual audience of young people and adults alike. We saw this with novels such as Markus Zusak's *The Book Thief,* published for teens but widely read by adults, and, on a more Harry Potter–like scale, with Cecily von Ziegesar's Gossip Girl books and Stephenie Meyer's Twilight series. Publishing lists got bigger in this first decade, yes (and are now shrinking again, reflecting the economic downturn), but the increase came largely in the form of more books for teens, not more books for the "zero to fourteen" age range served by ALSC and its award programs. The inauguration in 2000 of the Printz Award for young adult literature was an inevitable response to the renewed interest in books for teenagers, but one might guess that it, too, will inspire its own "Has the Printz Award Lost Its Way?" articles once publishing sets its sights somewhere else!

The publication of picture books may provide an object lesson to Printz-watchers. In the 1980s, with the proliferation of both young children and independent bookstores eager to sell to their parents, picture-book publishing thrived to excess, with one after another lavish edition of "Cinderella" variants placed before us. Now those children are grown, those bookstores are largely closed, and picture-book publishing is a riskier business. Caldecott contenders in this decade sit at an unhappy conjunction: fewer young children for whom to buy books and higher printing costs, plus lower margins and the vagaries of printing overseas, mean fewer new picture books being published. High costs encourage the economies of scale offered by large print runs, which means more mass-market-friendly repackagings of old favorites and picture books written by celebrities with parent-friendly brand recognition.

The past decade did, however, provide us with enough coulda-shoulda contenders for the Newbery and Caldecott medals to assure us that the awards still mean a lot: if nobody is outraged at the choices, then something is very wrong with your award. Silvey mentioned Rodman Philbrick's *Freak the Mighty* and Jeanne DuPrau's *The City of Ember* as two books embraced by children but ignored by the Newbery committee; my own list of misses includes Louise Erdrich's *The Game of Silence,* Ellen Klages's *The Green Glass Sea,* and Janet Schulman's *Pale Male: Citizen Hawk of New York City.* As far as the Caldecott goes, I would like to have seen some recognition for *I Stink!* by Kate and Jim McMullan, *Milo's Hat Trick* by Jon Agee, and *Fireboat: The Heroic Adventures of the John J. Harvey* by Maira Kalman. But all of us will and should have candidates for what we feel was unjustly neglected; I will reserve my outrage for the zeitgeist. However unmovable the laws of population and economics, and however unswayable an audience that wants what it wants, I am bothered that an increase in the number of children's books published has thus far resulted in fewer, not more, choices for our cherished medals.

NEWBERY MEDAL BOOKS, 2001–2010

Nina Lindsay

ANYONE WHO HAS been on the Newbery committee or has closely followed the award knows there is no such thing as "the" most distinguished contribution to American literature for children in a given year; rather, the rigorous procedures ensure the committee selects *one* of the most distinguished books, and recognizes others as "also truly distinguished" with Honor awards. That the committee has the option to give *no* Honors, but has never taken the opportunity to do so, confirms this.

Ten distinguished books can't establish any true patterns or trends, yet, as the Newbery Medal winners of their decade, they do establish a publicly recognized standard. Examining that standard allows us to ask whether the Newbery continues to expand and refine the definition of quality literature for children, growing in pace with the work it recognizes and fulfilling the vision of its initiator, Frederic G. Melcher.

In "Newbery Medal Books, 1986–2000," Kathleen T. Horning suggests that "children's books in general, as reflected in the Newbery Medal winners, seem to have truly come of age by the end of the twentieth century. Not only has the quality of the writing steadily improved over time, they have become structurally more complex and imaginative."[1] This "radical change" (so called by Eliza Dresang in her 1999 book of that title) continues in this decade's Newbery winners, though not perhaps as much as one would expect considering the changes in the field.

The blogosphere where much of the public discussion of children's literature takes place today didn't truly form until midway into the decade (*Read Roger* [2005] and *A Fuse #8 Production* [2006] being seminal). Blogs now provide a rich forum for Newbery predictions, controversy, and trend-spotting. Reality TV as we know it (*Survivor* 2000 and *American Idol* 2002), Facebook (2004), Twitter (2006), and handheld devices in every hand: these were not yet part of the landscape in the year 2000, when the Harry Potter phenomenon first took hold and the *New York Times* established a separate best-seller list for children's literature. Suddenly fantasy was popular, and popularity in children's books had a much greater cachet in the media. And yet while this decade's winners do showcase a breadth of excellence, the range is still comparable to that of past decades.

In 2001 *A Year Down Yonder* followed the success of its prequel, *A Long Way from Chicago,* which had been the sole Honor Book (a rare occurrence) alongside the widely popular *Holes* in 1999. So began a coincidental "trend" of historical fiction winners, following *Bud, Not Buddy* and carried forth by the next two years' winners. Though they share a genre, each is notable for different reasons: *A Year Down Yonder* for voice and humor, *A Single Shard* for character and tone, and *Crispin: The Cross of Lead* for plot and setting.

The selections from 2004 on disrupted this "trend" and expanded the range (starting with *The Tale of Despereaux,* its highly dramatic voice pitching time-honored themes of dark and light to a young audience), but toward the end of the decade, concurrent with a rise in online discussions and viewer voting in the media, notable controversies about Newbery medalists exploded—controversies remarkably similar to those of decades past.

Such was the "Lucky Scrotum Debate" of 2007. A surprise winner that caught many suppliers short, *The Higher Power of Lucky* should have assuaged naysayers who had found the previous two years' award winners "too old" (*Criss Cross,* a narratively complex coming-of-age story firmly within the award's age-level, but landing in many libraries' young adult sections), "too grim" (*Kira-Kira,* whose compelling humor-tinged voice perfectly suits themes of death and racial prejudice), or just "for too narrow an audience" (both are character- and theme-driven, and light on plot). *Lucky*'s nuanced characters and setting harken in tone to *A Single Shard* and *Crispin,* but Patron's very deliberate use of the word "scrotum" on the first page (intrinsic to the resolution of the theme) set off a minor furor that the *New York Times* promptly turned into a major one. Though *Lucky* is a very different story from either *Kira-Kira* or *Criss Cross,* detractors nevertheless saw these three as a triumvirate that indicated something dreadfully wrong with the Newbery: recent selections were not "appropriate" or "appealing" for all children.

Into that teapot, the 2008 committee introduced *Good Masters! Sweet Ladies!* The first nonfiction winner since *Lincoln: A Photobiography,* the first poetry since *Joyful Noise,* the book is actually the first dramatic work to win the Newbery. Though again extremely different from its three predecessors, this selection provoked further discontent about the lack of broad appeal in recent medalists, highlighted in Anita Silvey's article "Has the Newbery Lost Its Way?"[2] Silvey suggested that the decade's selections had less "staying power" than those of the 1990s, and that the committee was "mov[ing] away from the spirit and philosophy of those who established the award." The article provoked high-spirited debate on both sides in the blogosphere, though few participating may have realized they were reenacting a debate that has been present through the entire course of the award. For instance, Clara Breed wrote in 1942:

> The complaints about the Newbery Medal usually insist that the medal be something it is not. Elementary teachers say that the books chosen are too old, junior high teachers that the books are too young. An author of boys' books says the books are too feminine and too tender-minded. A parent objects that the selections too often have been books with foreign backgrounds. . . . Sometimes it seems as if all these people had joined hands and were chanting in unison "the Newbery books are not *popular*."[3]

Although it had been only five years since an indisputably popular title (*The Tale of Despereaux) had* won, the 2009 selection of Neil Gaiman's *The Graveyard Book* prompted the headline at *School Library Journal*'s website: "Finally! The Newbery Goes to a Popular Book!" (Within hours, the online "Finally" had been changed to "Surprise.") Gaiman's suspenseful homage to *The Jungle Book,* in which the nonliving teach a boy how to live, had already been on the best-seller lists.

Notably, at the end of a transformative decade for children's book marketing, the 2010 medalist *When You Reach Me* was not strongly marketed at first, but gained phenomenal grassroots buzz through the blogosphere. It heralded a return to the most "expected" type of Newbery book—a broadly appealing middle-grade novel—that is nevertheless genre-busting and speculative.

A different debate surfaced early in the decade about the proliferation of awards, particularly the Young Adult Library Services Association's

Michael L. Printz Award for young adult literature in 2000, and ALSC's Robert F. Sibert Informational Book Award in 2001. Though both were welcome additions to the podium, there were some concerns that the Newbery committee would henceforth ignore teen crossover and nonfiction titles. However, in 2004 *An American Plague* was awarded a Newbery Honor, as well as the Sibert Medal. In 2005 the feat was repeated by *The Voice That Challenged a Nation;* and *Hitler Youth* (2006) and *Claudette Colvin* (2010) were Honor titles for both awards. In 2005 *Lizzie Bright and the Buckminster Boy* was an Honor Book for both the Printz and Newbery. The Newbery Medals for *Criss Cross* and *Good Masters! Sweet Ladies!* also suggest that the Printz and Sibert have not deterred the Newbery committee from honoring titles eligible for multiple awards.

Authors of color are only modestly better represented in this decade's Newbery winners than in the past, comprising approximately 20 percent of the honorees. In 2002 Linda Sue Park became the second Asian American medalist, after Dhan Gopal Mukerji in 1928. (Only Laurence Yep had been to the podium since, twice, for Honor awards.) In 2005 Cynthia Kadohata swelled those ranks to three, and Grace Lin achieved another Honor award in 2010. The Honors circle also included the first Honor Book authored by a Latina—Margarita Engle—and five Honors for African American authors (Christopher Paul Curtis, Marilyn Nelson, and three to Jacqueline Woodson).

Ideally, the Newbery should encourage publishers to take a risk with a broad definition of quality. Among all the honored authors this decade, only five debut authors were recognized (Cynthia Kadohata, Kate DiCamillo, Cynthia Lord, Ingrid Law, and Jacqueline Kelly). Meanwhile, three authors among the medalists, and ten total among all honorees (counting Jacqueline Woodson twice) had been previously honored by a Newbery committee, approximately one quarter of the pool. Even so, could an Honor for a debut novel like *Because of Winn-Dixie* have been what allowed the author and publisher to take the leap to a book that was risky in structure, tone, and theme, in *The Tale of Despereaux*? If so, the award succeeds.

Despite the broadness of the award criteria, the vast number of books that were honored still fit a certain mold: fiction, generally realistic and "serious," for grades four/five and up. There is nothing in the criteria that calls for this type of book, yet many have come to expect it. So it's notable when books like *Carver, Show Way, Good Masters! Sweet Ladies!, The Surrender Tree, An American Plague, The Voice That Challenged a Nation, Hitler Youth,* or *Claudette Colvin* are honored to challenge the mold of genre. *The Tale of Despereaux, Show Way,* and *Where the Mountain Meets the Moon* are the only three titles that seem truly to dip below the fourth-grade watermark. Only a few more depart from the norm of realistic or historical fiction, despite a decade of Harry Potter mania: *The Graveyard Book, The Tale of Despereaux, The House of the Scorpion, Princess Academy, Savvy, The Underneath, Where the Mountain Meets the Moon,* and *When You Reach Me,* which notably sets a tone of realism despite its speculative theme.

Horning notes another type of radical change at the end of the twentieth century: books in which children "have been abandoned by their parents or even by society at large." She differentiates these bleak independence stories from old-fashioned orphan stories (which, oddly enough, are well represented among *A Single Shard, Crispin,* and *The Higher Power of Lucky*). This grimness is still evident in many of this decade's winners, though notably in titles in which other radical structural elements temper it: fantasy in *The Graveyard Book* and *The House of the Scorpion;* complex narrative and strong narrators in *The Tale of Despereaux* and *The Underneath;* melodrama and humor in *Joey Pigza Loses Control, The Wednesday Wars,* and *The Mostly True Adventures of Homer P. Figg.* (In fact, there is little true humor still to be found in the Newbery range.)

In a new century, with a heightened media presence for children's books, how different now is the standard set by these ten years' honored titles? Not very different. Children's books have "come of age." The methods by which we talk about them have. Yet the values that we seem to hold as marks of distinguished literature under the Newbery Medal continue to produce a certain type of book, with a standard margin for stretching boundaries. This decade's winners are slightly more inventive, slightly more diverse in authorship, and perhaps in genre and format, than in the past. Yet consider the kinds of works that have challenged our definitions of literature this decade. *The Invention of Hugo Cabret* was a groundbreaking Caldecott medalist alongside *Good Masters! Sweet Ladies!,* yet it had been "talked about" in the blogosphere for the Newbery. But Newbery criteria require that only text be considered, making it difficult to imagine any graphic novel winning, or many picture books. Is a work of literature still solely textually based? Can measures of excellence encompass different genres? If we continue to ask these questions, we should provoke the award to age gracefully, still honoring its "spirit and philosophy," and, most important, its readership. The range of best sellers and sleepers and underdogs in this decade's Newbery winners and their media reception spotlight Frederic Melcher's foresight in identifying librarians as the "jury which could give value" to the award, having "no commercial stake in the fate of any particular book."[4] But he also recognized, thirty years after establishing the award, that the charge of the Newbery committee is only half of the picture:

The growing value of the medals . . . has been due to the strict devotion to the standards the medals represent. Writers, artists, publishers and librarians can point out books of distinction, considered as they must be year by year, but only readers in succeeding generations can make them "classics."[5]

The Newbery committee has its charge, and in turn charges young readers. Some of whom grow up to join the Newbery committee, or even the stellar ranks of medalists.

NOTES

1. Kathleen T. Horning, "Newbery Medal Books, 1986–2000," in *The Newbery and Caldecott Medal Books, 1986–2000: A Comprehensive Guide to the Winners* (American Library Association, 2001), 24.
2. Anita Silvey, "Has the Newbery Lost Its Way?" *School Library Journal*, October 2008, 41.
3. Clara Breed, "The Newbery Medal: A Plea for Understanding," *Wilson Library Bulletin*, May 1942, 725.
4. Leonard S. Marcus, *Minders of Make-Believe: Idealists, Entrepreneurs, and the Shaping of American Children's Literature* (Houghton Mifflin, 2008), 86.
5. Frederic G. Melcher, "The Origin of the Newbery and Caldecott Medals," in *Newbery and Caldecott Medal Books, 1956–1965,* ed. Lee Kingman (The Horn Book, 1965), 2.

CALDECOTT MEDAL BOOKS, 2001–2010

Joanna Rudge Long

THIS CENTURY'S FIRST ten Caldecott Medal books are both brilliant and diverse. To compare them is to discover intriguing similarities and contrasts: just one winner (Beth Krommes) is a woman; only three (Krommes, David Small, and Chris Raschka) illustrated books they didn't write. With two new medals, David Wiesner now has three, a feat equaled only by Marcia Brown. Two books are nonfiction, the rest stories; each has an engaging narrative arc. For the first time ever, two are wordless. All are innovative explorations by artists long secure in their craft, which they employed with imagination and creative distinction to develop their books' worthy themes. Ranging from a toddlers' good-night book to a novel with appeal for teens, they address children from birth to age fourteen. Each exhibits a masterful artistry that may be most fully appreciated by adults, yet their ideas, narratives, and pictures all speak directly to the children who are their primary audience.

Nimble drafting plays starring roles: cartoon style, in Small's witty caricatures and in the broad lines that define Eric Rohmann's daft animals; in Mordicai Gerstein's delicate hatching and Krommes's elegant white scratchboard. Raschka's color blossoms joyfully unconfined; Wiesner's burgeons fantastically undersea; Jerry Pinkney's celebrates the creatures of Africa. White space, too, takes active roles, especially in Raschka's, Wiesner's, and Kevin Henkes's books. Curiously, two winning books (Henkes's and Brian Selznick's) are in black and white, joining only five out of the last century's sixty-three (three published by 1941). It's a refreshing reminder that, since printing's invention, book design has been a *graphic* art, with the harmonious melding of typography and printmaking invigorating its history. Such great illustrators as Wanda Gág and Fritz Eichenberg were in this tradition.

So is the 2009 winner, Susan Marie Swanson's *The House in the Night,* illustrated by Beth Krommes. Krommes's black-and-white scratchboard recalls the venerable art of wood engraving, though the book's golden highlights embody its themes—the night sky's beauty, the coziness of home. The nursery chant and trajectory to the wide world and back are traditional, yet Krommes's envisioning transcends the ordinary. The welcoming, hilly landscape and homey interior are composed of stylized details—simplified, orderly, decorative, their perspectives skewed to lead and focus the eye. Compositions feature diagonals that lead upward to the right, pause on significant features, and go on to a page turn. In surreal aerial scenes, the rural landscape's motherly curves resemble seams in a patchwork quilt. Gleams of yellow—delicately nuanced, lemon to gold—lend an entrancing, dreamlike glow.

In contrast, Kevin Henkes's *Kitten's First Full Moon* (2005) casts light on a world of silvery gray, realistically drained of the daytime spectrum. The book is actually printed in full color, warming the simple palette and subtly recalling what we remember—but can't see—by moonlight. Henkes's pacing is expert: he alternates active spreads, dominated by bold, action-defining lines against backgrounds of deep, texture-enlivened gray, with Kitten's thoughtful pauses ("the little bowl of milk, just waiting") on broad expanses of white. Just so is a cat immobile before its pounce; just so do gifted storytellers capture small listeners with a delicious surprise. Frames accelerate the action, and Henkes also uses them to develop emotions barely hinted at in the text. Safely home, Kitten finds her wish fulfilled, though not as she'd imagined: a true and satisfying lesson.

Brian Selznick's *The Invention of Hugo Cabret* (2008; black and white, except for its jacket) is a tribute to early films. From its solid black borders to its exploration of the dramatic possibilities of light, Selznick replicates the experience of watching old black-and-white movies. He leads the eye by focusing on significant details, by varying perspectives and points of view, and with sequences from distant vistas to larger-than-life close-ups. Wordless pages pass in swift succession to evoke a trek across Paris or into the train station's dark recesses; or pause for characterizations that suggest motives, elicit empathy, and convey emotion with a power beyond words. All this is cinematic, with white shining through dense black and rich grays to illumine the beautifully composed pages and to highlight significant moments like incandescent light.

Eric Rohmann's relief prints for *My Friend Rabbit* (2003) resemble woodcuts, placing the book in the graphic tradition; his emphatic black lines, however, are in the spirit of cartoon art. Where Selznick's Paris is evocative and atmospheric, Rohmann's setting (also bordered in black) is simply a narrow fringe of grass under a cloudless sky. The action that fills this space to its margins is propelled by Rabbit's boundless energy and determination. Abetted by Rohmann's compositional skill, Rabbit balances the outsized creatures he's commandeered in an unwieldy tower that defies both gravity and probability, to excellent comic effect. Delicate background colors keep the mood light; more saturated hues give the animals heft. Their eyes, though minimally defined, vividly express states of mind—consternation, indignation, hope, wonderment, bliss—as do their eloquently contorted bodies. Rohmann's few words relate this tall tale to a small child's world ("Rabbit means well. But . . . wherever he goes, trouble follows . . ."); but it's in his daft illustrations that the preposterous events come to life.

Where Rohmann's broad humor prompts guffaws, David Small's caricatures for Judith St. George's *So You Want to Be President?* (2001) elicit a more sophisticated response. An acquaintance with history renders his satirical political cartoons and nuanced facial expressions still more amusing: the incongruity of tailor Andrew Johnson pinning up Reagan's trouser hems, or a grim-faced Wilson dancing. From minimal sketches to full portraits, the familiar faces are instantly recognizable in Small's masterful limning, whether brush-broad or cobweb-slim. His stage-managing of cross-historical groupings is inventive, thought-provoking, amusingly detailed, composed with panache—and not always comical: Lincoln in his monument, sitting in stern judgment on two blameworthy successors, is a sober and telling vision.

"My intention . . . is to give children just what I want to give everyone: something . . . that provokes good questions," explains Mordicai Gerstein,[1] and so he does in *The Man Who Walked between the Towers* (2004), a thrilling true adventure that's also a poignant commemoration. Excellent picture-book art usually leads the eye from left to right. Paradoxically, Gerstein's compositions are perfectly balanced (their left-to-right devices judiciously understated): a visual metaphor for the high-wire artist's phenomenal equilibrium. Gerstein re-creates the World Trade Center and the space around it with lines as slender as Petit's cable as seen from the distant ground. His subtle gradations of color invoke a luminous cityscape of river and sky. And despite their symmetry, his spreads are anything but static: their vertiginous perspectives plunge us into a visceral awareness of gravity itself—the dynamic, inexorable power that makes Petit's feat so awe inspiring.

Norton Juster's *The Hello, Goodbye Window* (2006) also celebrates a place and its surroundings. Illustrator Chris Raschka renders Nanna and Poppy's home—heart of a three-generation family—in euphoric splashes of color. His deceptively casual added lines don't so much delineate forms as suggest their presence on the spacious pages, inviting readers to imagine them more fully. Sturdy type interacts with the glowing hues and bold drafting to produce lively, harmonious spreads. Though the childlike style of the art reflects a child-centered point of view ("I . . . take my nap and nothing happens until I get up"), Raschka's characterizations are keenly perceptive: activities in this welcoming house and garden are so freely creative that even the rules made by the indulgent but sensible grandparents contribute to the fun, and to the love.

"What if . . . ?" asks David Wiesner. What if the wolf blew *The Three Pigs* (2002) right out of their book to venture onto still-blank pages and seize their own destiny (and a new illustrative style)? Might they escape on a cleverly folded page (ironically, it depicts the wolf)? Wander into another book? What *is* a book? This one's a metafictional exploit and a brilliant demonstration: illustrations do transform stories. While making such playful additions as the dragon that figures in his altered conclusion, Wiesner also honors the spirit of the familiar tale, with its succession of clever escapes. His visual imagination, at once comic and profound, is superbly supported by his skill in integrating several styles into this thought-provoking whole.

Where *The Three Pigs* examines the nature of story, Wiesner's *Flotsam* (2007) explores the curiosity and wonderment inspired by a boy's observations of the real world. A camera extends his vision from the here and now to the past, the future, and some fancifully imagined ocean depths; and to further mysteries, revealed by magnification. Skillfully paced by the variety of its spreads and frames, the serenely horizon-wide book conjures the power of sea, sand, and unencumbered time during a day at the beach to free the imagination. This wordless book models seeing and thinking as intelligent, possibly wordless, activities: to discover, to decode, to ponder. Its protagonist is a real boy, and Wiesner's portrayal of him is vividly realistic, from his intent eyes and the ruminative angle of his bare feet to the enchanting piscine photographers who transport the camera to its next landfall.

Jerry Pinkney's wordless rendering of Aesop's *The Lion and the Mouse* (2010) crowns the decade. His sumptuous watercolors—keyed to the glorious gold of the king of beasts and his Serengeti home, to vivid jungle greens and sober mouse tones—are brilliantly arrayed over spreads and frames to play against the deep shadows and liberal white space that heighten the tale's drama.

Pinkney's African animals are realistic; yet their revealing postures and eyes bespeak complex reasoning and emotion. His art extends the fable at every turn, from the lion's bemused reaction to having a mouse run up his back and the mouse's dogged industry to a lovely Peaceable Kingdom, tucked under the jacket, that raises this particular drama to a universal vision of hope.

Crowns the decade indeed: like the other nine Caldecott winners, Pinkney's masterpiece has the craft, artistry, and appeal to keep it a favorite for decades to come.

NOTE
1. 2004 Caldecott Medal acceptance speech, *Horn Book Magazine,* July/August 2004, 408.

A Year Down Yonder

written by
Richard Peck

published by
Dial, 2000

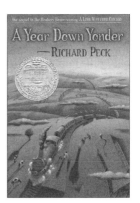

HORN BOOK REVIEW

This sequel to Peck's Newbery Honor–winning *A Long Way from Chicago* (rev. 11/98) is narrated by the formidable Grandma Dowdel's granddaughter Mary Alice, who is now fifteen and has been sent to live (or fend for herself, as she sees it) with Grandma after her father loses his job in Chicago—a casualty of the 1937 recession. Grandma is still dispensing her own brand of justice in her small Illinois town, and, as before, Mary Alice soon finds herself an accomplice to many of Grandma's brazen schemes—and even boldly hatches a few of her own. While the escapades are diverting, the seven stories, which span the school year, don't have the cumulative power of those in *A Long Way from Chicago*. Grandma, who was an indefatigable source of surprise and bewilderment to her grandchildren in the first book, doesn't come across as such a mythic figure this time around, perhaps because some of her shock value has worn off. The humor here is subdued but much in evidence, and a few overly sentimental moments don't detract much from the narrative. Peck presents memorable characters in a satisfying sequel, and those looking to be entertained once again by Grandma Dowdel will enjoy their visit.—*Kitty Flynn*

2001 NEWBERY ACCEPTANCE SPEECH

Richard Peck

Delegates to the American Library Association, members of the publishing community, members of the 2001 Newbery committee to whom I am so grateful, ladies and gentlemen:

Unaccustomed as I am to public speaking, I invoke my valued colleague, San Francisco's own, incomparable Peggy Rathmann. If she had not already said it to you before me, I would say it now. It takes a village to write my books.

I am grateful to my agent, Sheldon Fogelman, to whom my obligations go beyond the contractual.

I am grateful to Mary Tapissier, my British publisher at Hodder and Stoughton.

I am grateful to George Nicholson, once of Holt, Rinehart, and Winston. After the tense and silent summer of 1971, I took a first manuscript to him, hoping for advice. On the following morning, early, George rang up to say, "You may start your second novel."

I've just kept going, hoping to have the next book accepted before the last book can be reviewed.

I am here because of a colleague who was not nearly such a slow starter as I. She is S. E. Hinton. In the spring of 1973 she was unable to speak to the Indiana Library Association. I was called off the bench and onto the field to pinch-hit. I've never left it. That evening began nearly three decades of visits to young readers and their librarians who always, somehow, can tell me what my next book will be about.

I am grateful to librarians because they are the local representatives of all writers, living and dead. I'm twice grateful to those librarians willing to write grant proposals in their own time, grants for author-in-the-school programs. As a result, I never see a "typical" school. I see a school with a librarian willing to move heaven, earth, and the classroom teachers to bring writers and young readers together. It is always a librarian who fears no parent, because you can communicate with children or you can fear their parents, but you cannot do both.

Author-in-the-school programs mean a great deal to me, because if a living writer of anything had entered the classroom when I was in seventh grade, it would have given me permission to dream.

Many a better writer has accepted the Newbery Medal over these past eighty years. Many a better writer has been denied it. But no writer ever admired his writing colleagues more than I do, or learned more from them. They are names that should be on the lips of every American parent: Patricia Reilly Giff, Katherine Paterson, Paula Danziger, Will Hobbs, Walter Dean Myers, Lois Duncan, Sonya Sones, M. E. Kerr, Kate DiCamillo, Jerry Spinelli, Cynthia DeFelice, Chris Crutcher, Michael Cadnum, Graham Salisbury, Lois Lowry, Sharon Creech, Judy Blume, Marc Talbert, Jacqueline Woodson, Paul Zindel, Joan Bauer, Jack Gantos, and many, many more. Their work towers above the ruins of an educational system, public and private, in an era when literacy has become an elective and the librarian and the writer may be the only teachers in many young lives. Being a writer never improved anybody's mental health, and so I'm grateful for the companionship and therapy of my colleagues.

Only one hard truth beclouds this evening. I am the first writer to meet this moment after the lifetime of Robert Cormier. After his lifetime, but not after his life.

I'm here because of another colleague in our writers' village: Harry Mazer. In the fall of 1995, Harry sent forth a decree. He asked his colleagues to write short stories for a new collection he was anthologizing. It was to be a collection of gun stories. As you know, it became a book called *Twelve Shots*.

Now, I have not personally squeezed off a round since the rifle range at Fort Carson, Colorado, in January of 1957. And I had to wonder in my heart just how many librarians are members of the National Rifle Association, however much you may personally admire Charlton Heston. In fact, I wondered if Harry was slipping. But of course he wasn't. He'd included a postcard to send back, saying, Yes, I'll do you a story, or, No, I won't. I itched to send that postcard back saying, "Dear Harry, I'll give it a shot."

Trying to imagine what kind of stories Harry would get, I envisioned a lot of male-dominated yarns about how I killed a bear and it made a man out of me. In fact, a lot of overserious stories. So I gave myself an assignment. I'd write a comedy about a female character, just to give Harry's collection some balance.

I looked up from my desk, and there in the door stood Grandma Dowdel with a 12-gauge double-barreled Winchester shotgun loose in her trigger-happy hand.

I called my story "Shotgun Cheatham's Last Night above Ground." Then I ran it past my editor at Dial Books for Young Readers, Cindy Kane. She thought there was a book in it, a gathering of short stories building to a novel. That book became *A Long Way from Chicago*, which brought me to the Newbery-Caldecott dinner of 1999, though farther back in the room. When a book comes that far, the editor says what Cindy did: "We'll need another book about Grandma Dowdel, and we'd like it by Thursday." Thus, *A Year Down Yonder* began to be.

Real life is too contrived for fiction. The Delacorte editor of Harry Mazer's *Twelve Shots* has since become my editor at Dial: Lauri Hornik. In their discreet directiveness, Cindy Kane and Lauri Hornik are the best of editors. I thank them and Harry Mazer for this medal.

With another Grandma Dowdel book due, I saw I'd made a grave error in a career full of them. I'd let Joey, the narrator of *A Long Way from Chicago*, grow up. He was in World War II. And so a sequel was out of the question. Happily, Joey's younger sister, Mary Alice, was waiting in the wings. She told a different story. Joey expressed his awe at the power of a mighty grandmother and, perhaps, of all women. Mary Alice tells of finding in an unexpected place the role model for the rest of her life.

Now people ask, "Was Grandma Dowdel your grandmother?" Even librarians ask. We writers aren't given much credit for creativity. Did my grandmother fire off both barrels of a shotgun in her own front room? Did she pour hot glue on the head of a hapless Halloweener? Did she spike the punch at a Daughters of the American Revolution tea? Well, no. When you're a writer, you can give yourself the grandmother you wish you'd had.

And who is Grandma Dowdel? Since nobody but a reader ever became a writer, Grandma Dowdel marches in a long tradition. She is the American tall tale in a Lane Bryant dress. There's more than a bit of Paul Bunyan about her, and a touch of the Native American trickster tradition: she may just be Kokopelli without the flute.

But the setting for the stories is real, the town where my own real-life grandmother lived, a place called Cerro Gordo, named by the men coming home from the Mexican War. It was a town in Illinois cut in two by the tracks of the Wabash Railroad where people stood in their yards to watch the Wabash Cannonball go through.

A novel is a community, within the covers of the book. The smaller the town, the more meaningful is every inhabitant, unless that small town is a suburb.

Grandma Dowdel isn't the first of the great, granite elders to stalk through my pages. There's an elderly character in every one of my books: Uncle Miles in *The Ghost Belonged to Me,* Madam Malevich in *Are You in the House Alone?,* Polly Prior in *Remembering the Good Times.* And very shortly now in a new book called *Fair Weather,* a gnarled old codger named Granddad Fuller.

These ambulatory ancient monuments are there to offer wisdom and balance to a self-referential youth culture. They are extended family for young suburban readers and for young readers in cities where the elderly fear the streets. Most of all, the old survivors in my stories embody the underlying message in all fiction: that in the long run you will be held responsible for the consequences of your actions. A serious message, and so a comedy is called for.

Our readers find their role models and their lawgivers in their peer group leaders. Mary Alice finds hers in an elder, where I found mine. From my father, I learned nostalgia as an art form. My stories are set where he grew up, a paradise lost to him on the battlefields of World War I. Like all soldiers returned, he found the past wasn't where he'd left it. That only fueled his stories of boyhood until they merged in my mind with the stories of Mark Twain. I still see the stories of both these men through the mesh of a sun-warmed screen door on long-vanished, never-ending summer afternoons.

I am here this evening because I came from a home where no screens glowed, a home where there were bedtime stories because there was bedtime. I'm here because my mother read to me before I could read for myself. She had no intention of sending an ignoramus to first grade, and so she filled me up with words and opened the door to the alternative universe of storytelling, of fiction. I heard my first stories in my mother's voice. A satisfactory substitute for that technique has yet to be devised because most of who we are is decided in those first five fleeting years of life before we ever see school.

The narrative—language itself—is the gift of the elders. We are the elders now, the youngest writers and librarians among us. In only moments from now—a few semesters—our young readers won't be able to remember the twentieth century.

Powerful forces divorce the young from their roots and traditions: the relentlessness of the video game that is the pornography of the prepubescent, a violent virtual reality that eliminates the parent who paid for it. And the peer group that rushes in to fill the vacuum of the teacher's vanished authority and an awesome parental power failure.

We writers and librarians, we people of the word, spot for survivors in a generation who have learned the wrong lesson from their elementary-school years: that yes, you should be able to read and write; yes, you should be literate. But if you're not, you will be accommodated.

Thank you for fighting this good fight, school librarians who know that the beating heart of the school is the library, not the gym; public librarians who may just be the only adults on call for many of the young.

Thank you for stealing time from an increasingly intrusive technology to put the right book in the right young hand. Thank you for standing firm and hanging tough against the book censor who is so often the parent of a non-reading child.

Anyone who has reached this podium has traveled a long trail. Few have traveled a longer one than I have, across thirty years and thirty books. I am not a quick study. It has taken me this long to find the key that unlocks a Newbery: a naked woman and a snake. There is no accounting for taste, and I am grateful to the Newbery committee for theirs.

We read to know we're not alone. And that's why we write, too. Thank you for this moment, and for everything you will do for the citizens of the twenty-first century on your next day back on the job.

Richard Peck

THE CALL.

There are many great stories about Newbery Medal–winning authors receiving The Call. The Call can come at any time on that fateful day during the American Library Association's midwinter meeting. It is almost always a surprise. It is almost always received with an awkward and unrehearsed combination of disbelief and joy. It is always life-changing.

This year The Call came early on Monday, January 15th, but not too early. I didn't answer—Richard Peck did. Instead, I got The Message, left on my answering service at 11:27 a.m., which was nearly 1:30 New York City time. I picked it up a few hours later in my truck, driving my two children home from ice-skating at Santa Fe's new indoor rink. I heard a rather breathless but most familiar voice:

> Hello, Talberts. This is Uncle Richard calling. This is the first time I've been able to get to the phone this morning. And I just wanted to wish you a happy Martin Luther King Day and . . . to tell you I've won the Newbery. I'll talk to you later. Bye.

You may find this hard to believe, but we were all listening to the audio version of *A Year Down Yonder* as I was collecting my telephone messages. ("This is better than Harry Potter," my oldest daughter, Molly, had declared a couple weeks earlier while we were listening to *A Long Way from Chicago*—a Christmas gift from Richard. She's ten. In case you're visiting from Pluto or work for the *Horn Book*, this is a compliment not delivered lightly.)

I had to pull over to the side of the road because my eyes filled with tears. My girls were mortified. Guys who drive big red trucks do not pull over to the side of the road because they are crying for joy.

"Uncle Richard won the Newbery!" I managed to say. "For this book!" I pointed to the tape player, which obviously was not a book. This didn't do too much to reassure my girls. Neither did the words emanating from the tape player. From the speakers came narrator Lois Smith's voice, unabated: "Maxine was screaming for her life, and that snake was all over her. It looped around her shoulders . . ." Great as this image was (and now great in a Newbery kind of way), I turned the tape off.

In the stunned quiet of the truck, I listened to The Message again, to make sure I'd heard Uncle Richard correctly. I had.

The Message touched me nearly as deeply as if it had been The Call itself. And The Message was quintessential Richard Peck—full of his wry sense of humor, his sense of timing, his priorities, and his relationship with me and my family.

Richard has the most sophisticated sense of humor of anyone I know—at once disarming but instructive, at once humbling and ennobling, the punch line often delivered after a sharp intake of breath, the timing almost always flawless. It isn't acting. He *thinks* that way, in grammatical sentences that also have a point: sentences with beginnings, middles, and (almost physical) punch lines at their ends. Very much like his novels.

I believe Richard is naturally prone to thinking and speaking and writing clearly. He honed this way of thinking for many years by writing letters and speeches and novels on a manual typewriter, and now (reluctantly) on an electric.

Most conversation today is like fishing with a bobber, throwing the line into still water, sitting back, waiting for the fish (or ideas) to come. Richard's conversation is more like fly fishing. I don't know if he's ever fished at all, but I'm sure he would prefer running water—it is lively and it is going someplace specific. He would know where the fish are and where to lay the line so as to hook the exact fish (or idea) he wants. A conversation with Richard is always intelligent, purposeful, and fun. There is always something wiggling at the other end of his thoughts.

He writes the same way he speaks. And he hooks not only ideas but readers, young and old. Thank goodness, Richard's philosophy is one of catch-and-release. Readers aren't trophies to Richard, but living things that learn from being caught. They must then be set free to put this learning to good use, according to their own strengths and limitations.

The Message also demonstrated Richard's priorities. Much as I wanted it to be true, I could hardly believe we were the first people he'd called with The News. Yes, he dedicated *A Year Down Yonder* to me and my family. But when I telephoned him later, to tell him of the joy (and immortality) he'd brought to our lives, I was relieved to learn that indeed he'd called his mother first. Family should come first, although he is very much a member of our family.

To us he is Uncle Richard, not by blood, but by choice—my daughters' choice. What else could they call him? When he visits, they love being with him. To be on the receiving end of Richard's incisive gaze is to be understood and respected. It is a rare adult who can make children feel comfortable and at the same time not compromise the adult-child relationship. Richard is such a person. He listens, he respects, he cares, he understands, and he doesn't always agree. In fact, he often challenges. But like most children, my daughters like to be engaged, not pandered to. Richard engages. Totally. He is special that way. That is one reason why he is our Uncle Richard.

Another reason is that Richard Peck is my oldest and dearest author friend.

It is embarrassing for me to admit that I was not familiar with Richard's young adult novels when I began writing novels of my own. Children's literature was a big new world for me, and I had huge gaps in my reading (and still do). But, after I had written two middle-grade novels, a neighbor who had met him a year before told me that Richard Peck would be a good person to call for publishing advice. I immediately read *Representing Super Doll,* and was moved by everything but its title. This Richard Peck guy was obviously a master storyteller, a writer of substance, and, by the author blurb, had been prominent in the kid-lit business for a very long time—one of the founders of young adult literature. With my heart in my throat, I gathered enough courage one evening to call him. As I feared, he had no idea who I was, had read neither of my books, but he was the perfect gentleman. He listened to me, responded with courtesy, and even seemed genuinely pleased that I was sending him my first novel by way of thanks.

From that phone call has blossomed one of the most satisfying friendships of my life. I made a point of seeing him when I visited New York a couple of months later. By this time I'd read all of his novels, including two of his adult novels, and was impatient for him to write more. From the first, I was completely comfortable in his company. I was thoroughly charmed and flattered to be considered by him a colleague, and to be taken so seriously by him. He made it seem as if I were doing him the favor of visiting.

He returned the favor a few months later by visiting my wife and me in Santa Fe. As a born-again New Mexican, I took great pride in showing him my favorite places around town. Much to my chagrin, he showed me several places in Santa Fe that were new to me. That is so typical of Richard—his ability to reveal to people surprising new things about the places in which they live, and his ability to be comfortable wherever he is. Richard is a joy to have around the house. He's the kind of guest who, when asked if he likes pork chops, says, "Love 'em!" before the question has been fully asked. He loves to meet our friends and our family. He loves reading aloud to our kids. Clearly, he loves plain, old-fashioned visiting.

And he's a master at getting people to talk about themselves. I often feel like a blabbermouth after visiting with him, but I am always surprised and pleased by what I have learned about myself. Psychotherapy should be so much fun.

Good as he is at getting others to spill their guts, Richard is the kind of person who is fastidious about what he allows others to know about himself. He knows, respects, and honors personal boundaries in ways that are refreshing for someone who grew up in the sixties and seventies, when every little personal thing was fair game. But there are times when he allows glimpses of himself, and I am always honored when he lets me see the tired Richard, or the preoccupied Richard, or the unsure Richard, or the completely unguarded and surprised Richard.

I remember the time I surprised him with the news that he had taught a sister-in-law of mine in a wealthy Chicago suburban school. As it turned out, this surprise was not especially happy. He couldn't hide the fact that he had not enjoyed teaching my sister-in-law or her fellow students. Independently, she told me that she had not enjoyed having him for a teacher. But of course not. He actually expected his students to think and to defend their opinions. He set standards in an age when the highest standard in teaching was helping students feel good about themselves. He must have been a teacher to be reckoned with, and these students suddenly found they were not in command in his classroom.

Richard is so often in command of himself and his audience that it was a surprise to me to discover that he suffers from the same insecurities we all do. I remember sharing with him part of the rough draft of my first nonfiction book, a book about girls who live and work on ranches. He liked it well enough, except that he found the introduction rather stiff. And then, sitting at our dining room table, he read me a draft of his short story "Shotgun Cheatham's Last Night above Ground," which was to be included in the short story collection *Twelve Shots: Outstanding Stories about Guns,* edited by Harry Mazer.

Before Richard was finished, even the cat was moved enough to look up from his napping. "Do you like it?" Richard asked. His fingers were nervous. It was not a question begging for compliments. He really wanted to know, especially if I didn't like it.

But of course I did. I loved every word of it and told him so, hoping he wouldn't think I was just being kind. The story was everything we have come to expect from Richard: focused, funny, surprising, profound, real, and wise.

He allowed as how he was thinking of continuing the story of Grandma Dowdel, but he didn't know if he could do it. Typical Richard. Of course from that story came *A Long Way from Chicago.*

When he sent me a copy of the book, I read it and called him (after I'd sat for a moment, to allow myself to reenter the comparatively black-and-white world around me) and told him that, as much as I loved everything he'd ever written, this was his best book.

Others must have agreed. *A Long Way from Chicago* went on to become a National Book Award finalist and a Newbery Honor Book.

Success such as that cannot go unpunished. He was asked by his publisher to write a sequel and, with trepidation, agreed to do so. He told me that he feared the next book wouldn't be taken seriously because it was a sequel and, as anybody knows, sequels are usually mere echoes of the original, fainter and lacking distinction. He sent me one of the first copies that his publisher delivered to his apartment.

I read it and was astonished. Truly, *this* was the best book Richard Peck had ever written—which is saying a mouthful. Further, it was no more a sequel to *A Long Way from Chicago* than the New Testament is a sequel to the Old Testament. Chronologically, it takes place after *A Long Way from Chicago*. It shares the same setting and some of the same characters. But, emotionally, it is a prequel, giving us, through Mary Alice, a window into the kind of girl Grandma Dowdel must have been so many years before, shaped differently by different times and places but emotionally parallel to this budding young woman from Chicago. Could it be that *A Long Way from Chicago* is an echo of *A Year Down Yonder*? Perhaps.

I'm sure that some readers were disappointed that this wasn't another book about the magnificent Grandma Dowdel so much as it was Mary Alice's book. That Mary Alice went from thinking of her grandmother as an oddity and a hick to seeing her as a complex woman, at once tough and vulnerable, and with whom she shares many strong personality traits and values, was a marvelous achievement on Richard's part. I'm glad the Newbery committee agreed.

As we rush to canonize Richard, let me relate something I observed several years before any of this happened. I had called him to announce plans to visit New York City to meet a new publisher and editor and to see a couple of friends, including him. I was flattered when he told me that I shouldn't stay at a hotel, but at his apartment.

I slept in his office. The next morning, I sat at his desk, imagining what it would be like to be Richard. Unlike my desk, his was immaculate. Looking at it made me wonder what it would be like to have a brain that wasn't as cluttered as mine. Envy followed wonder. And then I looked straight up to the window that dominates the north side of his office. The season was fall, and most of the leaves had turned brown and fallen off in that brisk way of things that live in New York. A band of light had fallen across a squat, Greek revival building framed by a couple of nondescript buildings—all of them centered in the window. And in that light I could read the inscription that was carved above the columns supporting the building's limestone facade: "To Prepare Unto the Lord Perfect People."

I asked Richard about that building later in the day, when the light had moved on and the inscription was no longer readable from his office. It had been a school, he said. I asked him about the inscription. He claimed not to have noticed it before.

But how extraordinarily perfect. I'm sure that Richard spends as much time as any of us gazing out office windows. I find it comforting to think that his gaze might often linger on a phrase that describes what I believe motivates him in so much of his writing. It is amusing to imagine that his laser-sharp gaze may have carved those words in the stone where no inscription existed before.

Such an inscription may seem old-fashioned, even corny. But Richard doesn't shy away from old-fashioned ideas or values when they express a lasting truth. That is another thing I admire about Richard. Through his stories, he brings nobility into the lives of his readers. Through his stories, he makes the old new and the new old. And through his stories, he has touched each of us in profound, beautiful, and timeless ways, helping make the world a more perfect place.

Thank you, Uncle Richard, for the gifts of your stories and for your generous friendship.

THE **CALDECOTT MEDAL 2001**

So You Want to Be President?

written by
Judith St. George

illustrated by
David Small

published by
Philomel, 2000

HORN BOOK REVIEW

Sometimes you *can* judge a book by its cover—and this is one of those times. David Small has cleverly depicted the presidential faces on Mount Rushmore in a jovial cartoon style that makes them friendly and not formidable, an encouraging invitation to the witty observations within a narrative that felicitously begins, "There are good things about being President and there are bad things about being President." Arranging historical tidbits in an attractive buffet, this well-timed book offers anecdotes both cautionary and guaranteed to attract attention and arouse interest. Would-be presidents are apprised of the advantages of the position, which include having a swimming pool, bowling alley, and movie theater as well as never eating "yucky" vegetables—like broccoli. As a counterpoint to the advantages, a few negatives are also presented: presidents have to dress up, be polite, and never "go anywhere alone," and they have quantities of homework. Having examined both sides of the question, succeeding spreads offer tips for achieving the desired goal: having the right first name (six presidents were named James, four John, four William, two George, two Andrew, and two Franklin); having siblings; being born in a log cabin; joining the army; becoming a hero; being a vice president. The question of appearance is treated as a quasi-beauty contest featuring Warren Harding, who was handsome—but not a good president, as even he admitted.

The overall tone is upbeat, and the need for honesty in office is stressed by contrasting Truman and Cleveland with Nixon and Clinton, the latter two depicted descending, as in banishment, the steps of the Lincoln Memorial—a sad visual commentary. The conclusion, with its reiteration of the oath of office, is positively inspiring. Appended are a list of personages featured in the illustrations, brief biographical sketches of the presidents in chronological order, and a short bibliography.—*Mary M. Burns*

2001 CALDECOTT ACCEPTANCE SPEECH

David Small

I want to thank Connie Rockman and all fifteen members of the Caldecott committee for giving me this terrific award and for making possible all the honor and prestige it has brought me in the past five months. I also thank them, deeply and sincerely, for the opportunities the Caldecott brings in its wake. Public appearances in person, on TV, on radio, and on tape give us the gift of seeing ourselves, as well as seeing ourselves as others see us, which is really a great gift to have, so I thank you.

My congratulations to the other winners, and apologies for the banquet program. As the saying goes, "Do a caricature, lose a friend." Some of you are my friends and I don't want to lose you. Others I'd like to know better. I hope that my drawings haven't screwed up our relationship.

Thanks to Judith St. George for writing the smart, funny text that inspired my pictures for *So You Want to Be President?* As it happens, Judy and I met for the first time only a few months ago, long after the book was on the market, and I was happy to find she is as smart, as well-spoken, and often just as cheeky as her text is. I think I can speak for Judy, too, in expressing thanks to Patricia Gauch, vice president and publisher of Philomel Books. Patti is a savvy and—to use her own favorite word—sassy lady. She is sensitive, energetic, and a caring editor who helped in many important ways to guide and shape this book, and it was her idea to bring Judy's text and my illustrations together in the first place. I want to give very special thanks to my art director Cecilia Yung. Generally when you're working with an art director for the first time and you announce that you're planning to work in a new style, there is this long, dead pause on the other end of the line during which the art director is calculating how much money to offer you to kill the job. Cecilia didn't seem at all fazed that I wanted to take a fresh, looser approach to my art for this book and went along zestfully with everything I proposed. (Well, almost everything. And, okay, not always zestfully.)

There are several members of my family here tonight, among them my three stepchildren, Ginny, Mark, and David, who have been a wonderful support and encouragement to their evil stepfather these past five months, and who for twenty-five years, whether they know it or not, have been a source of great pride and satisfaction to me and their mother. Gin, Marko, L. D., I thank you and I love you.

I want to send thanks to George W. Bush and Al Gore for prolonging the election so that our book could stay on the *New York Times* best-sellers list for a few extra weeks. Nice work, fellas!

Thanks must naturally go to the great, hardworking team of marketing and publicity staffers at Penguin Putnam, and especially to Angus Killick, who was one of the first people to predict that this book would be a huge winner. Looking back over my career, I would like to give long-distance thanks to Alan Benjamin, whom I haven't seen for many years but who gave me my start in publishing in 1980. Alan persuaded Macmillan to take my first book and, during the short term he was senior editor at Crown, convinced them to acquire *Imogene's Antlers.* His inventive and twisted mind obviously recognized in me a younger brother.

Stephen Roxburgh, now the publisher of Front Street Books, was the other warped genius who gave me my second big boost up. Stephen brought both me and Sarah Stewart into the Farrar, Straus and Giroux corral and molded and guided a few of our early books. Stephen tends to flick off the table anything that did not meet his high standards and because of this I continue to learn a lot from him.

I'm proud to say that all those books Sarah and I have done with FSG are still in print. This is mostly due to the completely archaic and totally fiscally irresponsible publishing practices at Farrar, where good money that might be spent on things like swank offices and editorial assistants' salaries is lavished on the books they choose to publish. To all our friends at FSG, our deepest thanks.

Mary Rife of the Kalamazoo Public Library Children's Room was a fortuneteller back in 1982. When my first book, *Eulalie and the Hopping Head,* was published, she predicted that I would one day win the Caldecott. I merely laughed at her. Mary has been a friend and faithful supporter all these years. She is retiring from service soon, but she came out here from Michigan to be with us tonight.

Many blessings upon my wonderful agent Holly McGhee for being direct and tactful, for being such a mensch, and for always being on my side.

The last person I have to thank is really, ever and always, the first one on my list, Sarah Stewart, who is often my collaborator, my best and most honest critic, my friend, my darling, my soul, and also my wife. Without Sarah, I tell you this in all honesty, I would have been dead—spiritually if not literally—twenty-five years ago.

Patti Gauch reminds me that my sketches for *So You Want to Be President?* began to flood across her desk before the contracts were even signed. This shows how eager I was to do the project. The thing that excited me the most about this book was that it offered me the chance to combine the work I'd been doing for years as an editorial artist for publications such as the *New Yorker,* the *New York Times,* and the *Washington Post* with the work I'd been doing—also for years—in children's books. At last, I thought, the child and the adult in me could meet and shake hands.

One of the ways I have managed to duct tape together a living as an artist is this combination of careers—editorial and children's book art—each competing to see which could be the less lucrative. For a long time my life has consisted, on the one hand, of drawing (as it were) chickies, bunnies, and duckies, and having that work interrupted by magazines and newspapers calling upon me to draw caricatures of people like Tonya Harding, James Carville, and Linda Tripp. In 1987, for example, I was working on the finished art for a book about kangaroos and koala bears by Beatrice Schenk de Regniers when *Playboy* called me to join the interview team on the Jessica Hahn story. I dropped everything and flew to New York. For two full days, in a suite at the Plaza where Jessica Hahn was sequestered under a false name for her protection, I attended those disturbing interviews. At night I returned to my own hotel room and drew Hahn's memories of being sexually coerced by the Reverend Jim Bakker in a Florida motel. It's a wonder then, when I returned home and resumed work on my children's book project, that the kangaroos and koalas for the Schenk de Regniers story didn't end up looking like hucksters and degenerates. (Or maybe they did. That book was as well received as hoof-and-mouth disease on a boot heel, and has long since gone out of print.) This kind of mental and professional disconnect has been the hallmark of my working life for more than twenty-five years.

So, with the opportunity to illustrate Judy St. George's book about the presidents, my inner child and my inner adult finally did meet and sat down together to share the same box of crayons. Philomel Books became, then, the daycare center for this not-always-peaceful playtime. My inner adult, as it turned out, would not share, play fair, or cooperate. He wanted to hog all the art supplies and tended to express himself more forcefully than anyone else in the room.

One of the great problems for Patti Gauch and Cecilia Yung was reminding the editorial caricaturist—that is, the adult David Small—that he was working on a children's book and that, despite the many rich opportunities for sophisticated political satire offered by the subject matter, children would inevitably make up a great part of the reading audience. "It would probably be best, David, if you didn't have President Gerald Ford diving into that empty swimming pool." At the beginning of this project I often felt that my most potent ammunition was being taken away from me and that I was marching into battle armed with nothing but a slingshot and a bag of marshmallows.

It was the clash of two professions, a mix-up of métiers, an opposition of occupations, and for a while there it got pretty dicey. However, thanks to Patti and Cecilia, to their good sense and patience, I found a way to make the book funny without being vulgar, irreverent without being too offensive, and sharp without being savage. Hopefully, too, we found a way to help readers young and old take another look at the leaders of our country and see them neither as divinities nor villains, and certainly not as representatives of some impossible dream, but as men with both great abilities and great faults. In other words, to help people see these men as what every president has proven himself to be—a fallible human being.

As I told you at the beginning, it has been an amazing five months, and the Caldecott Medal has caused me to examine myself in a way and with an intensity I've never had before in my life. It has turned a big spotlight on me, and shown me the switch for turning on another big spotlight inside myself. One of the things that made this speech so problematic to write was my having to be careful to make a distinction between revelations that were enormous for me personally and ideas that would be appropriate to share.

Although I've had a lot of illumination shed on certain threshold experiences in my life, it would not necessarily be useful to drag these out in public. There is one point, though, that to feel good about myself I must make, and if it involves a certain measure of personal openness, so be it. Forgive me; it's not whining, it's the only way I know of to make this point effectively.

In all our travels this spring, to schools and libraries in cities from one coast to another, Sarah and I have been disturbed more than ever before by the nearly total eradication of the arts from the schools in America. Children who need the expressive outlet of art, music, dance, and playacting have none of it. At the best they listen to a visiting author or artist for forty-five minutes, and those people might as well be visiting from the moon, so remote are most children from the real, human, and very necessary activities of writing, of drawing, of playing an instrument. These things are deemed by school administrators as luxuries when they are in fact necessities. As someone so rightly pointed out, few people get chills from doing a math problem. Art and music are the things which speak to the human soul. These necessary tools of human expression have become the exclusive property of a small elite group when they should be readily available to all American schoolchildren.

Ask any teacher and he or she will tell you that the biggest troublemakers in school are often the best artists, that the most troubled boys (and let's face it, the kids who in recent years have unleashed the most serious damage have been boys) are also often the ones who draw obsessively in their spare time.

In the fall of 1967, when I was a substitute teacher in the Detroit Public Schools, I was sent for a few days to sub—that is, to babysit—for a class at the city jail for high-school-age criminals. Most of the boys I encountered there had been imprisoned for crimes like breaking and entering, but one among them was a murderer. Before I walked into the room I was told by a guard I would meet this young man who, for the sum of two hundred dollars, had shot and killed his friend's father. Nervously I prepared to come face to face with a monster.

When I finally saw him (a couple of the other students pointed him out to me), for a few moments I was taken aback by a complete reversal of expectations. Instead of the hulking, drooling demon I had anticipated, I met a boy who reminded me physically and spiritually of myself when I was in school. Thin and starved-looking, he didn't speak. Avoiding eye contact, he hung out around the edge of the crowded room, as far away as he could get on the periphery of things. Looking at this kid, I was suddenly thrown back into fifth and sixth grade at MacDowell Elementary, where hurtful words were hurled at me every day by students who took my underweight, underdeveloped body and my reticence to participate as a reason to cull me from their herd. Those names were leveled at me so often, I came at last to identify with them, believing that they branded my future. Furthermore, no one at home did anything to help or to alter that image of myself.

Now, in this young murderer I saw me and I asked myself, Could I have gone that route? There were big differences between him and me, of course, in class and in the opportunities afforded us. No doubt, by virtue of my circumstances at birth, I had more to look forward to than he ever had. I also had talent and ability in drawing that had been nurtured since a very young age. In my socioeconomic class, back in the fifties, it was acceptable that a child make art—lots of art, if he wanted to. At least I had that option, while I am pretty sure that that young man did not.

So, while it was difficult to see him ending up like me, I could easily see myself having ended up like him had I not had the option of the arts. Crime and violence know no class boundaries. But the arts in education do know class boundaries. We have seen flourishing arts programs in a few schools. There the hallways and classrooms are richly covered with paintings and filled with music, making these environments quite simply delightful to be in, as well as a delight to learn in. But these are for the most part in private schools in wealthy communities. But even wealth is not an indicator of a full education for the children. In March, while on book tour, Sarah and I were in emerging affluent neighborhoods with new elementary schools where there were no arts programs and the libraries had been lost to computer centers. In all too many schools across America, the halls are silent and the walls are empty but for a list of rules to follow in case of a fire drill. (When I see a wall full of colored-in xeroxed turkeys I also see emptiness. I am also underwhelmed when I listen to anyone extolling the virtues of the computer over things created by hand, as if drawing, painting, and sculpture are activities related to the Pliocene epoch.)

My school did not have the greatest arts program going, but at least it had one. If there had been no art room, no music, no school plays, an outsider like me would simply have been driven further and further underground. As it happened, because I was allowed to develop my art skills, by the end of seventh grade I wasn't being called those nasty names any more. Instead, the kids who used to call me a punk because I was bad at sports were calling me "David Small, the Greatest Artist of Them All!" Of course I was only the greatest artist at MacDowell Elementary School, but this made me feel different about myself and was a beginning step in a new direction. Our new world is full of terror and is shrinking in frightening ways. To dismiss art from the school curriculum—not only to do it but to allow it—is typical of a society trying to anesthetize itself from pain. But the inability to sense pain is a mortal danger in itself. Convicted murderer Gary Gilmore said, "Inside every killer is a little punk looking for revenge." Take "killer" out of that sentence and substitute "artist" or "outsider" and it still holds up. The fact is, self-expression erupts like a boil, whether it is in the Brooklyn Museum of Art or the halls of Columbine High. Self-expression is dangerous if repressed. Both the artist and the criminal can be punks looking for revenge for the wrongs done to them, so we must ask ourselves, What kind of revenge do we want to permit them? Would we rather have kids expressing their animus through acts of violence like those at Columbine or through a painting? It is up to us to choose which we would rather spend our money on, more prisons or more art programs in our schools. I choose art.

Over the past several months I have been asked repeatedly what it's like to win the Caldecott Medal. I think the answer to this question could possibly lie in a dream I had the other night:

In my dream I was inside my house, in the living room, waiting for my barber to show up. (To accommodate my schedule the barber was making a house call.) While I waited I noticed that there was a large tiger in the room with me. The tiger was prowling around, weaving in and out of the furniture.

Just then, the doorbell rang. It was the barber!

I reached into a desk drawer and pulled out a stun gun. With this instrument I knocked out the tiger. Then, grunting and sweating, I hoisted the heavy limp animal into the open case of the grand piano.

Just as I was closing the lid, the barber entered the room. However, as the lid came down I could see the tiger opening its eyes. Apparently I had not stunned it sufficiently.

Too late! The barber was already taking off his coat. He and I exchanged pleasantries and, getting straight down to business, he began to lay out his accoutrements. Meanwhile, the piano started to tremble, to rock from side to side, and to move a little on its wheels.

I said, "Excuse me," to the barber and left the room quickly. Then, through the door I heard, first the musical crash of the piano as it fell over on the floor, followed by the furious snarls of the tiger as it struggled free of the piano, and lastly, of course, the pitiable wails and screams of the barber as the beast fell upon him and ate him up.

This dream explains what it is like to win the Caldecott Medal: a huge, fierce and very handsome beast is let loose in your house; a few innocent people step in its path; and the only thing you can do is get out of the way and let it happen.

....

ILLUSTRATOR PROFILE BY PATRICIA LEE GAUCH

David Small

WHEN AN ILLUSTRATOR wins the Caldecott Medal, he or she joins a rare club of outstanding artists. The award means that the honored book is destined to be read and reread by children all over this country in mind-boggling numbers.

Winning the Caldecott Medal represents a peak in an artist's professional life. Delighted to have this approbation from the young audiences and professional world that he or she has been serving, the Caldecott winner breathes a pleased and contented sigh. It is not surprising that the artist takes stock, asking the simple question: How did I get here? How did I become an artist, creating this book at this time?

In David Small's case, everyone around him—friends and family—knew from the time he was a toddler that he would be an artist. He started drawing when he was two—anything that his young eye caught and wanted to put on paper. By six he had settled down to drawing cats, "because I wanted a cat." He sketched them "sitting, running, leaping" on every scrap of paper he could find.

Born in Detroit, on the bustling northwest side, not so far from the thriving if noisy automobile industry, he was the second son of a radiologist father and a music- and art-loving mother. From his earliest days, he cherished his solitude. "Grade school," he says, "was just one big interruption: I was concentrating on something inside of me. That's why I never liked TV. I was concentrating on the stories I was making up in my own head."

By the time he was seven and eight, he was covering sheets of paper with his own cartoons, making up his own strips with spirited and often witty interpretations in the spirit of Walt Kelly's Pogo, probably his favorite. "I didn't get most of the politics, but I loved the way the character was drawn," the artist says.

However, as clear as David Small's artistic future may have been from his family and friends' point of view, by the time David was eight he grew more and more intrigued by words, making up his own stories as intently as he created pictures. And by the time he was eleven, he knew that writing was what he wanted to do. In his teens, he could put it differently: Literature was a superior art form, fuller and broader. And harder. And because he always wanted to do the hard thing, his future was set: he would become a writer—no, he would become a playwright.

When he was seventeen, one of his plays was put on by a Detroit company, the Concept East. It was a "hot and steamy" Southern melodrama, conceived in part from stories and impressions left him by his Kentucky grandmother. It was received well, and he was encouraged.

Meanwhile, he kept drawing.

Even then a wry wit pervaded both his writing and his art, perhaps influenced by a father who had a cynical sense of humor. And perhaps, too, influenced by the increasingly troubled and torn environment of Detroit. Humor made up for a lot, he says.

The turn in the road for the Caldecott artist came unexpectedly. Not surprisingly, David Small chose to attend Wayne State University's Montieth College, an experimental college within the greater university, "run by a sociologist who thought if you gave kids blocks of knowledge and freedom, you would have a more complete person." In his sophomore year, one of his friends, a photographer by training, looked over his shoulder one day while he was doodling: "Those doodles that you draw at the edges of your pages are better than your playwriting," he said. And David listened.

Abruptly, at twenty, he took a right-angle turn and began studying art. First at Wayne State, and then at Yale University, where he received a masters degree in art and printmaking.

He describes his education as classical, but he has always been interested in the psychology of people and situations: Daumier and Goya and Redon were artists he admired for their interest in psychological states. They were artists with a dark side. Artists with a sardonic view of the world.

After graduation and for fourteen years, David Small taught printmaking, life drawing (his favorite subject), and design, first at Fredonia College in New York, then at Kalamazoo College in Michigan, but he continued to hone his appreciation for the sardonic. For years he worked as a freelance editorial artist, his drawings appearing in the *New Yorker,* the *New York Times,* and the *Wall Street Journal,* among others.

But it was in the field of children's literature that he gained his greatest popularity. Growing from draftsman to illustrator, he has illustrated twenty-nine picture books, six of them his own. He has celebrated the psychology of character and the relationship of environment to character in every single one—from *Imogene's Antlers* to *Fenwick's Suit,* both of which he wrote, to his 1998 Caldecott Honor Book *The Gardener,* written by his partner in life and art, Sarah Stewart.

The manuscript for *So You Want to Be President?* came to him as a surprise, but he contends that he had been waiting for it. His pleasure in political psychology, his old delight in Pogo, his sense of the sardonic, all were excited by the manuscript by author Judith St. George that celebrated the facts and foibles of our thirty-seven presidents. He began to illustrate the manuscript even before he signed a contract.

Sketching freely, wildly at times, he created page after page, tacking them up on his Michigan-farmhouse studio wall. Before the drawings were in the publisher's hands, visitors to the studio, looking at the sheets of ebullient drawings, were telling him that here was a book both wry and distinguished, a book that would make its mark.

From the moment it was published, the book garnered attention from reviewers, librarians, and teachers. Most commentary reflected the reader's delight that here was a book that integrated words and art, a genuinely *whole* book; and also a book that gave the reader a witty yet sure picture of the vulnerabilities and possibilities inherent in our American presidents. And a book that confirmed, somehow, the humanity in us all.

A Single Shard

written by
Linda Sue Park

published by
Clarion, 2001

HORN BOOK REVIEW

Tree-ear, a twelfth-century Korean boy, wants desperately to become a potter of celadon ware like the revered and talented potter Min. Though homeless and orphaned, Tree-ear wins the approval of Min, eventually becoming an indispensable apprentice to him. While the characters are somewhat flat and the plot slow, Park's story is alive with fascinating information about life and art in ancient Korea.—*Mary R. Holt*

2002 NEWBERY ACCEPTANCE SPEECH

Linda Sue Park

I would like to begin by proposing that we officially add a second "r" to the spelling of "Newbery." That way none of us ever has to see it misspelled again.

I understand it is traditional in this speech to discuss "The Call," so I am going to do that now and get it over with—because it was not one of my shining eloquent moments. I had gone to bed the night before with my fingers crossed for what I thought was the far-fetched possibility of a Newbery Honor for *A Single Shard*. That was as far as my dreams took me. So when Kathy Odean introduced herself and said something like, "We're delighted to tell you that *A Single Shard* has been named the 2002 Newbery Award book," I was utterly unprepared. I thought she must have said "*honored*." "Award?" I said. "Yes," she said, "we're so excited, we think it's a wonderful book." "The *Award*?" I said again. "Yes, the Award," she said. "That would be the winner, with the gold sticker."

At that point my knees buckled, which had never happened to me before. And I remember thinking, "I've read this! 'Her knees buckled'—so this is what it feels like!"

Kathy also explained that the speakerphone wasn't working, so she was the only one who heard me make a complete fool of myself in three words or less. About fifteen minutes after I'd hung up, the phone rang again. "Hi, this is Kathleen Odean again," and I was sure she was calling to say that there had been a mistake. But instead she said, "The speakerphone is working now, and we all want to hear you." So I am honored to have received The Call twice in one day!

Since that day I have been asked many times how I came to write a book worthy of that precious sticker. I would like to begin my answer here tonight by telling a story.

Once upon a time there was a young Korean couple. They had been in America for only a few years, and their English was not very good. They were living in the Chicago suburbs, and a city newspaper ran on its comics pages a single-frame cartoon that taught the alphabet phonetically. The young woman cut out every one of those cartoons and glued them onto the pages of one of her old college textbooks. In this way she made an alphabet book for her four-year-old daughter. And so it was that on her first day of school, that little girl, the daughter of Korean immigrants, was the only child in her kindergarten class who could already read.

That was how my life as a reader began—like so many stories, with a mother. Mine continued with a father who took me to the library. *He took me to the library.* (That was the Park Forest Public Library in Park Forest, Illinois.) Every two weeks without fail, unless we were out of town, he spent an hour each Saturday morning choosing books for my siblings and me.

A few years ago, I was thinking about how my father must have known very little about American children's literature when we were growing up. So I asked him, "How did you choose books for us?" "Oh—I'll show you," he said. He left the room for a few moments and came back with a battered accordion file and handed it to me. Inside were dozens of publications listing recommended children's books—brochures, flyers, pamphlets—and most of them were issued by ALA.

The importance of my library upbringing was brought home to me in an unexpected way with the publication of my first book, *Seesaw Girl.* In the summer of 1999, my editor, Dinah Stevenson at Clarion Books, sent me my first author copy, and as you might imagine, it was the most thrilling moment of my life (that is, until the morning of January 21!). I loved Jean and Mou-sien Tseng's cover artwork. It was unquestionably the most beautiful book that had ever been published. But . . . but . . . something was niggling at me, something wasn't quite right, and I had no idea what it was.

A few weeks later, I had my first book signing. A woman with a book bag approached the table and said, "I'm a librarian. I already bought two copies of your book for our collection—would you mind signing previously purchased copies?" Of course I didn't mind, so she pulled the two books out of her bag and handed them to me.

They were already covered with that clear cellophane, you know the stuff I mean.

And it was like a lightning bolt—*that* was what had been missing from my first author copy! That transparent cover was what made a "real" book!

A Single Shard has so many connections to reading and other books that it's hard to know where to begin. The idea itself was born when I was doing research for *Seesaw Girl*. I have done a lot of research for all of my books, because my childhood was pretty typically suburban American. My family ate Korean food and kept other aspects of Korean culture alive in our home, but I knew very little about Korea itself. And a crucial point, I do not speak Korean, other than those three phrases essential in any language: *anyanghaseyo* (hello); *komopsunida* (thank you); and *pyunsul odisoyo* (where is the bathroom?). I often feel the lack of my ancestral tongue keenly, but on the other hand, I try not to forget the flip side—that when I write, I am writing in my first language.

So I learned about Korea by reading and writing about it, and what I learned was so interesting that I thought I might like to pass it on, especially to young people. I do not believe you have to have children or be around children or act like a child to write for children. But I do believe that good children's writers share two characteristics with their readers: curiosity and enthusiasm. These qualities are what make books for young people such a joyful challenge to write and read: the ardent desire to learn more about the world and the passion with which that knowledge is received and shared.

In my reading I came across the information that in the eleventh and twelfth centuries, Korea had produced the finest pottery in the world, better than even China's, and I decided to set my third novel in that time period. As I was mulling over story ideas, my son said something like, "Why can't you write books like Gary Paulsen's?" He had loved *Hatchet* and wanted me to write an adventure story, a road book. So that is where the journey part of the story came in.

During the writing of the book, I got hopelessly stuck because I was not familiar with the part of Korea Tree-ear had to travel through. Photographs and maps were simply not enough, and I did not have the wherewithal for a trip to Korea. I was in writerly despair. And just at that time I came across a book called *Korea: A Walk through the Land of Miracles,* by Simon Winchester.

He will be more familiar to many of you as the author of the best-selling *The Professor and the Madman*, about the making of the Oxford English Dictionary, but years earlier he had written this book about Korea, which I had purchased and never read and forgotten about. I found it in a box at my parents' house. Not only had the author walked the length of South Korea in 1987, but he had walked *exactly* where I needed him to walk, from Puyo almost all the way to Songdo. He described the landscape and what it was like to walk so far over that specific terrain, and I had what I needed to complete the book. I am happy to have the opportunity to thank Mr. Winchester publicly here, for *Shard* would not have been the same story without his work.

The ending of *Shard* came to me in a single moment: when I saw the photograph of a beautiful celadon vase covered with cranes and clouds in a book of Korean art. I knew in that instant that the character in the book would grow up to make that vase. And for him to make such a remarkable work of art, he would need not only tremendous craftsmanship but also a great love for someone who had something to do with cranes. (By the way, when I first saw that photo, I thought the birds on the vase were storks. In early drafts, Craneman is called "Stork-man"!)

Much later, after the book was finished, I realized that the story owed a huge debt to another book: *I, Juan de Pareja,* by Elizabeth Borton de Treviño, which won the Newbery Medal in 1966. In that book, the orphaned black slave Juan de Pareja becomes an assistant to the painter Velasquez and is eventually freed by his master, which enables him to pursue his own painting career. The ending speculates on how a certain Velasquez work came to be painted, just as *Shard* speculates about that vase.

Juan de Pareja had been one of my favorite books as a child, and I read it again from time to time, always with great pleasure. Last winter I wrote an article for *Booklist* in which I listed what have proven to be the three most memorable books of my childhood and described what I had loved about them. I was startled to realize that two of the three titles featured black protagonists—Juan and *Roosevelt Grady,* by Louisa Shotwell—and that the third, *What Then, Raman?* by Shirley Arora, was about another dark-skinned child, a boy living in India.

In retrospect, it should not have been surprising. When I was a child, there were hardly any books featuring Asian characters. I did not realize it at the time, but I had obviously responded to the plight of "the outsider" in those three books. The relationship between Korean Americans and African Americans has a troubled history here in the U.S.; sporadic headlines over the years tell the sad story of animosity and even violence between the two. It seems to me that Korean Americans believe they do not have much in common with black Americans. My reading experience as a child proves otherwise, and it would be among my proudest accomplishments if one day my work plays a small part in helping these two groups feel more connected to each other.

Connections. Making connections has always been the most important element of story to me. Connections to another time and place and to my own ethnic background in historical fiction; connections to a character within the text; connections to people around us because of a text. A few years ago, my son and I were not getting along very well. I knew it was normal adolescent/parent stuff, but that did not make it any easier. I would like to read now from an e-mail I sent to another author after my son and I had finally gotten through that difficult time.

Here in part is what I wrote:

> It seems I have only one good memory of our relationship during that eternal year: your books. We talked about daemons endlessly, assigning them to each other, everyone we knew, television personalities, strangers, and so on. . . . We consoled each other when we lost Lee Scoresby. In a hundred ways the books gave us things to talk about during a time when it seemed any other attempt at communication was doomed to end in raised voices and slammed doors. . . . I admire many things about the series, and about your other books, too. But it is one thing to admire certain books and another to say they have truly made a difference in a person's life. Thank you most sincerely for the difference His Dark Materials has made in mine.

Most of you will have realized that the author is Philip Pullman, who recently won England's Whitbread Award for *The Amber Spyglass*. His books helped my son and me connect during a time when we needed it most. So it seemed a special serendipity that Mr. Pullman's Whitbread Award was announced on the same day as the Newbery.

Mr. Pullman answered me most graciously, and in another e-mail to a literature group, he closed his message with the exhortation to "Include! Include!" When I read that, my idea of the importance of "connection" was at once broadened. As well as connections—those straight lines of contact—"inclusion" seems equally apt, the idea of widening the circle. Widening the definition of "American" to include people with diverse ethnic roots, and widening the audience for books about all sorts of obscure places and times: these are vital forces in my work.

I write my books on what I call "The Pizza Model." Fifty years ago, pizza was a strange exotic food, the subject of ethnic slurs. Now, not only does it have coast-to-coast acceptance, but American chefs and eaters have made it their own: in Italy you would be hard put to find a Cajun-blackened-chicken pizza topped with mango salsa on a whole-wheat sourdough crust! In the same way, I think of *Shard* as an "American" novel. Its setting and characters may be twelfth-century Korean, but its author was concerned with the search for belonging and the drive to innovate, both very much part of the American experience. This strikes me as a fine parallel to both the Newbery Medal itself—named for an Englishman, yet now wholly American—and to American culture as a whole. It is one of our great strengths that we have such a richness of cultures from which to draw in the continuing evolution of our own.

Is it important that I am the first Asian American in seventy-five years to have been awarded the Newbery Medal? In some ways, yes. Seventy-five years is a long time—three or four generations. We all know now how important it is for young people to see themselves reflected in positive images from the culture around them. And I think it is even more important for those in the majority to see images of people of color in a variety of contexts, to move away from seeing them as "other."

However, I was pleased by Kathleen Odean's comment that the book's multiculturalism was not a factor in its selection. Certainly I did not write the book with an overt political agenda in mind. It has also been difficult for me to deal with the idea of becoming a sort of poster child for Korean Americans and for Asian writers in general.

I feel strongly that the author's bio should be kept separate from consideration of the text itself, so much so that for my first three books I declined to have my photo printed on the back flap. I wanted the books to stand or fall on their own, without help or hindrance from information about my ethnicity. And I still believe that this is the goal—the ideal we must strive for. But the response from Korea and Korean Americans demonstrates that we are still a long way from inhabiting that ideal world. I was stunned and humbled to learn what the award for *A Single Shard* means to so many people, young and old, complete strangers, who have written to tell me how proud they are that a book set in Korea by a Korean American had won this award—how they now feel included in a way that they did not before.

To "include!" also means to widen the experience of all children by giving them books they might not have chosen for themselves, in the hope that they will find their own connections within the pages. You librarians are the ones who have taken on this task, for which every reader and writer in the land is or should be grateful.

In the months since the award announcement, my own circle of inclusion has widened exponentially. I must take time here to thank those at its center:

my parents, Ed and Susie Park, who are so proud of me. My brother Fred and my sister Julie and their families, who have supported me in so many ways. My husband, Ben Dobbin, who has given me the two most precious gifts a writer can receive. First, the impetus to write my first book—as I recall, his words were something like, "For God's sake, would you stop yapping about it and just *write* it!?" And second, the time and personal space a writer needs so badly.

My children, Sean and Anna, have also given me that time and space, which is an even greater gift from a child. And they have given me the privilege of being their mother. I would like to thank Anna here for her unwitting encouragement: when *A Single Shard* was in manuscript, she was nine years old. I read it aloud to her, and every night she said the four words a writer most longs to hear: "One more chapter—please?" Writing friends in Rochester and elsewhere, and the online children's literature community, have provided companionship to balance the daily isolation. My writing partner, Marsha Hayles, is always at the other end of the phone line with time for sharing, and my agent, Ginger Knowlton, was a zealous supporter long before the big news.

Most of all I must thank the people at Clarion Books: Joann Hill and Debora Smith in the art department; Marjorie Naughton and Deb Shapiro in marketing; Managing Editor Jim Armstrong; they and all the staff make me feel like my books are the only ones they have to work on.

And no matter how long I speak or how much I write, I will never be able to thank my editor, Dinah Stevenson, sufficiently. She pulled my first book from the slush pile and has guided me every step of the way to this podium. I keep trying to think of new ways to thank her, but in the end I will have to accept what Tree-ear realized, that there are some things that cannot be molded into words.

To Kathleen Odean and the members of the 2002 Newbery committee, thank you for dialing that 585 area code on the morning of January 21—not once, but twice. I will think of you with amazed gratitude every day for the rest of my life.

I would like to close now with an image from Korean mythology. Koreans say that an eon is the length of time it takes for a heavenly spirit to wear a mountain down to a pebble—by stroking it with a feather. I love this image. All of us are here in this world for only a single stroke of that feather—but together we can wear away even the most intractable rock of a problem. And we can make our time count even more by touching the lives of others—especially the young people who follow us. So . . . Connect! Include!

Linda Sue Park

A FEW WEEKS before ALA Midwinter, Linda Sue Park sent me an e-mail: "I've gotten several e-mails from people congratulating me for the results of 'mock Newberys' that are coming in from library systems all over—*Shard* has been named an Honor Book a few times. I know I should be pleased, and I am, I'm thrilled to pieces, but it's also making me completely neurotic. Sometimes I wish people would just stop talking about it."

I understood perfectly. I have always been superstitious about awards, and I firmly believe that talking about them is a jinx. I thought that *A Single Shard* might have an outside chance at an Honor, but there wasn't much point getting excited about the possibility beforehand, because it could just as easily not happen. My honest answer was: "Committees are unpredictable. There is no way to anticipate the actual winners and honorees. Take what you're getting now as compliments from enthusiastic fans, because that's what it is. And that's *all* it is."

Linda Sue thanked me for my sage advice and claimed she felt much calmer.

Now, of course, the advice doesn't seem quite so sage. I can't help feeling that a truly perspicacious editor, which Linda Sue thinks I am, would have had some kind of sixth-sense warning of an impending Newbery. I didn't have a clue. One of the things that makes working with her such a pleasure is that she is so appreciative and complimentary that I have to be careful about my hat size. Perhaps my failure to predict the Newbery will disillusion her. But not entirely, I hope.

I have been working with Linda Sue since I signed up her first book, *Seesaw Girl,* in October 1997. Hers is an amazing true publishing success story: from unsolicited submission to Newbery winner in three novels. She told me once that certain other writers felt she had gone about it all wrong. Apparently, beginners are supposed to undergo a lengthy initiation period of submitting projects, having them rejected, and suffering. Linda Sue simply skipped that step.

In fact, according to the conventional wisdom and protocol of aspiring children's book writers, she did a number of things wrong. She sent her first query letter to twenty-two publishers without first researching the kinds of books they did. She said in the query letter that the children in her daughter's second-grade class loved the story. (Professionals learn they're never,

never supposed to say anything like that, even if it's true.) Moreover, she failed to enclose a self-addressed stamped envelope. While I was reviewing her manuscript for *Seesaw Girl,* she sent me a revision (she had waited a week and was growing impatient). And when I phoned to say I wanted to publish her book, she asked me whether there was any chance I was going to change my mind.

Linda Sue may have been a complete novice about submitting children's books for publication. But she knew plenty about children's books. An enthusiastic reader—her word is *maniacal*—from an early age, Linda Sue read indiscriminately and returned to her favorite books again and again. She retained a deeply ingrained sense of the pacing and structure of good middle-grade fiction, as well as some very specific memories. One of these that would become important later came from a collection of folklore retellings, *Tales of a Korean Grandmother* by Frances Carpenter—a reference to the fact that girls from noble families in seventeenth-century Korea were never allowed to leave their homes. This made a huge impression on her at age ten.

Something else that stuck in her mind came from one of the Little House books, which she probably read around the same time. The manuscript of her second novel, *The Kite Fighters,* had been accepted and was already moving toward publication when Linda Sue phoned me in something close to panic. Reading Laura Ingalls Wilder to her daughter, Anna, then nine, she came across a familiar paragraph and realized that she had unintentionally echoed its rhythm and structure in her manuscript. Did this mean she was an unconscious plagiarist—a kind of literary Jekyll and Hyde? No, I said, it meant she was the kind of reader who took things in very deeply, and I encouraged her simply to rework the offending paragraph.

After receiving a B.A. in English from Stanford University, Linda Sue worked in Chicago, went to graduate school in Dublin and then in London, married an Irish journalist (on the eighty-ninth day of her ninety-day fiancée visa), and had two children.

Linda Sue had been raised in the Midwest to be "more American than Americans." English had been spoken at home, and she learned only a few words of Korean. Living in London, her children got to know their Irish grandparents; the other side of the family was on the other side of the Atlantic. Making connections despite huge gaps between generations, between continents, between languages, is the theme of Linda Sue's poem called "Halmoni," which is the Korean word for grandmother:

She speaks; my mother speaks. The sounds crackle
and reach me always a second too late. I look down
at the babe in his swaddled sleep and find the answer.
Mother, please tell her that Sean is the Irish for John,
the man who baptized Jesus.
I hear Korean, then nothing, then the noise
of laughing and crying at the same time, Jong,
a wonderful, beautiful name, such a perfect choice.
She and my son will never meet, but as he grows
he will hear her voice on the phone
and learn to answer to Jong.

After seven years in London, Linda Sue, her husband, Ben, and the children moved back to the States. Now she wanted to share with her children the Korean side of their heritage. Realizing that her Korean background was something she'd need to learn about before she could pass it on, she began investigating Korean history. A writer all her life—poems, stories, ad copy, newspaper articles, annual reports—she found her research meshing with the story idea she had been carrying with her since childhood, about a well-brought-up girl in seventeenth-century Korea eager to escape, even temporarily, the confines of her upbringing.

Linda Sue began to write. She thought the story might be a picture book, but the first draft was three thousand words and the second draft six thousand. After four months, she had ten thousand words. To her surprise, *Seesaw Girl* had turned out to be a middle-grade novel. Depending on how you calculate, it had taken her either six months or almost thirty years to write.

She went on to write three more novels, each growing from a nugget of information about Korean history and culture. *The Kite Fighters* places in fifteenth-century Korea the story of two brothers, their rivalry in their traditional roles of first (important) and second (unimportant) son and their partnership in building and flying kites. Linda Sue's father, who told her about the Korean sport of kite fighting when she was a child, had been a second son and is a devoted kite flyer. Linda Sue considers this book in many ways a tribute to him, which made it all the more meaningful that it was he who drew the decorations that open each chapter.

The idea of a small country, Korea, being better at something—ceramics—than its larger and more powerful neighbors China and Japan appealed to her and became the basis for *A Single Shard*.

When My Name Was Keoko grew from a reference to young Korean men serving as kamikaze pilots in the Japanese army during World War II, and from her own parents' recollections of growing up in Korea under the Japanese occupation. The book's working title was *The Most Beautiful Tree in the World,* referring to the rose of Sharon tree that is the national tree of Korea, until Sean, then fifteen, stated flatly that no boy would read a book about a beautiful tree.

Doing the research for her books made Linda Sue "feel Korean." She began to see aspects of her upbringing—the emphasis on schooling, for example—in the context of Korean tradition. "Suddenly a whole bunch of my childhood made sense. I was illuminating my own past."

The response to her books makes it clear that she is illuminating the Korean past for many readers as well. She has a sharp eye for the telling details that bring the setting to life, and unobtrusively introduces and explains aspects of the culture that might seem alien, or arbitrary, to a young American reader. The bridge over the gap is often a process—embroidering a panel for a screen, inventing and constructing a Korean standing-and-jumping seesaw, building and decorating a kite, preparing clay for the potter's hand. The reader sharing these experiences with the characters becomes so deeply immersed in their world that it can be a surprise to look up from the page and find oneself at home. Perhaps the fact that Linda Sue was learning to feel Korean as she went along makes her an especially empathetic guide.

Another bridge between characters and readers is food. Linda Sue was a food writer at one time and has won cooking contests. She has passed her interest in food along to her family—her son's requested dinner menu for his fourth birthday included stuffed artichokes and calamari—and brings it to her books. We learn what her characters like to eat and what happens during meals. *A Single Shard* begins with hunger and a discovery of rice; Tree-ear's relationships with Crane-man and with Min's wife, Ajima, are partly expressed in terms of the sharing of food. The progress of the Japanese occupation and the war in *When My Name Was Keoko* is reflected in the gradual disappearance of familiar foodstuffs, and despite the privations of wartime, a broken friendship is repaired over popcorn.

As it happens, Linda Sue's editor is also interested in food. Our e-mails often touch on recipes and menus, and an embarrassing amount of time goes into deciding where we will have lunch when she comes to New York. These meals are always a lot of fun, as Linda Sue is adventurous and knowledgeable and serious about eating without taking it too seriously. She eats salad with her fingers. She's glad to share but only if everyone wants to. And if she orders a dish that a friend or family member loves, she will have part of it wrapped to take along and give away.

Linda Sue has the kind of effervescent generosity that can only come from a spontaneous pleasure in giving and sharing. Following the announcement that

A Single Shard had won the Newbery Medal, she came into the Clarion offices with a large paper shopping bag full of wrapped packages and a list of everyone at Clarion who worked on her books—the managing editor, the designer, the associate editor, the sub rights person, the part-time marketing assistant. . . . Everyone got a present, something made of celadon ware. It's a Korean tradition: good fortune is to be shared. It's also very much like Linda Sue.

On that same post-Newbery visit to New York, Linda Sue asked which store had the best petites department. *Petites?* I looked at her, noticing not for the first time that the top of her head is more or less level with my collarbone, and registered that she is indeed what clothing manufacturers call petite. It's an idea that takes some getting used to; her personality, her presence, is large.

Even now, months after the announcement, Linda Sue doesn't entirely believe that she has won the Newbery Medal. She prefers to refer to it as "the N word" or "the N." When she opened the carton of books she had ordered and saw gold seals on the jackets, she was amazed all over again: "Will I ever get used to this?" she e-mailed me. "Yes," I wrote back, "but probably not anytime soon."

I look across my office at the celadon vase ornamented with cranes and clouds that Linda Sue took out of her shopping bag in January and presented to me. I'm not used to this either, and I didn't see it coming—but I get to share it even so. That, to me, is good fortune.

The Three Pigs

written and illustrated by
David Wiesner

published by
Clarion, 2001

HORN BOOK REVIEW

David Wiesner's postmodern interpretation of this tale plays imaginatively with traditional picture book and story conventions and with readers' expectations of both. (Though with Wiesner, we should know by now to expect the unexpected.) Astute readers will notice the difference between the cover's realistic gouache portrait of the three pigs (who stare directly out at the viewer with sentient expressions) and the simple outlined watercolor artwork on the title page. In fact, the style of the illustrations and the way the characters are rendered shift back and forth a few times before the book is done, as Wiesner explores the possibility of different realities within a book's pages. The text, set in a respectable serif typeface, begins by following the familiar pattern—pigs build houses, wolf huffs and puffs, wolf eats two pigs, etc. But while the text natters on obliviously, the pigs actually step (or are huffed and puffed) out of the muted-color panel illustrations *without* being eaten. Escaping their sepia holding lines and the frames of their predictable storybook world, they enter a stark white landscape where they are depicted realistically with more intricate shading. The now-3-D-looking pigs, released from the story's inevitability, explore this surrealistic realm. The perplexed wolf remains behind in the two-dimensional pages, which, when viewed from the pigs' new vantage point, stand vertically in space, looking altogether like paper dominoes waiting to be knocked down. And that's what the three pigs do, with glee. The pigs' informal banter appears in word balloons in a sans serif font; a few striking wordless spreads feature the pigs flying (this *is* Wiesner, after all) across blank spreads on a paper airplane made from a page of their story. Obviously, there's a lot going on here, but once you get your bearings, this is a fantastic journey told with a light touch. The pigs encounter other freestanding story pages; they enter and exit a nursery rhyme and then a folktale, morphing into and out of each one's illustrative style. Saccharine, cotton-candy illustrations cloy "Hey Diddle Diddle" ("Let's get out of here!" one pig exclaims); precise black-and-white line drawings dignify a folktale about a dragon who guards a golden rose. The cat and its fiddle as well as the chivalrous dragon join the pigs in full-color, realistic definition, and eventually the five friends end up back at the pigs' story. After shaking the type off the pages, the animals re-enter the tale—but this time on the pigs' own terms. The last page shows them all happily ensconced in the full-page watercolor illustration, using letters of text to write their own happy ending while the wolf sits outside at a nonthreatening distance. Wiesner may not be the first to thumb his nose at picture-book design rules and storytelling techniques, but he puts his own distinct print on this ambitious endeavor. There are lots of teaching opportunities to be mined here—or you can just dig into the creative possibilities of unconventionality.—*Kitty Flynn*

2002 CALDECOTT ACCEPTANCE SPEECH

David Wiesner

So there I am, sitting at my desk early that Monday morning, getting ready to start working. The phone rings. I answer and a voice says, "Congratulations, you have been awarded the Randolph Caldecott Medal . . . for 1992."

When delivering my speech the last time I won the Caldecott, I never mentioned how I heard the news. Afterward, many people came up to me and commented on this omission. Why hadn't I followed the tradition? Well, now you know. It wasn't very interesting. I wasn't in the shower, awakened from sleep, or caught in some other noteworthy situation. I just answered the phone. I was alone in my studio; my wife, Kim, had already left for work; the Clarion staff was at Midwinter; and my artist friends were all still asleep. So after the initial flurry of phone calls, I, too, went to work.

This year, when the call came to inform me that I had won the 2002 Caldecott Medal . . . I just answered the phone again. Twenty minutes earlier and I would've been in the shower. Kate, your timing is a little off. The big difference this year is that I was not alone. This time, Kim, our son Kevin, and our daughter Jaime were there with me. In fact, the three of them were jumping up and down, holding hands, and skipping in a circle, chanting, "Daddy won the Caldecott! Daddy won the Caldecott!" Being able to share that moment with my family has been the best part of this experience.

The fact that I can use the phrase "the last time I won the Caldecott" is still hard to believe. To be honored a second time is an amazing feeling. I want to thank Kate McClelland and the entire 2002 Caldecott committee for letting me experience this all over again. Many people have made the comment that it must be nothing new because I've been through it before. I may be familiar with the process, but there is definitely nothing routine about it.

First frogs, now pigs. The animal kingdom has been very good to me. *The Three Pigs* is the culmination of nearly a lifetime of thinking about a particular visual concept. And it all started with Bugs Bunny.

I watched a lot of Bugs when I was a kid. There is one specific cartoon where, as usual, Bugs is being chased around and around by Elmer Fudd. But this time they run right out of the cartoon. We see the frames of the filmstrip flicker by, as well as the sprocket holes at the edge of the film. Bugs and Elmer finally stop, and they find themselves standing in a blank white space. They look around and then run back into the cartoon, which flickers, and then continues running normally. Even more than all the reality manipulation that was happening in the cartoon, I was fascinated by the idea that behind the "normal" reality lay this endless, empty, white nothingness.

I played with this idea in my artwork as I was growing up, and when I eventually realized that making books was what I was going to do, I looked for ways to bring this concept to those books. I wanted to be able to push the pictures aside, go behind them or peel them up, and explore the blank expanse that I envisioned was within the books. I had ideas for so many neat visual things that could happen. Characters could jump out of the story. The pictures could fall down, be folded up, crumpled; text could get scattered about. What I didn't have was a story. Every time I tried to turn these ideas into a book, I ran into the same stumbling block. If I created a story and then had the characters leave to take part in a new story, the reader would be left wondering what was happening in the initial story. To make this idea work, I realized that I needed a story that as many kids as possible would already know, so that when the characters took off, the reader would leave the story behind as well and concentrate on the new journey the characters would take.

So, I thought, what are the most universal stories around? In a way, any story would do. "Goldilocks"? "Hansel and Gretel"? And then, right on cue, up stepped those three pigs. Ever since I had pigs float away on the last page of *Tuesday,* I had wanted to use pigs as the main characters in a book. Here at last was my chance. Everything about "The Three Little Pigs" fit my needs perfectly. The pigs have every reason in the world to want to get out of their story. Every time it is read, the first two pigs get eaten up. This cannot be much fun. They were also clearly in need of a place where they could be safe, a place they could really call home. Interestingly enough, this pretty much described my family's situation at the time I was conceiving *The Three Pigs.* Circumstances led us to move from our home in Philadelphia, not something we had anticipated. For several months we knew we had to move, but we didn't know where we would end up. This uncertainty and sense of displacement very much fed into the story I was creating. I could really relate to those pigs. Fortunately, my family found what we were looking for—and so did the pigs.

Now that I had a story, I was ready to knock it down. When those pigs got behind the pictures they found themselves surrounded by a brilliant, white, overwhelming nothing. Up until now my books and the term *white space* had not gone hand in hand. This was about to change.

When I begin a new book, I always like to talk with the production department to find out how my idea can best be realized during the printing. Donna McCarthy and Andi Stern, masters of the printing process, have always assured me that if I thought it up, they would find a way to reproduce it. This time I think I gave them pause. There was going to be a lot of blank paper in this book. They were concerned that books would be returned under the assumption that there had been a mistake in the printing. And, in fact, there have been phone calls about just that issue. But in the context of the story, that emptiness creates as much of a sense of place as does an elaborately detailed illustration.

Many of my books have had few or no words, which left my art director, Carol Goldenberg, with little to do. This, of course, is not true. But it did often leave very little typesetting, something I know she loves. With *The Three Pigs* I decided to make up for all those years of neglect and see how many ways I could distort, crumple, and scatter the text to create a typesetting nightmare for her. In the end, it was fun. Painful, but fun. For her years of insight, commiseration, and always-welcome input, I dedicated *The Three Pigs* to Carol.

The word most often used in reviews of *The Three Pigs* has been *postmodern*. The word most often used by me while making the book was *fun*. I saw an opportunity to have some great visual fun, and I wanted to share that with kids who may have thought the way I did when I was their age, and the way I do now. The beauty of the picture book is that despite its seemingly rigid format, it is capable of containing an infinite number of approaches to storytelling. As a walk through any library or bookstore will confirm, those thirty-two pages get taken down a staggering variety of artistic paths.

Getting feedback from kids of any age is always great, but I particularly love hearing from kids in fifth grade, eighth grade, sometimes even high school. There comes a point with books when the words and pictures seem to part company. Whether with novels or textbooks, eventually the visuals fall by the wayside. I find this sad. The picture book at its best is a seamless blend of word and picture, where one is incomplete without the other. And unlike an image on a screen, the pictures in a book do not fly by in the blink of an eye. So I am heartened to hear from those older kids out there and to know that someone is continuing to expose them to this unique art form.

My creative process is a solitary one. It is something I get excited about, struggle with, succeed and fail at, and have a great deal of fun with. In the end, though, it comes down to me and that blank piece of paper. Despite this, there have been many people who have given me encouragement, advice, and inspiration that have added immeasurably to the direction and richness of my work.

First and foremost was my family. While I was growing up, they created an atmosphere where my interest in art was always taken seriously. My mother's approach was unconditional acceptance. She saved everything I drew when I was little. Finger paintings, pictures of kites with the tail made from string and pasta bows, and scrawl-like crayon drawings. The historical revisionist in me can now point to preprinted pages of vegetables I colored in during kindergarten and say, "Aha! *June 29, 1999*, started here!" Having these things to look back over is one of the greatest gifts I've ever received.

My father, a scientist, has said that since art was so outside his frame of reference, he felt he had nothing to offer me in the way of guidance. This turned out to be completely untrue. He was so excited by what I was doing that he investigated anything he thought could help me. Through family and friends, he found people in the art field for me to talk to. He researched art schools before I even knew such places existed. When I was about thirteen, he did something I'm sure didn't seem like that big of a deal at the time. One day when he came home from work, a truck pulled in behind him. In the back of the truck was a great big old wooden drafting table and an equally great old chair. They had been discarded at work, and he had brought them home for me. Taking up a large part of my room, this table became my own personal, private world where I could explore the outer reaches of my imagination.

And while most of the time they dealt with me as one does with the youngest in the family, my sisters and brother—Carol, George, Bobbi, and Pat—shared their own artistic knowledge and wholeheartedly encouraged me to further mine.

In art school, I met a lot of kids who had gone through huge family battles to be there or, possibly worse, had endured total indifference. I thank my family for creating such a nurturing atmosphere in which my talents were able to flourish.

Visual storytelling became the main focus of my work while in art school, although I wasn't really sure what form to apply it to. I first became truly aware of the picture book while taking classes with David Macaulay at the Rhode Island School of Design. It was there that I learned the technical process of book design and then was urged to push the boundaries of that design as far as made sense in the context of the story. Whether through his teaching or by the example of his remarkable work, David's enthusiasm for the possibilities of the picture book form was and is infectious. *The Three Pigs* represents my application of that creative spirit, and it was clear to me from the beginning that this book would be dedicated to David as well.

After art school I might have entered the illustration world without a real focus were it not for a moment of great serendipity. At the end of my senior year, Trina Schart Hyman came to speak about being a children's book illustrator. She stayed a second day to look at student portfolios. I was on my way out of the Illustration Building when one of my teachers said, "Aren't you going to talk to Trina?" I wasn't. I was considering children's books, but for some now-mysterious reason I was also considering things like science-fiction and fantasy book jackets and editorial magazine illustration. Thankfully, I did show her my work. At the time, Trina was the art director for *Cricket* magazine. As we finished looking at my portfolio, she said, "How would you like to do a cover for *Cricket*?" I thought this might have been some kind of a joke. But she wasn't kidding, and I did the cover, and I never thought about editorial or science-fiction illustration again. Thanks, Trina, for that risky and generous offer, which pointed me down the path to picture books without any wasteful detours.

This generous spirit has been a recurring trait among the people I've met within this field. I began to work with Dilys Evans as my agent a year after my graduation. This was also the end of Dilys's first year in business. Back then I spent many afternoons at her apartment/office. We would have tea, brainstorm ideas, and discuss work—or the lack of it. Dilys would hold impromptu seminars to fill in the large gaps in my knowledge of the history of children's books. During gatherings at Dilys's apartment I was incredibly fortunate to get to know Hilary Knight and Margot Tomes. Even now it amazes me. I was doing textbook work and little early readers, and they were genuinely interested in and supportive of what I was doing. It has been Dilys's mission from the beginning to help me do exactly what I wanted to do, and to find the best situation to do it in. I can't thank her enough for all these years of friendship and tireless support. It was Dilys who said that when I was ready to write my own stories, there was an editor she was sure would respond to my ideas. That editor was Dorothy Briley, and Dilys was absolutely right. Dorothy taught me many things during the years we worked together. She kept my focus on the important elements of making a good story without ever hindering my wilder flights of imagination. I will always be grateful to Dorothy for that guidance and encouragement at such a formative time in my career.

I was fortunate to have become friends with Dinah Stevenson during the time I was working with Dorothy. She had given me feedback during the making of most of my pre-pigs books, but *The Three Pigs* is the first time we have worked together as author and editor. It seems to be going well. Dinah and I had great fun making *The Three Pigs*. She asked tough questions and gave great advice. When, for a brief moment, I wondered if having the pigs fly around on a paper airplane was too weird, she responded, "No. Weird is good." Thank you, Dinah. I look forward to much future weirdness together.

Working at Clarion Books, I have found myself surrounded by people who were willing to do all they could to help me do what I love to do. In addition to those I have already mentioned, I'd like to say thanks to Nader Darehshori, Wendy Strothman, Anita Silvey, Joann Hill, and everyone on the editorial and art staffs who have made Clarion my home away from home.

Finally, to tie up some important loose ends, for encouragement and inspiration I want to thank, in no particular order, Jon Gnagy, Jean Shepherd, Jack Kirby, Jim Steranko, Robert Bernabe, Marcia Leonard, Barbara Lucas, the Ramones, Mike Hays, Julie Downing, and the entire Kahng family.

For years my wife, Kim, has been the only person who actually got to watch me work. That part is not a spectator sport. Over the last ten years this small circle has grown by two: our son Kevin and our daughter Jaime. There was a time when the thought of sharing those parts of my creative self with anyone seemed impossible. Now, to imagine it any other way is unthinkable.

ILLUSTRATOR PROFILE BY ANITA SILVEY

David Wiesner

IN JANUARY 2002 David Wiesner joined an elite circle, those who have won more than one Caldecott Medal. This "inner circle of the inner circle" includes Robert McCloskey, Nonny Hogrogian, Leo and Diane Dillon, Barbara Cooney, Chris Van Allsburg, and Marcia Brown (the only artist with three medals). Once an exceptional new talent to the field of children's books, David Wiesner has become a seasoned artist who has lived up to expectations. In a time fraught with difficulties in children's book publishing and in the nurturing of talented creators, why did David's artistic career evolve in a way that seems so right? What personal convictions and principles has he followed that helped lead to a second Caldecott

Medal? As David's publisher for several years and friend for many more, I tried to answer these questions. (For those seeking a more personal, traditional biography, see David Macaulay's essay in the July 1992 *Horn Book*. Written when David Wiesner won his first Caldecott for *Tuesday*, the sketch serves as a magnificent "Portrait of the Artist as a Young Man.")

In the decade since *Tuesday*, David has grown up in the children's book field and found his own voice. In *The Three Pigs* he pays homage to his mentors (L. Leslie Brooke, Howard Pyle, Trina Schart Hyman) without echoing them. His endearing shyness remains, but behind it one senses confidence and strength. Carol Goldenberg, David's art director for many years, describes him as "a regular guy who happens to be a genius." Part of that genius stems from the choices he has made in his personal and artistic life.

In a world of increasing change, David Wiesner seeks out and creates stability. He values and maintains his own nuclear family. Much like the family into which he was born, it nurtures and sustains him. His wife Kim Kahng, a valedictorian turned medical doctor, pursues her own career, still being present to support David. In this decade, they had two children, Kevin and Jaime. Functioning as an at-home father, David sees his children off to school or activities and waits for their return. For David, his family always takes precedence; one thinks of him first as a husband, then a father, and then the creator of books.

By his own choice, David remained loyal to the editor who discovered him. Dorothy Briley always maintained that David came into her life because of some old furniture. Dilys Evans, then working at *Cricket*, had decided to become an agent for artists, something new in the children's book field. While talking to Dilys one day, Dorothy noticed some extra chairs in her Lothrop offices. "Here," she said, "take these. You need them more than I do." Touched by Dorothy's largesse of company chairs, Dilys accepted the offer, promising to give Dorothy the first look when she found someone exciting to represent. And so, one day, Dilys brought Dorothy some of David's early drawings. Dorothy always had an uncanny knack for investment. She believed that David and her association with him proved far more valuable than office chairs.

Unlike many high-profile creators who write a book a year, David published only four books in the decade following *Tuesday*: *June 29, 1999*; Eve Bunting's *Night of the Gargoyles*; *Sector 7*; and *The Three Pigs*. At a point in his career when he might have capitalized on the Caldecott Medal and the money it can generate, David focused on making fewer books, crafted with even more care. David produced an enormous amount of work during this time, but most of it never saw the ink of a printing press. He abandoned a project tentatively titled "Spot" after about a year, deciding that the idea didn't merit a picture book. He developed "Moo" to the stage of finished drawings, when he realized that its theme was quite similar to the still-to-be-produced *Sector 7*. Yet *Sector 7* excited him more visually.

Dorothy Briley patiently saw David through the process, never pressuring him. She respected his creative process and the time needed for his work. By scheduling his books for a particular publication date only after David completed a book, she gave David the time he needed to make decisions—even the hard decisions of abandoning a project. As most editors do, Dorothy faced pressures from within her publishing house for "the next book by David Wiesner," but David never had an inkling of this. From his point of view, she just wanted what he wanted—the best book possible.

In May of 1998, Dorothy Briley died suddenly of a heart attack. As David lovingly and movingly spoke about Dorothy at her memorial service, he knew that he had arrived at an artistic crossroads. Because he had never trusted another editor with his work, he simply did not know what it would be like to create a book without Dorothy's gentle and sympathetic presence.

Fortunately for David, he still had much of what he considered his close creative team in place. As he said a couple of years after Dorothy's death, "By the time *Tuesday* was published, I was at the most enviable of places, a place that any artist would dream of. I was working with a team of people who I loved working with and who helped me create the best books possible. Dorothy Briley was my editor. Dinah Stevenson always read and looked at the books. Carol Goldenberg, my art director, and I could talk about every detail of the book, from type to binding. Donna McCarthy and Andi Stern in production were tremendously important in the process. They helped me find the best way to reproduce on the printing press what I wanted to create as art."

Dinah Stevenson, David's longtime friend and Dorothy's protégé, assumed Dorothy's job, to become David's editor and the publisher of Clarion. Even so, David felt extremely anxious about working with a new editor. For *The Three Pigs* David spent more time than usual on the book's early stages and prepared a complete book dummy. He photocopied his sketchbook layouts, added color, and sewed the pages together to make a small book. As they transformed a friendship into a working partnership, Dinah and David started to trim the forty-eight-page book to forty pages to keep a strong narrative line. With *The Three Pigs,* Dinah and David paid the ultimate tribute to Dorothy Briley. Bringing their own talents and what she had taught them to the project, they crafted a book that she would have been proud to publish.

(In the process Dinah Stevenson entered the record books herself as one of only six editors to win both Newbery and Caldecott simultaneously—an illustrious group that includes Walter Lorraine, Phyllis Fogelman, Jean Karl,

Ursula Nordstrom, and Margaret McElderry. Even the undisputed queen of the Newbery-Caldecott awards, May Massee of Viking, who captured more gold at ALA Midwinters than most Olympic teams, never won both awards in the same year.)

In a time when series predominate and all too often an author's new book looks depressingly like the last, David seeks a different approach and visual subject for each of his books. Although reviews and individuals commented on the innovativeness of *The Three Pigs,* in fact each of David's books has been a departure for him. As he did with "Moo," he will reject a book idea that appears to him too much like another. David takes risks, devotes the time needed to make a good book, and demonstrates an unshakable sense of purpose.

In a high-speed world filled with distractions, David maintains a laserlike focus on the task or the person at hand. A few months ago, we had an appointment to speak on the phone. When I called, Kim informed me that a family emergency had taken David out of town suddenly. An hour later, David called from the road, full of apologies, hoping to set up a time to talk that day. As we spoke later that evening, I knew he had experienced a grueling day and must be exhausted. Yet he treated our conversation as if it were the only thing that mattered. David unconsciously gives that precious quality of his undivided attention to others. Just as, when he is working, he focuses solely on the book at hand.

David does not evolve book ideas by taking polls or asking committees for direction. Nor does he consult with his editor, publisher, or public about the subject of the next project. He keeps his book ideas to himself at the formative stages. If he shares a work-in-progress at all, it is only with his wife and children. By the time anyone else sees a book, David has all of the story and visual elements fully worked out. Yet at the dummy stage, he shares the book with all who can nurture the project. He protects the artistic process, while inviting others into the bookmaking process. During editorial discussions, he listens intently, and then goes away to absorb and incorporate suggestions in his own way. During the actual printing of the books, he can, with the gentlest of comments, get press workers to reproduce precisely the tones and range of colors he desires. David possesses that rare combination of knowing exactly what he wants, while valuing the input and talents of others.

In an age obsessed with marketing, David allows his books to do the talking. Although he proves a charming guest at a conference, library, or bookstore, he travels infrequently to make public appearances. Because his energy, time, and talent go into creating books, each book becomes stronger, and readers react to its inherent qualities rather than the publicity about it. Although this course of action generally produces fewer initial sales, in the long run only the book and the way children respond to the book matter. David never forgets what truly matters.

A man who finds himself humbled by winning a second Caldecott, David cares that he is still producing books to which people respond. He learned long ago that if you fail in striving for quality, you have not failed. Fortunately, David knows how to succeed when producing children's books of quality. Rather than taking the conventional—or the easier, softer—way, he has stayed true to his own vision and his own principles. Because of that we can all celebrate his winning a second Caldecott Medal.

THE **NEWBERY MEDAL 2003**

Crispin: The Cross of Lead

written by
Avi

published by
Hyperion, 2002

HORN BOOK REVIEW

Falsely accused of theft and declared a "wolf's head" (whom any man may kill) after his mother's death, humble, pious Crispin flees the feudal village where he was raised and the steward who wants him dead. Taken in as an apprentice by a massive, red-haired, itinerant juggler who calls himself Bear, Crispin learns about music and mummery, about freedom and questioning fate, and about his own mysterious parentage that seems to be the reason behind the steward's continuing pursuit of him. Avi writes a fast-paced, action-packed adventure comfortably submerged in its fourteenth-century setting, giving Crispin a realistic medieval worldview even while subverting it with Bear's revolutionary arguments. Once master and apprentice arrive in Great Wexly for the Midsummer's Day festivities and some seditious intrigue on Bear's part, Avi slows down and offers both the reader and Crispin a chance to look around, but things speed up again with the reappearance of the steward and pursuit through the streets of the medieval city. The cause for the steward's enmity is finally revealed—Crispin is the illegitimate son of the local lord, who recently died without an heir—but the expected ending gets a surprise twist when Crispin trades this birthright for Bear's safety. From Crispin's initial religious dependence and inability to meet others' eyes to his eventual choice of his own path and freedom, the theme of self-determination is carried lightly, giving this quick, easily digested thriller just the right amount of heft.—*Anita L. Burkam*

2003 NEWBERY ACCEPTANCE SPEECH

Avi

I have lived a life of books. Family tradition says that at the age of five I breathlessly announced, "I can read! I can read!" Perhaps the book was *The Poky Little Puppy.* Maybe it was *The Story of Ferdinand.* Both were books I adored.

By the time I left high school I had already decided to be a writer. When assembling our senior yearbook (my school was so small we only needed a year-pamphlet), classmates used Shakespeare to define me by placing right next to my graduation picture Prospero's words: "[I was a] poor man, [but] my library / Was dukedom large enough." Indeed, I worked in libraries some twenty-five years.

Now, at the age of sixty-five, instead of contemplating retirement, I'm receiving from you the honor of this award. In granting it to me you have energized me, deepened my commitment—and alarmed me. For, once the immediate hubbub of the announcement subsided, all I could think was, "Oh my God! The next book better be really good!"

For most of us who write novels for young people, to win a Newbery is manifestly the summit of achievement. Its brightness seems to illuminate all of one's work. Indeed, the award is described as honoring the "most distinguished" work of children's literature.

I hope you won't think me churlish when I say in all honesty I am not comfortable with that word, *most.* Here tonight are many writing colleagues of mine who, I assure you, write as well as if not better than me. The notion that my book is better than the work of Nancy Farmer, Patricia Reilly Giff, Carl Hiaasen, Ann M. Martin, or Stephanie S. Tolan is doubtful. No question, there are kids out there who will like their books better than mine. More power to them. The democracy of reading taste, particularly among the young, is something I applaud.

Let's not forget that enduring books, such as *Charlotte's Web, Tuck Everlasting,* and *Hatchet,* did not win a Newbery. Nor have extraordinarily gifted writers like Walter Dean Myers won this award. Nor has the children's own choice (if one looks at best-seller lists), the nefarious Lemony Snicket, won this award. In the past year the Boston Globe–Horn Book Awards and the National Book Awards each selected different books. And what about all those state awards? To all this I say, bravo!

In a culture that is forever proclaiming (and selling) this or that as the best ever, a culture that promotes unanimity and conformity, I say let us celebrate diversity of every kind. Let us revel in the fact that there is so much good writing for young people that we cannot agree on a single best book. Let us celebrate how rich in talent we are. Why look back to a golden age of writing for young people when we are living in one right now?

We writers cherish the award because no one sits down to write a Newbery book. Indeed, no one deserves to win in a field where so many fine writers write so many fine books. It comes as a gift—a mix of luck, the right moment, the right people, and, I'm proud to say, a good book.

But, since you have bestowed this award on me, it appears I must answer the question that I quickly discovered is part of the established ritual attached to this prize: how did it feel to win?

I was in Philadelphia for most of ALA Midwinter, introducing another book. I was sick with some kind of flu and dared not eat for three days. It was bitterly cold, too, so I spent as much time as I could in my hotel room with a blanket around my shoulders working on a laptop on one project or another. The image of the lonely, sick writer in his garret almost fits.

When I was obliged to take part in proceedings and chanced upon Newbery committee members, they turned away in haste, eyes averted—as if I were some pariah. How humiliating! How depressing! I was so happy to get on the plane home that I arrived at the airport two hours early. Why stay for Monday's announcements and become even more depressed? Had I not recently worried that *Crispin* had not done as well as I thought it might? Had not my wife said to me as I left for Philadelphia, "If you think you might win an award, stay another day." And had I not answered, "Honey, if I were really smart, I'd stay home and write something good."

Where was I when the call came? I was sitting where every self-respecting writer who is also a parent should be at 5:30 in the morning—at my desk, working, editing my college-age daughter's application for a summer job.

In truth, when I got the news I was surprised, elated, humbled, and deeply moved. Once I accepted the news—it took a bit to believe—what did I do? I burst into tears. It required some time for me to sort out the meaning of those tears. Were they tears of grief? No. Tears of joy? Not really.

I have thought hard: The only vaguely comparable moment of ecstasy in my writing career occurred when I hooked up my first computer and discovered how to use a spell checker.

Indeed, those were tears of relief. My world was telling me an extraordinarily simple but powerful thing: I had been recognized as a good writer.

Why relief? Because, friends, writing is hard. And writing very well is very hard. Never believe any writer who suggests otherwise. Scratch the surface of any successful author and you'll find just below—in fetal position, sucking a thumb—is an insecure writer. Writing well for all of us is always a struggle.

How has the award affected me? First off, it immediately cured me of the flu. My daughter secured a better summer job (on her own). My wife said I was mellower around the house—for about a month.

To the extent that I thought about it, I had always believed that winning a Newbery might be like standing on a summit and having the world at your feet. It's not been that way at all.

Instead of an isolated, windswept, and splendid peak, I felt as if I had stumbled into a dark room. The lights go on and I discover a surprise party—for me. People shout, "Surprise!" and laugh at my bewilderment and joy. Who is there? All my friends, publishing colleagues, and you librarians, who are all excited with me, who, once the surprise is over, go on to have a really great party. To hear from so many writing and publishing friends that they were glad I had won was deeply satisfying and provided the sense of community and camaraderie we in publishing cherish.

At such a literary celebration, there is a natural tendency to focus on the individual author, the celebrity name on the book, even as our culture commemorates the myth of the isolated writer. There is some truth to both images. I work best in our Colorado mountain retreat surrounded by miles of stone-still wilderness. At nine thousand feet, there is none of civilization's chatter save what's in my head. But I am hardly working alone.

I think we need to celebrate more the collaborative nature of bookmaking. For of course there is another name affixed to the books: the publisher's name. Its one name encompasses many. While I have no qualms about saying the story is mine, every book that bears my name is an intensely cooperative work of art in which I, the author, play a part. It's no different in your libraries. There's the reference librarian front and center. The great skills of the technical service people are out of sight of the general public. But that reference librarian could not function without those others.

Bookmaking is a complex art and business. Many are involved. Most are invisible. It's a little like that credit listing at the end of a movie. You see the many names only if you bother to stay. A book does not provide such a list. All the same, there are dozens of real people involved.

To begin, I have the remarkable Gail Hochman as an agent. She's astonishing for any number of reasons. First, she holds the record for being New York City's fastest talker. Second, she's one of the city's smartest folks. She's also kind, funny, and—not beside the point—the best agent in town.

Then there are book designers, illustrators, marketing people, publisher, assistants, copyeditors, publicists, proofreaders, printers, binders—folks who are passionate about what they do but who, I suspect, are underpaid for all the care they put into their work. They, too, are skilled bookmakers who deserve our thanks and admiration, as do even the book reviewers. And of course there are thousands of booksellers and librarians who bring our books to the kids.

And while we writers travel upon the rough terrain of the earth in search of a destination, our editors—like astronauts—see the world whole. I may be the ship's skipper, but it is my pilot—my editor—who recognizes the dreaded shoals of clichés, the bays of bathos, the perils of prolixity, who guides the boat to a safe harbor.

Throughout my career I have been blessed with good editors. Over the years there have been some twenty-five of them. My early years were with the truly fabulous Fabio Coen of Pantheon Books. With Richard Jackson I have engaged in creative daring and gained a special friend. Anne Dunn and I crafted books that excited readers. Elise Howard trusted my visions and empowered them. I have laughed (and sometimes even worked) with Allyn Johnston and Anne Schwartz. Sally Doherty has always been a demanding editor and a good friend. And how lucky I was to have as editor for *Crispin* Donna Bray of Hyperion Books for Children. She is so smart, so articulate and discerning, so determined to get the best book possible out of me. Like the best of editors, she demands excellence while helping me get there—with a wry sense of humor that is always enabling. And of course she is patient when she has to read yet another of my endless revisions.

As for Hyperion Books for Children, they are in many respects a new kid in the publishing world, just ten years old. The image of Disney (the giant corporate entity) might mislead people, but this is one solid-gold publishing company. Small by today's publishing standards and led by Lisa Holton, they are tight, focused, and amazingly good at what they do—producing books of the highest quality for kids. I predict I won't be the last Hyperion author to be giving this speech.

My family is deeply involved in my life. Not, I hasten to say, with my work—but my life.

Jack, my youngest—though these days he's almost as tall as I am—once said to me, "Avi, sometimes I think of you as my stepfather, and sometimes I think of you as an author. But you know what, I like to think of you most as my stepfather."

In my book, that's the award of a lifetime.

To provide the full roster from eldest to youngest: There is Shaun, guitarist extraordinaire and chef supreme. Kevin, who is one tough marshmallow—and loving parent in his own right. There is Katie, who celebrated her high school graduation by parachuting out of an airplane—as smart, adventurous, and beautiful as they come. There is Robert, always his own man, who will take on any wilderness and conquer it. There is Jack with a heart as big as he is (and he's bigger today than he was yesterday) who—though he hardly knows how gifted he is, in class or on a lacrosse field—is our own All-American. Then there is my six-year-old granddaughter Ruby, who knows more about dogs than anyone in this room.

As for my wife, Linda Wright, she is nothing less than the smartest person I know—my best friend, my wife, my lover. Indeed, the only downside of this occasion is that I don't get to sit by her side.

The other day I was reading about the universe in the newspaper. What I discovered, to my astonishment, is that the scientific community has been able to identify only 4 percent of what the universe consists of. Think of it! Ninety-six percent of the universe is as yet unknown. They call it *dark matter.*

That extraordinary fact reminded me of something I once heard the writer Donald Hall say. He was trying to explain—by way of metaphor—what it is that a writer does, how writing works. It is a concept that, from the moment I heard it, I have cherished.

The writer in his writing, tries to create the letter *O.* But he does so by writing the letter *C.* Which is to say there is a gap. Where there is nothing. Dark matter, perhaps. The writer's words on the page create structure, character, and voice—but there are the gaps, the dark matter, the unknown, and the not written. It is the reader who fills this gap.

If the gap is too large, the reader cannot fill it. If the gap is too small, the reader need not fill it. But if the gap is just right, the reader fills it with self and the circle is complete. Thus, writer and reader have joined together to make the writing whole.

In other words, by surrounding what is not written by what is written the writer enables readers to see, feel, and experience some dimension of their own lives in the text.

How does the writer create this dark matter? As I once heard Paula Fox express it, he imagines the truth. Truth is always the harshest reality, even as it is the most liberating one. For the paradox of writing is this: the greater the writing, the more it reveals the ordinary. That is to say, great writing reveals what we know, but never noticed before. Great writing identifies that most elusive of all things—that which we have seen but had not noticed, that did not seem to exist until it was named. Nowhere is this done better than with children's books. Let us not forget it was a child who proclaimed, "The emperor has no clothes."

Here's my own key example:

Years ago, when I was a seventeen-year-old boy, living in New York City, I was coming home very late from some high school event. I was in the caverns of the city, in an empty subway station. It was 2 a.m. I was alone. I was tired. Standing there, I fell half asleep, my eyes still open. All of a sudden I saw a whole new world. In those nanoseconds, my culture, my biology, my sense of self vanished. In their place I saw the world as I had never seen it before—utterly empty, utterly devoid of meaning, a world that had no name, only matter.

It was a true epiphany.

For what I realized was that I—as is true for everyone in this room—create the world in which I live. Like Adam in the book of Genesis, we name everything. Writing is naming the world.

I love to write. Stories have been my passion, my life. What I truly adore is creating stories that, in my own jargon, work—stories that come to life for the reader, that name the world.

Crispin was my fiftieth book. Since 1975 I've published at least one book a year. Since *Crispin,* I've written and published more. But though I may be tired at the end of a day, I never tire of this great enterprise. I remain in love with the world of libraries, bookstores, and publishing. I have a passion for books, the smell of the ink, the turn of the page; for words; and beyond all else, stories. I love the whole process, from sitting down and writing the first sentence to seeing kids absorbed in my books, my story—not me.

For some twenty-five years I was privileged to have been allowed—as a librarian—to take care of stories. I've been writing some forty-eight years. Best of all, I've been sharing stories all my speaking life.

My friends, we live in a world in which there is so much that is bad. Plain and simple—*bad.* Harm is being done. The young and old are being ignored, kept ignorant, hurt, abused, and killed.

This enterprise—this writing, this reading, this world of children's books in which we are all engaged—is *good.* Plain and simple, good. My friends, we do no harm. We do good. And that, I think, is a very big thing. Oh yes, we may fail all too often. And I dare say there are a few less-than-sterling individuals among us—though surely none within this room. But—I repeat—we do good. It's not naivete that proclaims this. It's pride. That's what this celebration is all about—our collective goodness.

For whom do we do good? We do it for kids. Our mission is to bring the marvelous world of literature, of reading, to kids. What a glorious mission it is—helping kids to become themselves—empowering them to name their own worlds.

Here's something about *Crispin* you don't know. The book had an earlier working title, discarded for a variety of reasons, not least of which because I discovered it was the title of a well-known Victorian novel. But early titles, whatever their deficiencies, often indicate an author's emotional and narrative focus. Think of Robert Louis Stevenson's original title for *Treasure Island, The Sea Cook.*

The working title for *Crispin* was *No Name*. It functioned for me as a kind of metaphor for a kid who has no sense of self. There is this exchange in the book between Bear and Crispin in chapter 25.

> "I'll teach you music" [said Bear].
> "I won't be able to learn," I [Crispin] said.
> "Do the birds sing?" he asked.
> "Yes," I said.
> "Do they have souls?"
> "I don't think so," I said, somewhat confused.
> "Then surely you can sing no less than they for you have a soul."
> "Sometimes . . . I think I have none."
> For once Bear was speechless. "In the name of Saint Remigius, why?"
> "I have . . . I have never felt it."
> Bear gazed at me in silence. "Then we," he said gruffly, "shall need to make sure you do."

That's all we who write hope to do: create stories that will enable our young readers to find the stirrings of their souls.

I have long believed that as a parent one has essentially just two tasks. One is easy. One is hard. The easy part is to love the child. The hard part is to convince the child that he or she is loved.

We can do that, in part, through our great and shared enterprise: the wonderfully old-fashioned—some say obsolete—book. If we create books out of love, then surely to share them is part of that love.

Some of us here are story makers, others are story sharers. One way or another we provide stories for kids that will entertain, move, engage, and teach. Stories that say again and again that yes, life may be hard, or funny, or perplexing, always risky, but in the end, worth the living.

Dear colleagues, dear friends, you have chosen to bestow upon me this remarkable gift, this Newbery Medal for 2003. Moreover, you have done it most symbolically, for my fiftieth book, in my sixty-fifth year of life. I accept it with the deepest gratitude. In return I will offer a hope and a promise. My hope is that *Crispin* is not my best book. My promise is that I will always try to make the next one better.

To live a life of books is to know that life is its own sequel. May there always be more to come.

With a heart full of love and gratitude, I thank you.

Avi

IT WAS EARLY October 2001 when the bound galleys of *Crispin: The Cross of Lead* landed on my desk. Avi had worked for months on the book, through many revisions, which were now piled behind me in a stack the height of a small child. I was reluctant to throw them out (although I have since), despite their unsightly appearance. I wanted a record of all the changes we made, on the off chance we might decide at the last minute to substitute a paragraph from one of the many earlier versions. I also held onto them as a kind of monument to the intense revision process, which resulted in a book as tight and compelling as we thought it could possibly be.

I dashed off notes to Avi and his agent to send with their advance reading copies, and mailed out more to librarians, educators, and publishing friends. The next day Avi received his copies and called to express his thanks. When I said something about being anxious to finally get the book out into the world and see the reviews, he gently warned me against getting my hopes up. His books always receive mixed reviews, he told me. People who love his animal stories may not love his historical fiction, and those who admire his historical fiction don't cotton to his humorous or more experimental work.

I was a bit surprised. Was an author comforting *me* about reviews—*in advance*? Now this was unusual (and unnecessary, as it turned out). While I suspect that Avi is not completely immune to rave reviews, he did once share with me an anecdote about Sir Laurence Olivier's response to Charlton Heston regarding a play they had done together. Heston said, "Well, I guess you've just got to forget the bad reviews." To which Olivier is reported to have replied, "No, you've got to forget the good ones."

The advantage of working with an author on his fiftieth book is that he brings this kind of knowledge and perspective to the process. Avi's career spans more than three decades. His website bibliography reads like a menu for every age group and reading taste: early readers, picture books, young adult novels, and short stories; comedies, fantasies, and mysteries; ghost stories, animal tales, adventure novels; and, of course, historical fiction.

The stars in the lineup are the award-winners, and there are many. *The True Confessions of Charlotte Doyle* and *Nothing but the Truth: A Documentary Novel* were named Newbery Honor Books in 1991 and 1992, respectively. *The Fighting Ground,* about a Revolutionary War skirmish, was a Scott O'Dell Award winner, and *Encounter at Easton,* also set in colonial America, garnered a Christopher Award. In *Poppy* (winner of the Boston Globe–Horn Book Award) and its companion books, Avi created a cast of beloved animal characters. Many other books are great favorites with readers. *The Barn* is a spare, classic story of family and community. *"Who Was That Masked Man, Anyway?"* written entirely in dialogue, reflects Avi's boyhood love of radio shows.

A career in literature might have been expected of him. He grew up in Brooklyn, surrounded by the readers and storytellers in his book-lined home and exposed to the rich diversity of New York City. It seems that almost every member of his family engaged in writing or other creative pursuits. Two of his great-grandfathers, his parents, a maternal aunt, cousins, his twin sister—all writers of one kind or another.

Avi's success is remarkable, however, when one considers that this was the same young man whose high school English teacher told him, "You can't write!" The same boy who slogged through school, whose syndromes of dyslexia made it difficult for adults to see the talent behind the errors and misspellings. But Avi continued to write anyway.

These are all facts readily known about Avi. What may be less well known is that his experiences, personal and professional, have given him a great respect for and sensitivity to his audience and a steadfast determination to remain true to his creative vision. And as everyone at Hyperion has discovered, he approaches the publishing process with energy, grace, and a collaborative spirit.

An editor's first book with an author is always a learning experience. The process for *Crispin* started early in 2001, when he called to tell me about a novel he'd written that he thought I might like. It may have been titled "No Name," or "Wolf's Head," or even "Crispin" at that point (if only I'd kept the first draft!), and was set in fourteenth-century England. Avi had been reading Barbara W. Tuchman's *A Distant Mirror: The Calamitous 14th Century* and listening to taped lectures by Teofilo Ruiz, a scholar of medieval history (and the person to whom *Crispin* is dedicated). He was intrigued by the fact that during this tumultuous time, the modern era was born. I was intrigued, too. It is difficult for us living in the twenty-first century to imagine what it was like then, to be so completely defined by your station in life, to be denied the many choices and freedoms we Americans take for granted. This awakening of individual consciousness seemed to be the perfect metaphor for any young person's coming of age.

Reading the first draft of the manuscript that eventually would be called *Crispin: The Cross of Lead,* I was transported immediately to the narrator's small English village. I felt the damp rains, smelled the rotting wood and leaves thick on the forest floor, and most of all experienced the monotonous, backbreaking, hopeless lives of the villagers, who worked from dawn till dusk, day after day, for no personal gain. Crispin's change of fortune was dramatic, his triumph immensely satisfying. And the main characters were vivid and memorable. Once again, Avi had managed to inhabit a completely foreign time and place and make it at once authentic and accessible.

We wanted to get to work right away, and I was prepared to work quickly—but perhaps not quite as prepared as Avi was! He took my suggestions, added his own inspiration, and would usually return a full revision within a week. Sometimes I'd be working on a line-edit of a draft and receive a whole new one via e-mail, often with just a brief note—"Better, I think." E-mail, fax, and over-night courier have certainly made the process of working with authors faster and easier. But with Avi, these technologies sped the revising and editing along so much that I had the sense of watching a book being written in real time.

There were many small changes to the manuscript that now seem inevi-table—such as making Lord Furnival's given name Crispin—and that added a layer of resonance and connection. And it's hard to believe that in an earlier draft, the titular "cross of lead" was not even part of the story. While some things in the novel changed very little, the beginning was rewritten so many times that I would sometimes hesitate—did I dare ask him to revisit it *yet again*? But he was never in the least unwilling, and in fact seemed energized to start over and get it right. For Avi, the process of rewriting seemed to be more than just fixing what was written—it was discovery. It is this sense of curiosity and discovery, of the writing being as much of an adventure as the story, that comes through in his books and makes them immediate and engaging.

In *Crispin*, the eponymous narrator claims his name for himself, stripping it from its association with his lord, and begins a new life. How very fortunate for all of us that, once upon a time, Avi claimed a new name for himself as a writer and embarked on a life's work of creating literature for children. It is a joy and an honor to celebrate with Avi this gift of the Newbery Medal for his fiftieth book. What more can I say, except—here's to the next fifty!

My Friend Rabbit

written and illustrated by
Eric Rohmann

published by
Roaring Brook Press, 2002

HORN BOOK REVIEW

When narrator Mouse's well-meaning but trouble-prone friend Rabbit gets Mouse's airplane stuck in a tree, his solution (a precarious tower of reluctant animals that almost reaches the airplane) causes even more problems. The book is visually exciting—Rohmann's hand-colored relief prints make fresh and innovative use of picture book space—and broadly humorous.—*Martha K. Parravano*

2003 CALDECOTT ACCEPTANCE SPEECH

Eric Rohmann

What a strange feeling to be up here, standing here speaking to you. For the past few months I have found myself in unknown territory. The truth is, I'm living my usual life, but all things have the tinge of unfamiliarity. Consider me surprised, overwhelmed, perplexed, astonished, exalted, joyful, and humbled by all that has occurred.

In the breakneck, headlong months of making a book, when you are deeply involved with little choices, when you are propelled by the buzzing energy of the work, when moments of panic rise in the shadow of the deadline, there is not a lot of time for wondering what will happen when the book goes out into the world. In the studio, day to day, you ask yourself small questions. Have I put too much red in that blue? Is the leg of the alligator drawn awkwardly?

While working, you never consider that one day people will look closely at your finished book—the result of all those decisions, mistakes, and discoveries—and say, I think this deserves the Caldecott Medal. The imagination encourages such fancies, but the work is always more pragmatic. And then you get a phone call early one January morning.

And speaking of that call, the phone rings at half past six, and I rise to answer. (The verb rise may be a touch too active. On this cold, dark January day I awaken slowly, my limbs bending like stale Twizzlers.) Through the cobwebs of early morning, I hear a voice on the other end of the line—a voice way too enthusiastic for 6:30 a.m.

The voice says, "This is Pat Scales of the American Library Association." My first thought is that I have overdue books.

And then I think I hear, "Your book, *My Friend Rabbit,* is the recipient of the 2003 Caldecott Medal."

Silence. If this were a movie, you'd hear a ticking clock, raindrops on the windowsill, a heart beating.

I say, "You mean an Honor award?"

"No, the medal."

"The silver?"

"No, the gold."

I'm *arguing* with Pat, trying to convince her that this can't be, but she's resolute and I fumble for some articulate response, a meaningful reply, some eloquence equal to the moment, but I got nothing. Silence. More ticking clocks. *My* heart beating.

Even now I'm not sure I know how to respond to this great honor with anything resembling coherence.

I must confess that a few years back I dreamed I was speaking before a crowd much like all of you tonight—and I knew it wasn't my recurring anxiety dream about public speaking because this time I was wearing pants. I stood before the audience and an important man in a blue suit announced that I had won the Caldecott—and the Newbery, the Nobel, the Pulitzer, the National Book Award, a Guggenheim Fellowship, and the Heisman Trophy, an Oscar, an Emmy, a Tony, the Stanley Cup, the World Cup, the Grey Cup, the Pillsbury Bake-Off, and Best of Breed, Westminster Kennel Club, a Grammy, a Juno, the Boston Marathon, the Great Texas Chili Cook-off, and runner-up, Playmate of the Year.

Don't kid yourself, there's something in all of us that wants to be visible from space. But there is also a part of us that is ever-cautious and disbelieving. This doubting part of me is well developed, made muscular through extensive use.

Artists and writers are lucky this way. We start with a blank sheet of paper, work until we think the thing is finished, then wake the next day and start all over again. If you're serious, the work teaches humility early and often.

Which leads me to another dream. I had this one during graduate school, the night before I was to read my very first story in my first ever writing class. But in the dream I'm in the fourth grade—Mrs. Cerny's room—and I'm late for class.

"Sit down, Eric," she says.

I look around and don't recognize any of my classmates.

A bearded kid in a fisherman's sweater sits in Nina Oakrant's seat. Another kid, dressed in a white suit, sits behind me at Alan Holtzman's desk. I turn to him. He looks like Mark Twain.

He *is* Mark Twain. And the bearded kid is Hemingway, and next to him is Faulkner, and Poe, and Melville, and Hawthorne, and Emily Dickinson.

"Now we will read our stories," Mrs. Cerny says.

One by one the other students read their stories aloud. Stories of courage and human frailty, profound tales of man and nature and the struggles of the heart and soul. Then I read mine, a story about a lost shrimp named Binky. *Binky the Shrimp Comes Home.* The last thing I recall before I wake is glancing around the classroom, the other kids smiling, holding red pens in their hands like drawn swords.

At the time this felt like only a bad dream—I was a novice in a class of graduate writing students—but the dream now appears to have been happily prophetic. Binky probably won't show up in a book anytime soon; then again, every once in a while I wonder how he got lost in the first place.

As a boy, sometime around the fourth grade, I began to read anything that used pictures and words to tell stories. The Sunday funnies, picture books, the illustrated instructions for a model battleship, the airline safety information card (located in the seat pocket in front of you), but I mostly read comic books. I thrilled at all those colored panels and word balloons. And it wasn't just the drawings, it was also that, page by page, the story unfolded before me. Comics always awakened my imagination, drew me into the stories, and suggested further adventures. I was right there with Tarzan or the Green Lantern. Like most kids, I could move between the world of stories and the world around me. I spent my weekends and afternoons after school in the forests and fields just beyond the creek that ran in front of our house. I'd imagine I was in exotic, wild places or on some far-flung planet. The pictures I made at the time were bits of stories, images from a larger, ongoing narrative. My first comic was called *Steve Star—Good Guy of the Galaxy.*

It was also during this time that I became curious about the natural world. I recall that I could never pass a fallen log without turning it over to see what lived underneath. In an effort to understand the things I'd discovered, I began to draw. The pictures I made took place in imaginary worlds by way of the fields and forests across the creek. One time, while playing on the bank of the creek, I mistook a snapping turtle for a rock—its prehistoric head slowly tilting, jaws opening to warn me away. I thought that I'd never seen anything so fierce and wonderful. That same day I drew a comic about a kid who discovers a dinosaur emerging from the drain in his grandmother's kitchen. It was Thanksgiving, and no one believed the kid's story—that is, until the beast ate Uncle Earl, who was a bit of an overeater himself. I recall one wordless panel of Uncle Earl sleeping on the couch dreaming of dinner. The drooling dinosaur loomed above, thinking the exact same thing. When I was a boy, the world around me was always a point of departure.

It makes sense that that boy became this man. I still use pictures and words to tell stories, but now my medium is the picture book. And the medium is unlike any other. Although the picture book may look like a typical book—paper pages, between two pieces of cardboard—it's unique in many ways. A picture book is not just a container for text and illustrations. When you make a picture book, you use words, images, and the book form—the book's shape and heft and physical quality—to suggest the reader's path of movement through the story: right to left, up and down, in and out, page to page. If a painting is two-dimensional and a sculpture is three-dimensional, then a book brings in a fourth dimension—time. The picture book is a sequence of moments that move through time.

The picture book is a physical object. The reader holds the book in her hands, she turns the pages, forward and backward, as fast or slow as she wants. Reading a picture book involves the eye, the mind, and the hand. When you turn the pages, your imagination—your thinking, feeling mind—fills the moments between page one and page two. Imagine a boy holding a paintbrush and a can of green paint. Behind him stands an elephant. If the image is well-made and the story is well-told, the reader is curious, anticipating and wondering what's next. Turn the page and you see the boy standing beside an unhappy, dripping, green elephant.

When I was working on the storyboard for *My Friend Rabbit*, I'd make small sketches inside a rectangle that represented the border of the finished book. Then I'd place that sketch on a larger sheet of paper and draw the action going on outside of the book. When Mouse looks up at the plane stuck in the tree, we don't see the plane, but we understand that he sees the plane. The reader fills those spaces, and the story is told. Not only by the person who's made the book but also by the reader. The story is incomplete without the reader, and therefore making a picture book isn't only about what you put in, but also about what you leave out. Making a book is a collaborative act. At some point you have to trust the child reading the book.

And kids will see things.

I was drawing at the Brookfield Zoo one morning when a girl, she must have been six or seven years old, asked if she could see my sketchbook. "Hippos are my favorite animal," she said.

I showed her a drawing I had made of a sleeping hippo earlier that day, and she said, "Which one is it?" I must have looked puzzled because she continued, "There are two hippos in the pen. Two big brown ones."

I recalled the hippos sleeping in the mud, and said, "I'm not sure. It's hard to tell them apart."

"One has a cut on its ear," she said.

After my talk with the girl, I walked back to look at the hippos, and she was right about the cut on the ear. This is the way children see—fully, with attention to subtlety and engagement with detail. Children are not visually sophisticated—I mean, they don't have the experience or vocabulary to describe the complexities of what they see—but they are visually aware, more so than most of us adults because it's what they do. A child's primary job from birth to eight years old is to observe the world, to learn how things work. Children are hard-wired to be curious.

Over time, I've found that children are the best audience. They are enthusiastic, impulsive, generous, and pleased by simple joys. They laugh easily at the ridiculous and are willing to believe the absurd. Children are not ironic, disillusioned, or indifferent but hopeful, open-minded, and openhearted, with an inquisitive yearning for pictures and stories. To a child, every day is a great invention.

I want to thank Pat Scales and all the members of the Caldecott committee. Thank you for looking at my book and seeing something there. Although I have to admit that a little part of me says, "What were you thinking?" all of me is humbled, thrilled, and deeply appreciative. Also, I want to thank everyone at the Association for Library Service to Children for all their support and assistance.

My congratulations and admiration to the other winners—Peter [McCarty], Tony [DiTerlizzi], and Jerry [Pinkney]. I couldn't ask for better company.

To my family, who never seem surprised when good things happen to me. I treasure their enduring, unconditional support. And then again, my father, who loves only realism in painting, reacted to my news by saying, "They gave an award to the cartoony one?" Those who love you always keep you from getting beyond yourself.

To my friend Simon Boughton, who also happens to be my editor at Roaring Brook Press. He took a chance on me a few years back and published *Time Flies*. When I spoke with him about making hand-colored relief prints for *My*

Friend Rabbit, he never blinked. I treasure his steadfast confidence in my abilities even when I doubt myself. The simple truth is my books are far better for having worked with Simon.

Thanks to Lauren Wohl for the seemingly effortless way she turns difficulty into success. And to all my friends at Roaring Brook who put *Rabbit* on their very first list. Incidentally, if anyone here has a manuscript titled *The Little Publisher That Could,* now might be a good time for submission.

Thanks to my agent, Ethan Ellenberg, who also took a chance on a green, unproven artist. I've come to rely on his insight and good sense. Thanks also to Isabel Warren Lynch and Tracy Gates, who were in on this book at the very beginning and provided invaluable ideas and guidance.

To Harold Boyd, the best artist I've ever known. And not just because of his drawings and paintings, but also because he taught me—by example—how you can live a life as a working artist. He revealed to me what today seems so obvious: that telling stories with pictures is the way I engage the world.

To all my friends who have encouraged me in spite of my capricious temperament. Especially to my friend Bob Erickson, for listening to me howl and lament ever since graduate school. When I told him of this award, he said, "I feel as if I've won something." And to my friend, the writer Candace Fleming. When I was confused about the ending of *Rabbit,* it was Candy's keen sense of story and her perceptive eye for humor that rescued the final page from the brink of ordinary.

Thanks to the kids who send letters, enlightening me to all the things in my books that I hadn't seen, and for providing me with an endless supply of one-liners. To James, the seven-year-old boy who suggested that on the cover I replace the plane with a Torah scroll, put a yarmulke on Mouse, and call the book *My Friend Rabbi.* And to another boy, Steven, who—in a nod to the comic possibilities of spellcheck—wrote, "Congratulations on your award. The rabbit book is good. You must be very impotent."

Finally, I spend a lot of time with my friends Mark and Mary Anne Loafman and their sons Nicholas, Ethan, and William. A few years back, after dinner one night, the three boys and I got the idea to build a tower of toys. Our building materials were cardboard bricks, toy trucks, action figures, and stuffed animals. We made the pile as high as possible and topped the swaying, precarious structure with a stuffed toy lion. Then we devised ways to knock it down. The boys called the game "Dead Simba."

I'm sorry to say that I have never had a lightning bolt moment of inspiration. For me, and I suspect for most artists and writers, revelations come slowly, one after the other. You draw a line and then respond to the line. No heavenly flashes, but a slow brightening.

The falling pile of toys did not give me the idea for the tower of animals in *My Friend Rabbit,* but when I made the first tentative drawings of a bear atop a goose atop a rhino atop an elephant, I recalled those nights playing "Dead Simba" and knew that if that moment was so funny in real life, it had a good chance of being funny on the page. When I made the drawings, those joyful nights with the Loafman boys returned unbidden and clear—the brightening I spoke of—a confluence of imagination and memory. When I look back over the past few months, that's what the Caldecott has felt like. Receiving this honor has been another kind of brightening, also unexpected, that has cleared away the chaff and chatter of doubt and uncertainty, making me more sure of my choices, reminding me of the good and true reasons I make books for children. Thank you.

....

ILLUSTRATOR PROFILE BY PHILIP PULLMAN

Eric Rohmann

MY FIRST VIEW of this gentleman's work was on the cover of *Publishers Weekly,* seven years ago or thereabouts. Alfred A. Knopf was publishing a book of mine, which they called *The Golden Compass* (the British title was *Northern Lights*), and they'd paid to have it featured on the cover of that magazine. I arrived in New York for a pre-publication tour, and there was my publisher holding up *Publishers Weekly* to show the title of my book against the background of the most amazingly beautiful painting, which, as I say, I'd never seen till that moment.

"Who did that?" I said.

"Eric Rohmann," said Simon Boughton proudly.

He might as well have said "Theophrastus von Sparkenpumpe." I'd never heard of him.

"Well, he's very good," I said.

"I'm glad you said that," said Simon, "because you're going to meet him tomorrow."

What would have happened if I'd hated it, I never found out. But there was no chance of my hating it. The cover designed by Mr. Rohmann (I'm going to call him that from now on, because he is very respectable now) showed the face of the young heroine, Lyra, as she sat on the back of the armored bear Iorek Byrnison, with her dæmon Pantalaimon in the form of a mouse close by. Mr. Rohmann had done something miraculous with Lyra's face. The story depicts her poised between childhood and adulthood, on the very cusp of adolescence—and poised between several other things as well. She is very definitely a girl, and her world is a more traditionally run place than ours; but she's also what used to be called a tomboy. Mr. Rohmann's picture shows her exactly balanced between a past and a future, between safety and danger, between one world and another, between a thousand possibilities in one direction and millions of possibilities in another. It's a face full of dreams and full of wonder. It is Lyra as she truly is, better than I could ever have hoped to see her pictured.

So I was prejudiced in favor of Mr. Rohmann even before I met him, which I did in Chicago at a dinner (that tour was full of fancy dinners where I met lots of very nice booksellers and tried to engage their interest in a book that wasn't even published yet) to which he, Mr. Rohmann that is, had traveled a long way by train, and in his fine, modest way he traveled home by train as well, even though most artists of his distinction would merit a limousine.

I was glad to be able to pay tribute to him in the few clumsy and nervous words I spoke at that dinner. And I am even more glad to pay tribute to him now that his genius has been recognized with the highest honor the American book world can pay to its illustrators. Setting aside my personal esteem for the gentleman, which is unbounded, I have to say that as a worker in line and shape and color he is unsurpassed. (I shall have more to say about lines in a couple of paragraphs.)

The first book I saw that was illustrated throughout by Mr. Rohmann was *King Crow*, by Jennifer Armstrong. *King Crow* abounds in sweeping panoramas, dramatic compositions, and beautifully rich and glowing colors; but what stood out at once for me was the draftsmanship. Anyone who can get a dog to look like a dog, a crow to look like a crow, or a hand to look properly articulated with an arm that in turn fits onto a shoulder that in turn looks as if it has a proper structural relationship with a backbone—is someone who deserves respect.

(It strikes me that "the toe bone's connected to the . . . foot bone, and the foot bone's connected to the . . . ankle bone, and the ankle bone's connected to the . . ." is a good description of the ideal curriculum for a life drawing class.)

Anyway, I've tried drawing those things myself, and it's *hard*. When you look at a page of Mr. Rohmann's work, you see not only the expression of a great innate talent but also the consequence of solid work and study and thought. I mean *toil*, the daily engagement with the tools, the never-ending struggle to make two dimensions represent three, the fresh-every-day effort to persuade the color to flow where you want it to and to preserve its warmth and brilliance all the way through the printing process.

Take Mr. Rohmann's *The Cinder-Eyed Cats*. The story is a charming fantasy—a dream, really, all moods and wishes. The success of it was always going to depend on the quality of the pictures, but there was no risk that it wouldn't succeed. Mr. Rohmann's command of the medium had reached the point where he was able to draw any animal, from any angle, doing anything. As for the color, the whole book is suffused with a warm tonality that glows off the page: the tints are exquisite. Look at the various kinds of white he finds for the clouds on the spread beginning, "Quiet now the sea-blue sky. . . ." Look at the colors in the morning sky: a perfectly controlled wash of tints from lemon to lavender, so that wherever you look on the page you know that it's *right*—but you can't see how he's done it.

What it produces in the reader is a sense of effortless control, the experience of watching a technique so perfect that it seems to be just happening, as a bird sings. It isn't, of course, but that's what it seems like.

Not many *lines*, though. I do like lines.

And then came *My Friend Rabbit*.

At first glance, you wouldn't think these pictures were by the same hand at all. Instead of the beautifully smooth and modulated painted surface of his previous work, here was a heavy, chunky, thick black line printed from a relief block. The man was *carving* this stuff. Not only carving it but hacking into it with force and vigor, leaving little jagged bits uncut, to catch the ink and sparkle blackly on the page; and then painting the result in bright, vibrant colors that blow through the book like a March wind. This wasn't smooth in the least. It shook and quivered and banged and rattled. I don't know what Mr. Rohmann calls this technique, but I *love* it. It reminds me of the woodcuts of William Nicholson: deep black, solid color; power and simplicity and wit all bound up in one unforgettable image.

But the roughness (if I can call it that) hasn't compromised the accuracy of the drawing at all. In fact it enhances it. In one of the Little Nemo strips by the great Winsor McCay, there is a picture—just one frame—showing six Bactrian camels (the two-humped variety) harnessed to a chariot and all colliding with one another and falling over in a heap. Every single limb is in the right place, and the perspective is immaculate, and *everything works*. Now since the world began, no one has ever seen that happen; but McCay could draw it perfectly. In *My Friend Rabbit*, Mr. Rohmann has nine animals all doing something similar, and everything works, and it's all done in a thick, bold, hefty line that you could tow an oceangoing ship with. It's funny up close, and you can put it on a table twenty feet away, as I have just done, and it's still funny—it still works.

The man is a genius.

I haven't space to do more than mention his many other qualities: handsome, generous, witty, and debonair, he is like Ivan Skavinsky Skivar in the old song, who "could imitate Irving, play poker or pool, and perform on the Spanish guitar." But enough of that. When I heard that he'd been awarded the Caldecott Medal, I gave a yell of delight that is still echoing around the ancient rafters of this house.

Well done, Mr. Rohmann! Well done, Simon Boughton, who published *My Friend Rabbit*! Well done, Caldecott committee! Well done all round!

The Tale of Despereaux

Being the Story of a Mouse, a Princess, Some Soup, and a Spool of Thread

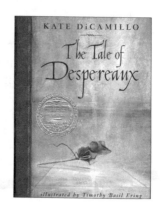

written by
Kate DiCamillo

illustrated by
Timothy Basil Ering

published by
Candlewick, 2003

HORN BOOK REVIEW

Despereaux Tilling is not like the other mice in the castle. He's smaller than average, with larger than average ears. He'd rather read books than eat them. And he's in love with a human being—Princess Pea. Because he dares to consort with humans, the Mouse Council votes to send him to the dungeon. Book the First ends with Despereaux befriending a jailer who resides there. Books two and three introduce Roscuro, a rat with a vendetta against Princess Pea, and Miggery Sow, a young castle servant who longs to become a princess. Despereaux disappears from the story for too long during this lengthy middle section, but all the characters unite in the final book when Roscuro and Miggery kidnap Princess Pea at knifepoint and Despereaux, armed with a needle and a spool of thread, makes a daring rescue. Framing the book with the conventions of a Victorian novel ("Reader, do you believe that there is such a thing as happily ever after?"), DiCamillo tells an engaging tale. The novel also makes good use of metaphor, with the major characters evoked in images of light and illumination; Ering's black-and-white illustrations also emphasize the interplay of light and shadow. The metaphor becomes heavy-handed only in the author's brief, self-serving coda. Many readers will be enchanted by this story of mice and princesses, brave deeds, hearts "shaded with dark and dappled with light," and forgiveness.—*Peter D. Sieruta*

2004 NEWBERY ACCEPTANCE SPEECH

Kate DiCamillo

About thirty miles west of Orlando is a small town called Clermont, and in that town is a library called the Cooper Memorial Library. When I was seven years old, the librarian there, a certain Miss Alice, stepped out of her office one day and stood beside me and put her hand on my shoulder and spoke the following words with a great deal of force and volume.

"Kate," Miss Alice said to the person at the circulation desk, "is a True Reader! Therefore, the four-book maximum will be waived for her! She may check out as many books at a time as she likes!"

Miss Alice's hand trembled on my shoulder as she said these words. Or perhaps my shoulder trembled beneath her hand. I cannot say.

All I know for certain is that her words, spoken so passionately, so fiercely, shaped me and helped me define who I was. Who was I? I was a True Reader!

I know, emphatically, that Miss Alice's words are a part of the miracle of my presence here tonight. I also know, emphatically, that it is a miracle that I am here tonight at all.

And, in keeping with the nature of miracles, I am properly awed by it. I cannot explain it. I can, however, joyfully point to the many people who are a part of the miracle: Kara LaReau, my patient and daring editor who read the first seven pages of this book and said exactly the words I needed to hear: "More, please"; everyone at Candlewick Press who believed in my small mouse; Timothy Basil Ering, who brought the mouse to life; my mother, who read to me; my friends, who listened to me. Thank you.

And to the Newbery committee: thank you, thank you, thank you. Thank you to each one of you for this miracle. Thank you, all of you, for believing in the power of stories.

Speaking of stories, I would like to tell you one. I grew up in Florida, but before Florida, until I was five years old, I lived in a house on Linden Lane in Philadelphia. The house was a large mock Tudor, and within it there were two stairways: the front stairs, which were light and bright and grand, adorned with a chandelier and lit further by tall windows above the landing; and the back stairs, which we called the servant stairs. These stairs ran from the kitchen to my brother's bedroom, and they were dark and dismal and full of cobwebs and smelled of mildew and rot.

Also, according to my brother, the servant stairs were inhabited by trolls and witches. Because of this, my brother kept the door in his room that led to the stairs closed. He shoved a chair up against the door. He checked often to make sure the chair stayed in place. But sometimes, on weekend mornings, when he believed that the trolls and witches were sleeping, my brother would pull the chair aside and open the door and run down the servant stairs and emerge, triumphant and out of breath, into the kitchen.

I was four years old at the time of this story. My brother was seven, and we had a father who was a storyteller and a joke teller. Also, our father could laugh like a witch. The sound was terrifying: a high keening, a cackle that was almost, but not quite a scream. The witch's laugh made me shiver. It made my brother's teeth chatter, and this disgusted my father. He considered my brother a coward, and he told him, often, that he was too afraid of too many things. One Saturday, my father said to me, "Let's fix your brother. We'll give him a *real* scare. We'll hide in the servant stairs. And when he runs past us, you grab him, and I'll laugh like a witch."

Now you have to understand: no one knew better than I did how afraid my brother was of those stairs. No one knew better than I how much the witch's laugh terrified him. And the combination of those two things—the dark stairs; the witch's joyful, murderous scream—would, I thought, be enough to kill him.

No one knew better. But this is what I said to my father: "Okay."

I knew that if I said, "Let's not do this; it will scare him too much," my father would say, "Oh, you're just like him. You're a big scaredy-cat, too. What's the matter with you guys? You're no fun."

I wanted my father to think that I was brave. I wanted my father to think that I was fun. And so I said nothing.

Instead, I stood at the bottom of the servant stairs. I held my father's hand. I listened as, upstairs, my brother moved the chair aside and opened the door. I could have called out to him. I could have warned him. But I said nothing as he descended the stairs toward us.

I was four years old. And I knew that I was committing an act of great treachery.

That's it. That's the whole story. And it's not, I know, much of a story, but I'm telling it here because there are people who believe that stories for children should not have darkness in them. There are people who believe that children know nothing of darkness. I offer up my own four-year-old heart, full of treachery and deceit and love and longing, as proof to the contrary.

Children's hearts, like our hearts, are complicated. And children need, just as we do, stories that reflect the truth of their own experience of being human. That truth is this: we all do battle with the darkness that is inside of us and outside of us. Stories that embody this truth offer great comfort because they tell us we do not do battle alone.

When I was five years old, we left the house in Philadelphia, but the stairs in that house stayed inside of me. They were carved in my heart, just as the memory of my treacherous act was imprinted there, shaping the person I became.

In Florida, however, two wonderful things happened. I learned to read. And then, safe within the magical confines of the Cooper Memorial Library, I met people in books who had conflicted, complicated hearts like my own. I met people who fought against their own jealousy, rage, and fear. And each page that I turned, each story that I read, comforted me deeply.

I have wanted, for a very long time, to tell the story of me and my brother and the servant stairs. But it was not until I sat down to write this speech that I realized I had, unwittingly, told the story already. It's all there in *The Tale of Despereaux*: the dungeon stairs and the castle stairs, the chandelier and the tall windows, the sibling betrayal and the parental perfidy.

Despereaux's story turns out differently than mine, of course. And part of the reason that it does turn out differently is that Despereaux reads, in a book in the library, the story of a brave knight. And at the moment when he must make a difficult decision, the mouse decides to act like that knight. He decides to act courageously in spite of his fear.

This is the other great, good gift of stories that acknowledge the existence of darkness. Yes, the stories say, darkness lies within you, and darkness lies without; but look, you have choices.

You can take action. You can, if you choose, go back into the dungeon of regret and fear. You can, even though there is every reason to despair, choose to hope. You can, in spite of so much hate, choose to love. You can acknowledge the wrong done to you and choose, anyway, to forgive.

You can be very small, as small as a mouse, and choose to act very big: like a knight in shining armor.

But none of these things, none of these shining moments, can happen without first acknowledging the battle that rages in the world and within our own hearts. We cannot act against the darkness until we admit it exists.

Thirty-five years after I stood at the bottom of those stairs and said nothing, I have started to forgive myself for not speaking up. I have begun, too, to forgive my father for what he did, for making me complicit in my brother's suffering.

This forgiveness that I am slowly approaching is the gift of the stories I have struggled to tell as truthfully as I can. And it is the gift, too, of each truthful, complicated, tragic, celebratory story that I have read.

Four years ago, when he was eight years old, my friend Luke Bailey asked me to write the story of an unlikely hero. I was afraid to tell the story he wanted told: afraid because I didn't know what I was doing; afraid because it was unlike anything I had written before; afraid, I guess, because the story was so intent on taking me into the depths of my own heart.

But Luke wanted the story. I had promised him. And so, terrified and unwilling, I wrote *The Tale of Despereaux.*

Recently I had to make a very difficult decision. I had to be brave, but I did not want to be. I had to do the right thing, but I did not want to do it. Late at night, as I lay in bed agonizing over this decision, a friend called me up. She had received a letter from one of her students. The letter was written by a group of third graders at Talmud Torah in St. Paul, Minnesota, who had just finished reading *The Tale of Despereaux.* Each child said in one sentence what they thought of the book. I'd like to read you a few of those sentences:

> "You taught us how to do what is right the way Despereaux did."—*Chaim*
> "You inspired me to have courage."—*Jonah*
> "You inspired us to believe in ourselves."—*Gabi*

And my favorite:

> "I think that it was an all-right book."—*Ernie*

At the exact moment when I needed it, those kids gave me the courage I lacked, the courage they had gotten from a book that I had written even though I was afraid.

And this, finally, is the miracle of stories: together, we readers form a community of unlikely heroes. We are all stumbling through the dark. But when we read, we journey through the dark together. And because we travel together, there is the promise of light.

Einstein said, "There are only two ways to live your life. One is as though nothing is a miracle. The other is as though everything is."

Tonight, I choose to believe that everything is a miracle. It is a miracle that I am here. It is a miracle every time I find comfort and courage in books. It is a miracle that we can live in this world long enough to learn how to be brave, long enough to learn how to forgive.

I accept this award tonight. I know that I don't deserve it, but I accept it . . . for all of us—True Readers, Unlikely Heroes—in honor of our shared journey toward the light.

Kate DiCamillo

SHE'S A FIREFLY, this Kate DiCamillo, and who would want to catch a firefly? Having caught one in a jar, who would think that this captured thing was what he was after? I like my fireflies best in the wild, on the wing, out there in the tall grass at the edge of the woods. This account, on behalf of Kate's friends, is therefore only a glimpse.

She's a loyal friend, our Kate. She forgives us our failings, which remind her that we are as human as she. Our wooden legs amuse her. They provide her with proof that, as she suspected, life is not only a dire enterprise but also a hilarious joke, a game played by half-wits, all of us, doing the best we can—a best that, at best, is farce. At the same time, she witnesses the paradox that a man or a mouse may transcend absurdity and rise to heroism.

Kate takes delight in the incongruities of mankind, that glorious ruin. Nothing pleases her more than a man dressed up in an Easter Bunny suit smoking a cigarette out behind the strip mall. Well, one thing pleases her more—the ramshackle wreck who enters the restaurant where she and I are eating sandwiches. As he sits down behind me, Kate's eyes sparkle at the incongruity between this unfortunate and the grandiose view of humanity with which we all delude ourselves, but she observes with such empathy that tomorrow she will make of him a poignant anti-hero, a revelation of our universally woeful condition.

She's a scamp, Kate DiCamillo is, who loves to scare the horses and shock the prigs. She can belch like a truck driver, and the most outrageous remarks issue from her mouth, but those who prove to be neither horses nor prigs hear the wisdom and tenderness that follows. A phone call or an e-mail comes from her that begins, "Listen to this!" Then, in the manner of someone presenting a Ceylon sapphire in a satin-and-velvet box, she offers a gift: a paragraph from Isak Dinesen, a story from Russell Hoban or George Saunders or Alice Munro. Kate is better acquainted with contemporary literature than anyone else I know. "Listen to this!" she says, and we do listen, for what follows might be something as wonderful as lines from Antonio Machado's poem "Last Night," in which the speaker dreams that bees have built a hive in his heart and are "making . . . sweet honey from my old failures." Writers need the promise that Machado's dream offers, as they struggle to overcome their failure to gain acceptance for their work and to satisfy themselves. The promise means so much to Kate that she commissioned a friend who has a gift for needlework to stitch Machado's lines into a woolen wall hanging, which Kate then gave away to a writer friend.

Five years before I met her, Kate confronted a question like the one Mary Oliver asks in "The Summer Day":

> *Tell me, what is it you plan to do*
> *with your one wild and precious life?*

Kate answered that if she were ever going to write, she had better begin.

Having begun, she was a dogged worker. To make a living in Florida, she directed shuffleboard at a trailer park, or said, "Look down, and watch your step," to a never-ending line of thrill seekers at Disney World. Such jobs, of course, were never her real work. In the seven years since she and I met in Minneapolis, she has earned her bread at a book warehouse, sold hot dogs at a park, and tended the children's department at a used bookstore. Her many menial jobs enabled her to rent a small apartment and to feed herself, primarily on bean sandwiches. (Her cooking skill might add up to boiled water or a fried egg, if she owned a kettle or a skillet.) She didn't have the cash, though, to buy a cup of coffee in a shop, or enough to repair the defunct heater in her tin-can car when the temperature in Minneapolis was thirty degrees below zero.

Her true work was her writing. Before she went to the book warehouse every morning, she woke up at four thirty to write. Every morning, without fail. She read about writing. She studied the methods of the writers she read. She collected rejections, 470 at last count. (Yes, 470. The bees have made sweet honey indeed from her old failures.) When *Because of Winn-Dixie* found her, she was ready for it. She knew then how to write it and how to cope with rejections and lukewarm editorial responses. At about the same time, she won a large grant from a Minnesota institution, the blessed McKnight Foundation, for a short story she wrote for adults.

When *Because of Winn-Dixie* came along, Kate said she had found her voice and her métier. The first time she read from the novel in my hearing, it was worthy of publication. Before anybody else had laid an eye on it, the work was so astonishing in its voice and originality and in the quality of its craftsmanship and the depth of its emotion that I said to her, "You're going to be famous."

Among her many virtues is the fact that Kate never writes the same book twice. Her versatility has enabled her to depart in voice and mode from each of her successes, with *The Tiger Rising*, and *The Tale of Despereaux*, and the several other books that are progressing now toward publication. Yes, she continues to write, every day when she isn't in a plane or a hotel, for what has her success won her if not the wherewithal to write whatever her spirit moves her to say?

Kate DiCamillo's friends rejoice in the recognition the world has given her. We try to protect her from writer's envy, including our own, and from her own highly developed devotion to duty, for she is beloved among us. As Mr. White told us, in *Charlotte's Web*, "It is not often that someone comes along who is a true friend and a good writer." We are grateful that sometimes Kate casts her firefly light on us.

The Man Who Walked between the Towers

written and illustrated by
Mordicai Gerstein

published by
Roaring Brook, 2003

HORN BOOK REVIEW

"Once there were two towers side by side. . . . The tallest buildings in New York City." Another September 11 book? No—and yes. Gerstein's story takes place in 1974, when the World Trade Towers' construction wasn't quite finished. Philippe Petit, the French street performer and high-wire walker, couldn't resist the temptation to dance between the twin towers. "Once the idea came to him he knew he had to do it! If he saw three balls, he had to juggle. If he saw two towers, he had to walk! That's how he was." Gerstein is in top form, pulling the reader into his story with a conversational style extended by playful pen and paint illustrations. Like Petit, Gerstein conceals much careful planning behind an obvious enjoyment of his subject. As the book starts, rectangular paintings are set well inside the edge of each white page. When Philippe and his co-conspirators, disguised as construction workers, toil through the night setting up the wire, the area between the illustrations' borders and the edge of the page fills with a gray-blue wash, providing the visual equivalent of foreboding background music. As dawn breaks and Philippe gets ready to step onto the wire, the blue fades away. Now we're ready to be exhilarated and terrified—and on two successive foldout pages, we are. The first heart-stopping image shows Philippe from above as he moves to the middle of the wire. The tiny buildings below him seem terrifyingly distant while on the far right his destination, the top of the tower, is shown with exaggerated perspective, taking our eye down, down, and off the bottom of the page. Next we see the same scene from the ground with the book turned on its side. People on the street look up in surprise and fear while a cop calls for assistance. The denouement takes us back to solid ground and back to the rectangle-on-white illustrations. Philippe is arrested, as we knew he would be, but the kindly judge sentences him to perform in Central Park. Finally, the last pages bring us to the present ("Now the towers are gone"), showing the current empty skyscape. "But in memory, as if imprinted on the sky, the towers are still there." And so they are on the last page, translucent against the clouds, with a tiny Philippe on his wire connecting the towers to each other and the past to the present.—*Lolly Robinson*

2004 CALDECOTT ACCEPTANCE SPEECH

Mordicai Gerstein

I think that being human is probably the most difficult, incomprehensible, and sometimes seemingly impossible thing in the world. And I believe that all of us who live the lives of human beings every day, bravely, as well as we possibly can with the cards we're dealt, should hear our phones ring one morning and answer them to hear what sounds like thousands of librarians cheering for us, telling us we've won the great prize. This should happen to everyone, as it seems to have happened to me.

I say *seems* because even now, months later, it's still hard to believe that I'm standing here full of gratitude and a feeling that if I were to lift both feet off the ground at the same time, I would not fall.

Disbelief struck me dumb when [Caldecott committee chair] Kathy East called me with the news. When I was finally able to speak, much to my surprise I heard myself say, "I have always loved librarians!"

And it's true. Ever since my first visit to the Wabash Avenue branch of the Los Angeles Public Library when I was four-and-a-half and took home my first book, *And to Think That I Saw It on Mulberry Street,* by a Doctor named Seuss, I have loved librarians and libraries and books. Books are still one of the greatest of all human inventions. In a book you can hold the imagination of another person in the palm of your hand and explore it at your leisure—true magic. I am very grateful to be part of this magical world of books, and, especially, of books for children.

I am often asked, "How do you write for children? How do you know what they'll like?" I'm always surprised by the question because I'd never given it much thought. I feel as if I'm being asked, "How do you write for penguins? Or wombats?" The shocking truth is: I myself was once a child. In fact, all of us, without exception, either are children or have been children. Many people seem to forget that children are ourselves as we were and as we are and not a different species. Maybe it's as Wallace Stevens wrote:

There is so little that is close and warm.
It is as if we were never children.

I think being in touch with your childhood keeps you in touch with what really matters to you, and who you really are. My earliest years are still as vivid and important as anything that has happened since. I was surprised to learn that this is not true for everyone. Tragically, many people have had childhoods best forgotten. But essentially, I'm sure I haven't changed much since I was four.

I have a snapshot of myself then, smiling proudly, brush in hand, beside my first easel, on which stands my very first painting—a bowl of flowers. Well more than sixty years later, I am still at it. Same smile.

My dear mother Fay, now long gone, cut photos of famous paintings from *Life* magazine and made a scrapbook museum for me, with artists ranging from William Blake and Michelangelo to Picasso and Cézanne. Lying on my belly on the floor, I studied those pictures over and over and over again till they all became part of me. I've found that the books I loved then, I still loved when I later read them to my children; they were still important, still meaningful to me as an adult. *Alice in Wonderland* is almost everything I love in a book: hilarious, scary, full of surprises and bizarre characters, all in a strange and bewildering world. It could be the story of my life. As a child I was interested in almost everything, and as an old man I am interested in absolutely everything. And one of the things that interests me most is that special, overwhelming feeling that I remember first having when I saw the full moon for the first time—wonder.

From wonder into wonder
Existence opens.

So writes poet Witter Bynner in his translation of Lao Tzu.

Remember being a child, and the full moon will always provoke wonder.

The important question for me has not been how to write for children but how to write *anything*. As a painter, animated-film maker, and illustrator, I came late to writing, and it was in order to make picture books. I am always looking for subjects that puzzle or disturb or amuse me, subjects that make interesting pictures. I make books for people, most of whom happen to be children, and I try to address the most essential parts of all of us.

In creating a picture book, I try to make the sentences and pictures as clear and simple as possible. I feel that in the simple and obvious, paradoxically, one can find the utmost complexity and ambiguity. What could be simpler than a soap bubble? And what could be more mysterious and complicated?

My books come from many sources: myths and legends, biographies, and my imagination. *The Man Who Walked between the Towers* came off the streets and out of the sky.

In the 1970s I saw a young Frenchman perform on the sidewalks of my New York neighborhood. Philippe Petit was a high-wire walker and unicyclist whose juggling was as witty and full of surprises as Charlie Parker's solos. When I picked up the *New York Times* one day and saw that Philippe had walked a wire between the Towers, I was thrilled to my toes and thought it was one of the most wonderful things anyone had ever done.

Later, in 1987, a *New Yorker* article about Philippe reminded me of his walk, and I started playing with a story about a boy who bicycles to the moon on a tightrope. My editor told me that it was simply not believable, which surprised me. It seemed quite plausible to me, but I put the story away.

Though I no longer lived in New York City on September 11, and lost no friends or relatives, I experienced the destruction of the Towers in a personal way, as did all New Yorkers. I still consider myself a New Yorker, just as I still consider myself a Californian, and now a whatever-you-call-people-from-Massachusetts. The Towers were part of my home, my furniture. Over the years, I'd seen them in different light and weather from different parts of the city. I'd passed them on my morning runs and painted watercolors of them in the evenings. The idea came to me that instead of concocting a fictional parallel to Philippe's walk, I should tell the story of what actually happened; it was less believable and therefore more truly wonderful!

The text came to me quickly. When Roaring Brook agreed to publish it, I learned that Philippe was about to publish his own book for adults about his walk, *To Reach the Clouds*. I was able to get an advance copy and found that it was a fascinating, hilarious, and moving true account of a young man's years-long obsession and struggle to carry out something beautiful and impossible.

Best of all for me, the book was full of photos and diagrams that were invaluable for making my pictures. The story of Philippe Petit's walk is, for me, one that addresses the question, "What is a human being?" He proposes that we are creatures who can leave fear behind and walk through the air—that life can be exciting and fun and may be lived in learning to do the impossible; that the human imagination has no bounds. For Philippe, the Towers were there for no other reason than to provide two anchors for his wire, just as for a spider the most heroic statue is only a place to spin a web. Entrepreneurial and architectural imagination created the Towers; Philippe's imagination transformed them into his art; and other imaginations destroyed them, showed them to be as ephemeral as Philippe's walk.

Books take us to places we will never go and let us be people and creatures we can never be. I didn't want to just tell the story of the walk—I wanted the book to be the walk between cardboard covers. I think of a picture book as a hand-held theater, entered by opening it and operated by turning its pages (no batteries, you don't have to plug it in); I wanted this book to cause real vertigo, to put the reader, child or adult—and of course myself—on the wire.

I admit there are differences between adults and children, wonderful and often maddening ones. Children do need adults; I think children make us become the adults they need. We must give them love and nourishment and books, which, as we know, are part of a healthy diet. My intention in all my books is to give children just what I want to give everyone: something beautiful, magical, funny, and soulful; something that provokes good questions—questions about what an incomprehensible, beautiful, and seemingly impossible thing it is to be a human being in this incomprehensible, beautiful, and seemingly impossible world. What could be more difficult and more wonderful?

So here I am, still that child standing proudly and happily beside his easel. I simply have a bit more experience, which hasn't kept me from believing, more than ever, that life should be fun!

And what fun it is, after all the countless hours alone in my studio talking to myself, to be standing here telling all this to you. I want to first thank the members of the committee, for honoring my book, and then all of you, for listening. My heartfelt thanks to Simon Boughton, my editor and publisher who embraced *The Man Who Walked between the Towers* wholeheartedly, and to Filomena Tuosto, our designer, who helped make the book as effective as it is. My continuing thanks to Joan Raines, my longtime agent, champion, fairy godmother, and friend, who sent the book to Simon, despite my telling her, after two turndowns, to put it away and forget it because I wanted to make books that everyone wanted. Joan, sadly, could not be here today, but she wept like a baby when she heard the news of the award, and that made me cry, too.

My thanks always to my dear wife and love, Susan Yard Harris, and our dear and beautiful daughter, Risa, for their love and support on the crazy, careening, roller-coaster ride that has been my picture book career. In 1996 Theron Raines, Joan's partner and husband, described my ups and downs prophetically. He said, "I wish Mordicai would stop going over Niagara Falls in a barrel and walk across the Grand Canyon on a tightrope!" I've had those words taped over my desk for the past eight years.

My eternal gratitude to Philippe Petit, who is also a marvelous writer, for doing what he did and still continues to do, for all of us.

I feel, thanks to the award, a new sense of freedom, and I see at the horizon of my imagination picture books barely-dreamed-of waiting to be born . . . and I wonder what they'll be. Thank you.

....

ILLUSTRATOR PROFILE BY ELIZABETH GORDON

Mordicai Gerstein

ON THE WALL near my desk is a small, framed, pen-and-ink drawing of a boy, arms (or should I say wings?) outstretched, tousled head of feathers, surrounded by a paddling of helpful ducks. It is from *Arnold of the Ducks,* and in many ways it symbolizes for me the very essence of Mordicai Gerstein. It is signed Christmas 1982, but *Arnold* was not the first book I worked with Mordicai on. He was the illustrator of *Frankenstein Moved In on the Fourth Floor* by Elizabeth Levy. His black-and-white drawings for that very funny book delivered the perfect combination of levity and fright for young readers. He understood Liz's story exactly the way the children who read the book would. He really believed the neighbor could be Frankenstein. His drawings expanded and elaborated on the text, helping make the book a true page-turner for the chapter book set, leading the reader from beginning to end at just the right pace. Mordicai didn't simply illustrate Liz Levy's book—he worked with her to make text and art seamless. He was a true collaborator (and worked with Liz on dozens more books, including the winningly clever Something Queer series).

But back to *Arnold of the Ducks*—for it was the first book that Mordicai wrote as well as illustrated. That little pen-and-ink drawing is a masterpiece of expressive line. Those ducks are positively reveling as they help Arnold keep his feathery garb in good working order. Their puffy cheeks, so absolutely duck-like, convey completely their pride and love for this new member of their family. Arnold's smile, his posture, the crinkles around his eyes, really just a few sketchy lines, let the reader know exactly how Arnold feels. From a distance, the drawing is perfect, but a closer look shows the work behind the perfection. There are white-out marks hiding stray or unnecessary lines, even a cut-out patch where Mordicai redrew part of Arnold's hand. Just as you don't see the hard work and hours of painstaking practice that went into Philippe Petit's soaring act of daring between the Towers, you don't see the hard work and hours of painstaking practice that go into Mordicai's own soaring acts of daring, acts that define each and every book he writes and illustrates. In *Arnold,* we also see the seeds of a subject that Mordicai would explore in greater depth in both *The Wild Boy* and *Victor,* that of the feral child. He was also exploring—in my opinion—the core of intuitive behavior that children have in abundance but most of us sadly lose when we grow older.

There have been many joys in working with Mordicai. He is a lovely, gentle man, with a twinkle in his eye and a way of looking at the world around him that is not exactly square on. His work in animation and filmmaking gave him, I think, the ability to look at story from many perspectives. In his book *The Room,* which grew from an experimental film he did in the 1960s, Mordicai gives us not only the story of an ordinary room but also the story of all the people who live in the room over time, and even a bit of the story of the city the room inhabits. In this ordinary room a little girl sees fairies, and families with children and a dentist with ducks come and go while the city grows outside one of the room's windows and a pear tree endures outside the other. Mordicai fills this simple little room with all the explicit detail that makes even the most ordinary life extraordinary. There's humor here, too, both high and low, as in all of Mordicai's books. At the end of *The Room,* the reader has chuckled and sighed and is ready to be the next to take the "for rent" sign out of the window.

Mordicai is interested in everything! He's an accomplished cook, an intrepid bicyclist, an avid reader of all things from poetry to history, and, of course, a painter and sculptor. He is a deeply spiritual man who brings an academic's eye and mind to his exploration of the stories of the Bible. When he finds a topic that piques his interest, he researches it with all the fervor of a dogged detective. His more than thirty books are a reflection of these interests. From *The Room* to *Tales of Pan* to *The Gigantic Baby* to *What Charlie Heard,* Mordicai moves his readers to tears and laughter and a sense of wonder about the world. There is the "aha" of recognition coupled with the exhilaration of worlds not yet explored. Didn't you always know there was another world under your sofa, down there with all the dust bunnies (*Behind the Couch*)? Didn't you know that the months have personalities all their own (*The Story of May*)? Didn't you really believe that dogs and cats are smarter than people, proud of themselves for making *us* take care of *them* (*The New Creatures*)? Thank goodness that Mordicai knows these things, too. Thank goodness he can give them shape and a story so that we can nod and tell ourselves, "Yes, I always knew that was true."

As an editor, much of my satisfaction involved working with both text and art, helping—through questions, suggestions, and pointed comments—to make the work become fuller, tighter, more cohesive. But the particular pleasure of working directly with the creator of those words and pictures is like nothing else in the world. And for me, working with Mordicai was heaven. First of all, he has these *ideas*! Second of all, he loved talking about these ideas. And most important of all, he loved to work *with* his editor. Perhaps because he was secure in what he ultimately wanted his books and characters to be, there was always good, freewheeling discussion about his assumptions, about the effect each word or sentence or picture might have on the reader, about the internal integrity of his flights of imagination. Working with Mordicai made me a better editor. I knew he would listen to my observations and suggestions and then gently sift them through his own slightly skewed way of looking at the world. He used only what really seemed true to him, what really strengthened his own original vision of his book.

I called Mordicai the day the Caldecott Medal winner was announced: "About time!" I said. "So it took a Caldecott Medal for you to call!" he replied. And even though I haven't worked on a book with him in years, all the delights of working with him came flooding back. Not just the editorial discussions, but also his absolute niceness and deep-down goodness as a person. I remember all the talks we had, whether about bicycling or his wife Susan and daughter Risa (the love and pride he had for them so apparent); the joy he got from living in a town filled with other fine writers and illustrators; even the inevitable shared sorrows from the illnesses and deaths of friends and family. In *The Shadow of a Flying Bird*, Mordicai promised me—as well as all his readers—that the Promised Land is waiting for us. In *The Mountains of Tibet*, he showed us the rich satisfactions of living a full life (although at the time, it was the feminist twist at the end that I loved so much). And in *The Man Who Walked between the Towers*, he shows us all how memory helps the joys of life remain strong.

Thanks, Mordicai, for being a good friend, a fine writer, an exquisite artist, an impeccable observer of human nature, and an all-around terrific nice guy!

Kira-Kira

written by
Cynthia Kadohata

published by
Atheneum, 2004

HORN BOOK REVIEW

In this debut novel for young people from adult writer Kadohata (*The Floating World*), Katie Takeshima's first-person voice is compelling and often quietly humorous as she describes her family's move from Iowa to Georgia and her older sister's subsequent struggle with lymphoma. Katie worships her sister; it was Lynn who taught Katie her first word (*kira-kira*, Japanese for *glittering*) and Lynn who "said she would teach me everything in the world I needed to know." But the sisters become less close the year Katie is ten, as fourteen-year-old Lynn starts to grow up; worse, though, is that Lynn starts feeling sick. Katie's shrewd descriptions of people—relatives, friends, strangers—make startlingly vivid this novel that captures both the specific experience of being Japanese American in the 1950s and the wider experience of illness and loss. Like Meg in Lois Lowry's *A Summer to Die*, Katie is able to see what her family has lost and also what they've gained through her sister's death, leaving readers with a glittering sense of hope.—*Jennifer M. Brabander*

2005 NEWBERY ACCEPTANCE SPEECH

Cynthia Kadohata

I was looking recently at my increasingly messy night table, and I noticed a white strip sticking to the wood. I scraped at it and realized it was a piece of soft, foamy tape that I had been wrapping on my broken glasses. But because I didn't want to appear on the *Today* show with tape on my glasses, I'd finally gotten them fixed in a mall in the frenzied hours after the call from the Newbery committee. I ended up wearing my contact lenses on the show, but I still would like to thank the committee for the fact that I can now unembarrassedly go out in public with my glasses.

Reading some speeches by former Newbery winners, I noticed that Christopher Paul Curtis mentioned he was the first Newbery winner to wear dreadlocks. That got me thinking about what might be my own first, or what might distinguish me from the others. The answer came quickly. I believe I hold the distinction of receiving the earliest Newbery phone call ever.

My son, Sammy, was seventeen months old in January, and he doesn't always sleep well. On the Sunday night before "the call," I went to bed as exhausted as ever. It wasn't a situation where I thought I might be receiving a phone call soon. On the other hand, like just about everybody else in children's books, I knew who Susan Faust was. When the phone rang at 4:26 a.m., I thought it might be a friend who lives in Japan. Her son had just started school in America, and she had been calling a lot with concerns over his big move.

When I heard the words, "This is Susan Faust," I don't know if you would say I screamed exactly; it was really more of a screech such as you might hear from a seagull. When Susan said I was the winner of the Newbery, the seagull seemed to become completely hysterical. It flapped its wings and jumped up and down. Susan talked, I screamed some more, and we hung up.

I believe she told me not to tell anyone about the Newbery yet, since the public announcement hadn't been made. I'm ashamed to admit that I quickly called my brother and sister. My brother sleepily said, "Is it an emergency?" I said, "It's a good one." He said, "Did you win the lottery?" I said, "It's better."

After that a number of people called to talk to the seagull. They told me I was flying to New York that day to be on the *Today* show the next morning.

As I talked on the phone I kept noticing how the floor needed vacuuming, just as it had the day before. I thought, *Everything's exactly the same, yet everything's totally different.*

My boyfriend, George, came with Sammy and me to New York. We missed our first flight and ended up settling into our New York hotel room at two in the morning. Sammy and George seemed to be snoring within minutes. I remember feeling annoyed at how noisy they were. I had set the alarm for seven so I could shower before the car picked me up the next morning.

Every so often that night I would glance at the clock and think things like: *If I fall asleep by three, I can get four hours of sleep. What if I'm only imagining all this? It would be so embarrassing if I only thought I'd won the Newbery, and I really hadn't. But if I were imagining all this, I wouldn't be in New York. But what if I'm not really in New York? Wait a second. Obviously, I'm in New York.*

. . . If I fall asleep by 3:30, I can get three-and-a-half hours of sleep. The last time I remember seeing the clock, it was 3:40.

When I arrived at the studio the next morning, Kevin Henkes was sitting on a couch. I sat next to him. Two weeks earlier, I had been on the phone with the royalty department at Simon and Schuster, begging them to overnight a check to me, and now I was sitting next to *the* Kevin Henkes. Was the world going completely insane? I seem to remember several people shaking my hand and saying, "I've read Kevin's book, but I haven't read yours."

Later that day I walked back and forth several times from various goings-on to my hotel room. The temperature in New York was thirteen degrees, and I was dressed California-warm and wearing shoes with heels. By the end of the day, I was loaded down with a bouquet of white roses, a battery-operated Teletubby, and a bag full of Simon and Schuster books for Sammy. My shoes were growing tighter every second. George was wearing only a windbreaker. Sammy was completely covered up in a pile of coats, scarves, and blankets. The only way you knew he was in the stroller was by the wailing emanating from beneath the blankets. We must have looked pretty pathetic, because several people asked whether we needed help. And, this being New York, some people just shouted out their advice: "Get that baby inside!"

At the hotel, Sammy didn't care much about the Newbery. He wanted to be fed. He wanted to play in his bath. He needed to work off some energy walking up and down the hotel hallway. That night he and George again seemed to be snoring within minutes. And again I lay in bed awake, with thoughts nearly exactly the same as I'd had the night before.

The next evening we were back in Los Angeles. During the car ride home from the airport I felt a sort of quiet elation; it was maybe the first time since Monday that I felt quiet inside myself. The freeway was calming, like water rushing around me. Just as I was starting to feel satisfied, and maybe even self-satisfied, regurgitated orange airplane food appeared all over my clothes. Sammy looked up at me with a puzzled expression and orange lips.

I looked at George. He too seemed puzzled. He said, "Monday was supposed to be a perfectly normal workday."

I had never seen George as stressed as he'd been the previous three days. Let me explain something about George. He has the body type, the courage, and the heart of a bear. He is a police officer. People have shot at him. He once crawled into a fiery building to save a woman. He has chased killers through the streets. He once said to me wistfully, "Nobody has tried to kill me in a long time." But this was different. This was the Newbery. The astonishing thing about the Newbery is that it spans your life: you first read a Newbery book as a child and you're still reading Newbery books when you retire. So the very word "Newbery" encompasses the world you live in today and the world you left behind.

People have asked me, "Where did you get the idea for your novel?" I have basically been answering, "From the world I left behind."

My first real-life home was Chicago, where I was born in 1956. My family moved to Georgia for a while, then to Arkansas for seven years. As in *Kira-Kira,* I really did talk with a heavy Southern accent. My sister's name was Kim, which I pronounced "Kee-uhm," and I never said, for instance, "You should see that cloud," but rather, "Y'all should see that cloud." And the entire staff at the hospital really did come to look at my brother because they had never seen a Japanese baby before.

My father says we were raised rather freely in Arkansas. We didn't wear diapers when we played in the back yard, just did our thing whenever and wherever we felt the need. When my mother told my father to make us soft-boiled eggs, he fed us raw ones instead because, he says, "You didn't seem to care one way or the other." My nickname was Nee, and I liked dogs, playing chess, reading, and complaining. Today I like dogs, reading, and complaining.

When I think of my father in Arkansas, I think, *my father worked.* When I think of my mother, I think, *my mother read.* When my mother began taking us to the library, she discovered a love of reading at the same time we did. Someone once said to me, "The problems between your parents began when your mother started reading." My mother quoted Kierkegaard and the Bible with equal fervor to my sister and me. She made us read *Scientific American* articles we scarcely understood. I remember one article about peer pressure and another about monkeys who became warped because they didn't have love. One of my favorite childhood memories is of when my mother became obsessed with the stars. She made charts of the constellations and lay with us in the backyard at night to look at the clear skies of our small Arkansas town. One of the family activities I remember most vividly is burning our garbage together in the incinerator in back at night, the ashes sparkling through the air as the fire warmed our faces. All of that is part of my real-life home, as well as my home as a writer. Out of our homes, I believe, grow our stories.

My father worked as a chicken sexer, separating the male from the female chicks at hatcheries. Some weeks he worked one hundred hours, and some days the only time we saw him was when he was asleep. I remember peeking into my parents' bedroom at 2 p.m. and giggling as he snored.

As an Army veteran, my father had learned chicken sexing under the GI bill after the war. Because of the brutal hours in his profession, he took amphetamines to stay awake and tranquilizers to go to sleep. But he made enough money to buy us a house. Later, when my parents divorced, he said he laid in his tiny apartment with sheets on his windows and believed that his life was over.

When I say *Kira-Kira* grew from "the world I left behind," I'm usually referring to those years in the South. But in writing this speech, I realized another impetus from a world left behind. One day, near the start of what I expected to be my senior year in high school, I walked off my Hollywood, California, high school campus and didn't return. Something I haven't mentioned in interviews is that I was a high school dropout. And I believe the way I felt when I dropped out was a little the way Katie Takeshima felt when her sister got sick, like she didn't know what to do or where to go. My English teacher, Mrs. Stanley, had given me an A. But mostly my grades were bad, my attendance was worse, and I had just been told by the administration that I was being held back a year. Mrs. Stanley was one of those people you meet every so often in life who seem to have been sent from a divine source to guide you. But Mrs. Stanley retired, and I didn't return to high school.

My mother worked as a secretary by day and attended law school by night. When I told her I'd dropped out, she told me I had to either go back to school or get a job. Thus began my brief careers as a salesclerk and a hamburger waitress. I was a bad salesclerk, but I like to think I was a splendid waitress, with just the right balance of good manners and sassiness.

After I'd dropped out, I sought out the library near my home. Seeking it out was more of an instinct, really, not a conscious thought. I didn't think to myself, *I need to start reading again.* I *felt* it. I rediscovered reading—the way I'd read as a child, when there was constantly a book I was just finishing or just beginning or in the middle of. I rediscovered myself.

At eighteen I began attending a two-year college. I decided to major in journalism because I thought it was more "practical" than English. To quote Joan Didion, "Was anyone ever so young?"

Many of the students at the journalism program in the two-year college were older. Most were like me: people with a lot of confusion and a little hope.

After finishing the program at the two-year college, I transferred to a university. The students were different: younger, with a little confusion and a lot of hope. One summer during school I worked as a salesclerk at Sears. I proudly told the other salesclerks that I wanted to be a writer. They laughed loudly, and one said, "What are you going to write about, working at Sears?" And I confess I thought they had a good point. What would I write about? Other people suggested I "write a best seller."

A couple of years after I got my degree in journalism, I moved to Boston to be near my older sister. But before I left Los Angeles, I decided to take a bus trip through parts of America. I think I felt I needed to conjure up some spirits. Whenever I wrote anything for college, I would listen to music or smell perfume from long ago, anything to conjure up the writing spirits.

So I bought a month-long Greyhound pass and started with a ride to Oregon, which I'd never visited.

I remember walking on the beach talking to a former Coast Guardsman who had recently returned from being stationed in Alaska. As we strolled on the sand, he told me that his best moment ever was saving the life of a five-year-old boy. He gave me a green glass fishing float that he said he had found on a beach in Alaska. He believed the float had traveled across the Pacific Ocean. I still have that float. I like to think it once belonged to a fisherman in Russia or Japan.

I met an old woman on the bus who said she had left Oklahoma during the Dust Bowl years to pick fruit in California. She said she was sick and in her eighties, and this was the last trip she would ever take. She told me she'd known a lot of people who'd died over the years. I told her I'd never known anyone who'd died, and she was so surprised she threw her head back and it hit the window. I told her she'd lived a fascinating life, and she said I wouldn't think so if I'd been there. She emanated kindness. We hugged when she got off at Amarillo, Texas, and she said something like, "I hope you have a nice life." That was nearly a quarter of a century ago. In fact, I can imagine myself saying something similar today to a young girl on a bus, trying to understand who she is and why, and where she should go.

Later that night on the bus, I opened my eyes and saw smokestacks amid an explosion of greenish fluorescent lights. It was a factory, and it was an astonishing sight rising from the barren flatlands. From somewhere in back a man called out, "This is America!"

What those words conjured up in my heart was a sense of what it meant to me to be an American in general, and in particular, an American writer. It did not mean shared history or even shared values with other Americans, but a shared landscape. What all of us shared were the factories, the deserts, the cities, the wheat fields. That sharing was an immense responsibility we had to one another.

I understood then that I could write about my section of that shared landscape.

One of your first realizations when you win a Newbery is that you didn't win it alone. Many things have to happen over the decades in order to reach the magical moment. Twenty years ago, I was going to grad school and living in the attic of a big house on Pittsburgh's south side. I already had one roommate, and my second roommate arrived one late summer day. Her name was Caitlyn Dlouhy, and she later became my editor at Atheneum Books for Young

Readers. Caitlyn alleges that I didn't come down to say hello that first day, and also that the first time she saw me I was wearing a glamorous silk robe—and my glasses were held together with tape.

Caitlyn is one of my closest friends and one of the most beautiful, happy people I have ever known. I wrote this novel because of her prodding. She has changed my life equally with her editing and with her happiness.

I want to thank the Newbery committee for the incredible honor and the incredible miracle of this award. Not long after they called me I was standing at the edge of a swimming pool watching one pink and one yellow rubber duck float around in the water. Sammy was playing beside me. I watched him for a minute, and when I looked up again I couldn't see the pink duck anywhere. I felt a moment of panic and maybe even despair. I thought, *My God, I'm in an alternate universe now. There is no pink rubber duck in this universe, and I haven't won the Newbery.* Being transported to an alternate universe seemed no more or less amazing than winning the Newbery.

I want to thank George, who has sustained me fervently and whose belief in me has often been greater than my belief in myself. I'd also like to thank everyone at Simon and Schuster, who published a book for no other reason than that they believed in it. In particular, thanks to Susan Burke, Caitlyn's assistant and future editor extraordinaire; Michelle Fadlalla, Jennifer Zatorski, and the entire talented marketing and publicity teams; the magnificent Russell Gordon; Jeannie Ng; Rick Richter; and the incomparable Ginee Seo.

Although my son is still too young to understand this, I'd like to say a few words for him on this night that is so important to me. When I was in Kazakhstan adopting him, another single woman and I told each other that the international adoption process was the hardest thing we'd ever done. Do you know why we said that? Because we hadn't become mothers yet.

My plane ride home from Kazakhstan was scheduled for something like 4:20 a.m. I didn't sleep at all that night. Right before I passed through the airport's gates, I turned to say goodbye to the adoption agency's driver. Before I could say anything, he shouted out the last two sentences I would ever hear from him. The first sentence was, "Once you pass through those gates we cannot help you anymore." He pointed to a door beyond the gates. The second sentence was, "If they take you into that room to shake you down, do not give them more than twenty dollars!" I believe I had about $1,800 in cash on me, since nearly all transactions in Kazakhstan, including paying apartment rent and adoption-related fees, were conducted in cash. I passed through the gates, staring fearfully at that door. But the guard smiled at me, and after more than seven weeks in Kazakhstan, I was on my way home.

I had a two-hour wait in the airport, a seven-hour ride to Germany, a four-hour layover in Germany, and a twelve-hour flight to Los Angeles. Sammy cried inconsolably nearly the whole way. On the first flight, I tearfully approached a man I thought I'd heard speaking English and said, "Are you an American? Can you help me?" He was. He did. On the second flight, a man told me that because of Sammy's crying the entire airplane was talking about me. A beautiful and generous family from Finland watched Sammy while I slept.

There were many moments after our return when I told myself, I cannot do this. I am not a mother, and I cannot be a mother. I have three more novels scheduled to be published by Atheneum. In the fourth, I quote from the ancient Chinese philosopher Chuang Tzu. For my son, I'd like to quote from Chuang Tzu now:

> Once I, Chuang Tzu, dreamed I was a butterfly and was happy as a butterfly. I was conscious that I was quite pleased with myself, but I did not know that I was Tzu. Suddenly I awoke, and there was I, visibly Tzu. I do not know whether it was Tzu dreaming that he was a butterfly or the butterfly dreaming that he was Tzu. Between Tzu and the butterfly there must be some distinction. But one may be the other. This is called the transformation of things.

At some point, without even realizing it, I became a mother who only dreamed she was not. This is called the transformation of things.

I also need to thank my family. When either second or third grade—I forget which—was coming to an end, I had fallen in love with the reader we used in school. I told my parents that I would not return the book. I loved it too much. I cried. I ranted. I raged. I wanted that book. Finally my parents decided that my mother, who'd taken typing in high school and owned an old manual typewriter she practiced on, should type up the book before we returned it. I still remember the Xs all over her typing errors. A few years later I got a Christmas gift from my family. It was a notepad with the Lucy character from Peanuts. A frown furrowed Lucy's brow. The caption read, "No one understands us crabby people." That gift proves that somebody did understand me. So I really need to thank my family for their understanding, and I hope that I've returned it.

I also have to thank my dog Shika, who lies by my side every moment that I write.

I've moved many times in my life. Whenever I move to a new place, I call the phone company and the gas company. I don't like to drive so I figure out the transportation system. And I figure out where the nearest library is.

I read voraciously until I finished eighth grade. Then I hardly read at all for three years. I look back on 1973, the year I dropped out of school, with the belief that libraries cannot just change your life but save it. Not the same way a Coast Guardsman or a police officer might save a life, not all at once. It happens more slowly, but just as surely.

I started out tonight by discussing what distinguished me from other Newbery winners. I believe what we all have in common with one another and with everybody in this room is that we search out libraries like heat-seeking missiles. And another thing we have in common: our parents could not have afforded to buy us all the books we read as children. Our parents walked across the doorway of that first library holding our hands because they knew our futures resided in that building, as I believe the futures of my son and indeed of all Americans reside in those buildings.

Libraries fed our passion as children, and feed it still.

AUTHOR PROFILE BY CAITLYN M. DLOUHY

Cynthia Kadohata

SHE WAS THE mysterious woman in the black silk robe who lived in the attic. The door leading to the attic was always closed, and once every so often, I'd hear pacing. Somewhat more often, I'd hear the low hum of an electric typewriter. But it was the silence that was startling. I'd been there for two days, and had so far only caught a single glimpse of my housemate late at night, running down the stairs in a black silk robe.

We were in the same graduate writing program. On the third day, as I struggled to finish a short story to bring to my first writing workshop, the mysterious upstairs roommate chose to come downstairs at the Exact Same Time that I did. She was in the black silk robe. She wore glasses held together by a knot of tape. She sort of nodded at me, then glided off toward the kitchen. That was how I met Cynthia Kadohata.

I didn't see her again until that first workshop—led by Lewis "Buddy" Nordan. That first class consisted primarily of our being told that we would read stories from our fellow classmates each week and critique them the following week. We had to be ruthless, ruthless, but not opinionated. Basically, we couldn't say, "I think this story stinks." We had to say, "This story stinks because . . ." Buddy then gave us a brief summary on each of the three short stories he was passing out for next week's class. The third one, he told us, was titled "Snow" and was about a racetrack. I grimaced. I had not even a remote interest in reading about racetracks. My mind jumped ahead to next week, on how I would position my critique. "This story stinks because it's about a subject that is completely uninteresting to me."

Things grew worse. When the trio of manuscripts reached me, I saw that the one on top, "Snow," was written by Cynthia Kadohata, my mysterious attic roommate. Wonderful. Just wonderful. I was going to hate it and I'd have to completely avoid her until class (which didn't actually seem that difficult since I'd only seen her once in five days, anyway).

It was an assignment, so I of course had to read it. But I only needed to read the first paragraph to know—it was stunning. This was written by a girl who was in a graduate writing program, just like me. But not like me. Not like me at all. I *wanted* to be a writer. This attic roommate *was* a writer.

There are a few times in your life when you meet someone whose skill helps you recognize your own range. When you meet these people, there's no envy—because you can't envy the gifted. You either are, or you're not. Cynthia Kadohata, I knew after reading that short story, was gifted. Gifted with a clear, brave, pure voice, with a way of looking at the world that brought a freshness to her every sentence, and with an ease to her prose that seemed effortless. But I knew it wasn't effortless. Over the months, I grew to learn that the seemingly endless quiet up in the attic was the quiet that comes with intense focus.

I can't quite remember when we actually became friends, but the obvious connection, writing, wasn't what did it. Still, suddenly we were playing weekly backgammon and Trivial Pursuit tournaments and consuming horrifying amounts of Tostitos with sour cream. She taught me how to use chopsticks. I showed her the shortcut to the grocery store. We argued over which was the ideal breed of dog (she *loves* a good argument). I learned she could work herself into terrific furies. I found out she laughed a lot and danced wildly in her attic, but barefoot, with the music very low. She wrote her first short story when she was a deeply philosophical nine-year-old, contemplating the dejection that quickly follows opening presents at Christmas. And she sent her stories out—to the *New Yorker,* the *Atlantic Monthly,* the *Paris Review.* No one else in the program yet dared, but Cynthia did. She was that sure of herself. Or that hopeful.

Tobias Wolff tried to lure her to the Syracuse writing program; Columbia successfully lured her to New York with a scholarship. I finished my thesis in Pittsburgh. We wrote each other, called each other, usually very late at night.

We'd talk about anything but writing. And then, in one phone call, she just happened to mention that the *New Yorker* was publishing one of her stories. I'd expected her to be screaming with delight. Instead, I screamed for her. Cynthia, uncomfortable with the praise, deflected my enthusiasm.

Years went by; there were more short stories in more exemplary magazines. I'd congratulate her; she'd hem and haw and change the conversation. Cynthia moved a lot when she was a child; her parents swung from Chicago to Georgia to Arkansas to Michigan, from apartment to house to motel to house to motel, searching for better work and a better life for Cynthia and her older sister and younger brother. And it seemed that Cynthia herself couldn't relinquish that peripatetic lifestyle. She moved again and again, and when she wasn't moving, she was traveling through the badlands and prairies of America on a Greyhound bus, just to see. To search for connections that would inspire her writing, connections that might make her think of a home she never really had. So sometimes there'd be gaps when I'd have no idea where she was, what she was doing. Then one day she called to say she'd written a novel. Would I look at it? She just wanted to know if I liked it or not, even though it had already been bought by Viking. I read it, thought it was gorgeous, and told her so. She thanked me, and then about a year later sent me a first edition of her debut adult novel, *The Floating World*.

Another year went by. Cynthia was living in Los Angeles at this point. I should have been living in New York, but in my first month there, interviewing for an entry-level publishing job, I'd broken my ankle so badly I had to go back to Massachusetts so my parents could take care of me. About three days after the surgery Cynthia called and asked if I'd read something else for her. This time she didn't want to know if I liked it or not—well, she did want to know that—but she also wanted to know where the story wasn't working. It was another novel for Viking. Would I write up some notes?

I was flabbergasted. *She* wanted *me* to write up some notes? I felt so honored.

I began working on the manuscript the day it arrived. I wrote copious notes on about the first twenty pages before I allowed myself a break. The next day, I picked up the manuscript again and realized I couldn't remember a word I'd read. I looked at my notes, and they made not one bit of sense. I'd learned a very valuable lesson—you can't edit while on Percocet.

Determined to do right by the trust Cynthia had placed in me, I took no painkillers the next day. A week later, I had my dad mail off what I thought was a brilliant editorial letter to Cynthia.

And I heard nothing. Cynthia called, sure, to see how the old ankle was doing. But she said nothing about the letter. She'd call again, to say she was sending me a book she was sure I'd love, and still say nothing about the letter.

I decided that somehow it never got to her, and she was too polite (Cynthia is exceedingly polite) to mention it, not wanting to seem as though she were pressuring me to hurry up and get my notes to her. So I decided to check. "Yep, got your letter," she said, then immediately changed the subject. I tried not to panic. But I knew. She was furious. We continued checking in with each other for another six months, never once mentioning The Letter. Every time I'd put down the phone, I'd think, Phew. She didn't explode this time. But. It was coming.

And it did. And, as with most things with Cynthia, not in the way I'd expected. One day I picked up the phone to hear her already in mid-rant. Cynthia will often begin a conversation halfway in—by which I mean she's so intent on getting right to the point that she sometimes forgets the formalities of hello/how are you/it's me Cynthia, and instead launches full steam into whatever she needs to talk about. She was *furious*. She'd just reread my notes on her novel, six months after receiving them. Six months after slamming them into a drawer after deciding I couldn't possibly have been more off-base in my assessment of her work. But today, she'd been feeling particularly masochistic and had decided to reread my letter. And she was furious because she realized she now agreed with almost everything I'd written.

And I realized I might just have a future in editing.

Fast-forward to Cynthia's wedding on the top of a volcano in Las Vegas. She'd asked me to be a bridesmaid. I was an assistant editor in a publishing company and couldn't possibly afford the plane ticket. But by now my parents had met Cynthia several times and had unofficially claimed her as a second daughter. A few days after I'd told them that Cynthia was getting married, an envelope arrived containing a check and note that said: Go to Cynthia's wedding. I went. The bride wore a sarong, a huge sunflower in her hair, and may have been barefoot. As I said, Cynthia never does anything quite as expected.

During this time, I'd had the supreme good fortune of working at Laura Geringer's imprint at HarperCollins. As I read through the never-ending piles of submissions, I kept thinking of Cynthia. Every one of Cynthia's novels, while published by adult divisions, actually featured an adolescent or teen protagonist. Her voice was so true. Her prose could be heartbreaking without ever slipping into sentimentality. She created characters you felt you'd known forever. As I rejected yet another poorly written manuscript, I came to a decision. Cynthia would have to write a book for children. She was born to do it. And I was going to pester her ceaselessly until she did.

And so I began. After days of mental rehearsals, I slipped my idea into a conversation. "Gee, I keep thinking about how much I loved Olivia in *The Floating World,* and she's only twelve. Have you ever thought—"

She was in the middle of a new novel.

I waited until she finished the novel and asked again.

She was taking a screenplay class. *The Floating World* had been optioned for film, and the director wanted her to try her hand at writing the screenplay.

I waited another year.

She was still working on the screenplay. Also, her brain was bloated from eating too much over the holidays.

I waited another year.

She was writing another screenplay. But yes, she'd love to speak at my wedding.

I moved to Atheneum. The move made me all the more determined.

But this time I took a different tack. I would lure her with a box of books. Books by Bruce Brooks and Elaine Konigsburg and Frances O'Roark Dowell, books by Katherine Paterson and Phyllis Reynolds Naylor and Hilary McKay. Books and books and books. I could barely haul that box to the mailroom. Oh, and I wrote a note. "Read these." I'd like to think I added something encouraging such as "You can be *this* good," but I'm afraid I probably didn't.

And then, once again, I waited. Finally, I received an e-mail from her: "How dark could a YA novel be?"

I nearly fell out of my chair. She was thinking about it. She was thinking about it! I practically cartwheeled into my then-publisher Ginee Seo's office. "Cynthia Kadohata is thinking about writing something for children!" I shouted. Ginee knew I'd wanted to work with her for years. She was as gleeful as I was, and said that if Cynthia could put a story idea into a proposal, we could give her a contract. I dashed off an e-mail to Cynthia. She responded immediately: "How do you write a proposal?"

After a few more days, another e-mail arrived, titled "Proposal, or something I think might be a proposal." It was not a proposal. It was a gorgeously written sixteen-page piece in the voice of a little girl, Katie, who was telling the reader about how her older sister Lynn would dangle her mother's rhinestone necklace in her face and repeat the words *pika-pika* (a word similar in meaning to *kira-kira*).

Cynthia is a novelist to the core of her being. She is absolutely incapable of summarizing a story. She could not write: "This is a book about two sisters; one eight and the other twelve." Instead, she had given me paragraphs, then pages. She had given me the opening chapter of *Kira-Kira*.

It took ten years of nudging, but at last she was going to write a children's book.

It's a tricky thing, editing a very good friend. When I'm editing her, I have to be her editor first, and I can't think about her feelings. I have to be honest about what doesn't work, and that can be upsetting. As I had learned, Cynthia could be, shall we say, *touchy* about criticism at first, even criticism with the very best intentions. So I sent out my first editorial letter on *Kira-Kira* with a certain amount of fear in my heart. I didn't know if I could take another six months of furious silence.

I won't ever know how many darts were thrown at my picture as she read my letter. I only know that with a single revision, Cynthia brought forth elements in *Kira-Kira* that I could never have known to ask for but that were simply perfect. For instance, I knew her much-beloved Doberman was failing while Cynthia was writing the book. She somehow transformed the personal heartbreak of watching her dog die into Katie's lonely agony over her sister, into that scene where Katie chases wildly, desperately, after the setting sun, climbing higher and higher, not wanting the last day her sister was alive to end. And I knew she knew very well, as Katie in *Kira-Kira* does, what it was like to feel "other." When Cynthia's family moved after seven years from Arkansas to Michigan, her drawl was so thick that the teacher recommended speech therapy so people could understand her. Her strongest memories of her father are of him working impossible hours so that his family could finally have a home of their own, much as she has Katie's parents work and sacrifice for their children in *Kira-Kira*.

Cynthia once said that every piece of writing strikes a balance between experience and imagination. This is certainly true for her. She mines personal experiences and weaves them with singular imagination, giving us worlds we'd never know otherwise. Imagine not knowing that we were once a country where an entire hospital would turn up to see a newborn Asian baby. Yet this very thing happened when Cynthia's brother was born, and a similar scene takes place when Katie's little brother is born in *Kira-Kira*. Imagine not knowing that we were once a country where women in some jobs were not allowed to take even a bathroom break while they were working. Her father's descriptions of the working conditions in the poultry plants in the 1950s brought this horrifying fact to Cynthia's attention. Cynthia in turn brings it to ours as we read about the pads the female poultry plant workers had to wear, as they were denied any breaks during the day. Yet once you've read about this in Cynthia's novel, you'll never forget. That's the power of words under the power of a gifted writer.

I find that gifted writers are usually gifted revisionists. Gifted revisionists are an editor's dream. Cynthia admits, now, to a bit of storming around the house, a little old-fashioned pouting, when she receives a revision letter. But I suspect such letters best serve to get her creative ire up. *I'll show her!* she probably thought just before moving the scene in which Katie's father smashes the car with a two-by-four to later in the novel so that it would have that much more emotional impact. She'll never duck an opportunity to make her work stronger. She is fearless in the face of hard work.

Cynthia writes when life is good, she writes when life is bad. She writes when life is terrifying. Last June she flew to Kazakhstan to bring home the baby boy she was adopting. She was going alone, as a single mother. She had $12,600 strapped to her waist—for the orphanage fees, for rent, for unexpected necessities. She was scared. She went anyway. The trip was supposed to last three weeks. Bureaucracy she struggled to understand in a language she didn't understand pushed three weeks to four, to five, to six, to seven. She hunkered down in a flat with a single light bulb and brown water spurting irregularly from the sink and bath pipes. And when she wasn't with the baby during the Baby House's visiting hours, she wrote. And wrote and wrote and wrote. By hand. She came home with her son, Sammy, and her next novel. A children's book.

She is a writer who has always wandered, searching for a place that feels like home—for herself, and for her writing. Since adopting Sammy, Cynthia hasn't moved once. I'd like to think she might stay where she is for a good while with her new family. And I'd like to think that maybe Cynthia has also found a home in children's books, in writing for children, within a community of artists who share her passion. When she finished *Kira-Kira,* I asked her if she would like to write more for children. Without a moment's hesitation, she shouted (yes, she shouted), "YES!" She'd never had something come so naturally. She loved it. So yes, the mysterious woman in the attic, the surreptitious dancer, might just be home. For that, and for her many gifts, including the great gift of her friendship, I will be forever grateful.

Kitten's First Full Moon

written and illustrated by
Kevin Henkes

published by
Greenwillow, 2004

HORN BOOK REVIEW

Henkes takes a break from his signature mice—and from illustrating in color—to tell this sweet story about a kitten who thinks the full moon is a bowl of milk. The black-and-white forms, with subtle gradations of gray, are larger and more solid-looking than Henkes's usual work, with less interior line. Nevertheless, the kitten, whose white fur glows against the charcoal-gray sky like the moon she desires, is sprightly and expressive as she fails repeatedly ("Poor Kitten!") to get at that milk. Small children, for whom the rhythmic, action-oriented text is just right, will appreciate the gentle slapstick of the kitten getting a firefly on her tongue when she tries to lick the moon and getting drenched in the pond when she tries to drink the moon's reflection. Anyone who has ever watched a cat spasmodically pounce and chase for no apparent reason will enjoy the imaginative, unpretentiously poetic method Henkes reads into this madness.—*Christine M. Heppermann*

2005 CALDECOTT ACCEPTANCE SPEECH

Kevin Henkes

The picture book texts I love most are those that are so succinct that not one word can be extracted and not one word need be added. Those that get right to the point and are not overly long. And so I thought it would be fitting if tonight I simply stood before you and borrowed from a character of mine by remarking, "Wow! That's just about all I can say," and then sat down.

However, more than one person has informed me that a speech is, in fact, not a picture book. And so I will elaborate.

It was Kitten's first full moon.
When she saw it, she thought,
There's a little bowl of milk in the sky. And she wanted it.

In the life of a young child there are many firsts, one right after the next, in a row that seems to stretch to eternity. I recently read through the scrapbooks my wife and I have kept for our children, starting from their births. The word *first* appears on nearly every page in the earlier books, sometimes more than once.

These are some of the "firsts" we noted: First bath. First feeding. First visitors. First car trip. First night away from home. First smile. First time sleeping through the night (not to happen again for about five-and-a-half years). First cold. First flight. First rainbow. First blown kiss. First haircut. First snowfall.

As a child gets bigger, so, too, do the firsts. Here are a few more: First word. First steps. First sentence. First day of school. First time zipping up a jacket with no help.

The list goes on and on. The magnitude of each first, each act, is staggering when you consider it. Think of them, these firsts, and think of the child experiencing them.

A child—someone who is egocentric, but powerless. Someone whose knowledge is limited, but whose imagination is vivid. Someone whose experience is limited, but who has curiosity to spare. These combinations are complex and difficult by their nature. They provide the perfect setup for a child to misinterpret with great certainty. Northrop Frye wrote, "Nearly all of us have felt, at least in childhood, that if we imagine that a thing is so, it therefore either is so or can be made to become so." A blanket on a chair at night *can* be a bear. An illustration in a book *can* be as physically real as the book itself. The moon *can* be a bowl of milk.

Back to firsts. The sociologist Erving Goffman made the following observation: "To walk, to cross a road, to utter a complete sentence, to wear long pants, to tie one's shoes, to add a column of figures—all these routines that allow the individual unthinking competent performances were attained through an acquisition process whose early stages were negotiated in a cold sweat."

These negotiators are who I write and illustrate picture books *for*. They are also who I write *about*. And Kitten, of course, is a child. She is myopic. She is curious. She is persistent. She wants and wants and wants. She makes mistakes. She misunderstands. She gets hurt. She is confused. She is scared. She is also a symbol, a symbol that says: childhood is anything but easy.

Another first. This time, mine. My first trip to New York City. I was Kitten, and Greenwillow Books was the moon.

It was twenty-five years ago next month that I, at age nineteen, flew from Wisconsin to New York in search of a publisher. I was armed with a map of Manhattan (photocopied from a book at my local library), three portfolios filled with what I thought was my best artwork, a dummy for what would become my first picture book, and a list of my ten favorite publishers. Greenwillow Books was my first choice, my number one.

Just to make sure that I wouldn't be late, I arrived at 105 Madison Avenue, Greenwillow's then-home, about an hour before my morning appointment with Susan Hirschman.

I don't really remember Susan looking at my work, although I know she did. Mostly I remember talking about favorite books, many of which we agreed on. And I remember Susan asking, "How old are you? Where are you staying? Why did your mother let you come?" (I think she thought I was twelve.)

Then Susan asked where I was going for my next appointment, and when I told her, she said, "We'll just have to take you before they do. Let's call your mother and tell her we're going to publish your book."

The moon, a bowl of milk—call it what you will, I'd found it. And so I was taken in by the Greenwillow family—my only publisher in twenty-five years. I walked about a foot above the ground for the rest of my stay in New York.

I suppose you could say that, like Kitten, I was naive. Remember, I was nineteen. I truly thought I would go to New York and come home with a contract for a book. That I did so is a miracle. And I will be grateful to Susan forever for that. Would I have the same confidence now, at age forty-four? I doubt it.

During my early Greenwillow years, I'd travel to New York once or twice a year, usually for a week. Susan would often find an empty office in which I'd write. Some of my early books were composed and polished in New York. If I happened to be in town when my art director, Ava Weiss, was going to press nearby, she'd take me with her. Ada Shearon was managing editor, and Libby Shub was senior editor. I learned so much from these four women about all aspects of American trade publishing for children. I was hungry and they were willing to share what they knew.

The Greenwillow staff changed very little over the years—one of the many things I love about Greenwillow. It truly has a family feel to it. Phyllis Larkin joined Greenwillow during what I call my "middle Greenwillow years." And now, of course, Susan, Ava, and Phyllis have retired, and Virginia Duncan is the publisher and also my editor.

I think of *Kitten's First Full Moon* as a bridge book, a link from Greenwillow before to Greenwillow now. *Kitten* began with Susan and Ava, but by the time

I finished it, I was working with Virginia and my new art director, Paul Zakris. The influence of all four of them is surely present. The book wouldn't exist without Susan and Ava, and it wouldn't be the book it is without Virginia and Paul.

Books have many beginnings; sometimes they're difficult to pinpoint. But I know this: I've always been drawn to picture books for the youngest child. I love their simplicity and their poetic nature. When I became a parent, this attraction intensified, and so I tried my hand at creating board books. I also became interested in simple concept books and tried without success to write one. One failed attempt was all about circles—a ball, a bowl, a button, a plate, a marble. One of the lines read: "The cat thought the moon was a bowl of milk." The book idea didn't work, but I liked this line and it stuck with me. Over time—several years—the line expanded and finally became the words for *Kitten's First Full Moon*.

As I was rereading my son's and daughter's scrapbooks to prepare this speech, I stumbled upon what I think might be another link to how *Kitten* began. The entry that made me pause was in my son's scrapbook, describing his first rainbow. This is what I wrote: "There was a huge rainstorm today . . . You watched from the window. Soon, the sun broke through the clouds and we all went out to look at a magnificent rainbow—your first! It was a double rainbow—one arc curving over the other. I wonder what you must think of it—colors in the sky that aren't usually there."

Obviously, a rainbow is not the same as light reflected off the moon, but a few key elements are similar to those in the book: a very young child, a natural phenomenon, the sky. But most important and interesting is my comment at the end of the entry: "I wonder what you must think of it—colors in the sky that aren't usually there." It's this kind of musing that allows a writer to see things differently, to see things the way a child might—to see, perhaps, the moon as a bowl of milk.

From the start I pictured this book with black-and-white illustrations, bold sans serif type, a square trim size, and soft, creamy paper. I love to use color—even bright color—in most of my picture books, but for this book color seemed unnecessary. I thought that by keeping everything as simple and spare as possible, a better, tighter, more complete book would result. I liked the idea of having a white moon, a white cat, and a white bowl of milk surrounded by the black night.

When I draw, I usually use a crow-quill pen, which makes a rather thin line. This time I wanted a much thicker line, and I wanted the line to vary in thickness, so I drew with a brush—a technique I'd never used in any of my other books. This allowed me a freedom I'd not previously experienced while doing finished art. I'd been used to scratching away for hours making small marks.

With a brush I could make broad strokes and long continuous lines. I could define shapes with a single motion.

The art was prepared using black gouache for the line and black and gray colored pencils. But the book was printed in four colors on a full-color press. This gave the illustrations a richness and depth they wouldn't have had if the book had been printed with black ink only.

Although the finished art is very dissimilar to hers, I thought of *Kitten's First Full Moon* as a sort of tribute to Clare Turlay Newberry all the while I worked on it. The black-and-white illustrations of cats in her books, including *Mittens, Pandora,* and *Marshmallow,* are masterful. I've always admired them. And although she isn't given a name other than Kitten, I secretly think of my heroine as Clare.

I also admire the work of Jean Charlot. His illustrations for Margaret Wise Brown's *A Child's Good Night Book* and *Two Little Trains* are some of my favorites in any children's books. His line work is simple, direct, and, in my mind, perfect. I am struck by his ability to capture the essence of something beautifully, without one bit of excess. That's what I strove for in *Kitten.*

And, of course, I was thinking of the great Wanda Gág.

Here's another first. 1985. My first ALA. Coincidentally, the first ALA Annual Conference I attended was in Chicago, twenty years ago. My in-laws lived in the Chicago area, so Susan asked if my wife, Laura, and I would like to go to the Newbery-Caldecott banquet. Laura and I sat at a table with librarians, most of whom were from Kansas, if I recall correctly. None were children's librarians. They were adult card catalogers (perhaps there's a new term now). I had published only four books at the time, each of which had sold about a hundred copies (half to my mother), and no one at the table had heard of me or my books. After the speeches were over and people were rising to leave, one of the women pulled a catalog card out of her purse and asked me to sign it. She had an open face and a kind smile. I did as she requested. And as we parted, she said, "Who knows, maybe one day you'll be up there winning a medal."

For making exactly that happen, my deepest heartfelt thanks to Betsy Hearne and the 2005 Caldecott committee. I cannot adequately express how much this honor means to me.

Thanks, also, to my parents and siblings, who were there for my "firsts"; to my other family, the Dronzeks; to all my friends at HarperCollins; to everyone from my Greenwillow past; to everyone at Greenwillow present, especially Virginia; to Will and Clara; and to Laura, my first, last, and everything in between.

Thanks to the librarians and members of the American Library Association—all of you who have understood and supported me and my books all these years. Ginny Moore Kruse and the late Gertrude Herman were there for me from the start. I had intended to name more names, but if I did, we'd be here until tomorrow. I thank you all from the bottom of my heart.

And, last and most, to Susan—you gave me my work life and so much more. From "firsts" to last—one last story.

A young man who works in the art department at Greenwillow gave a copy of *Kitten's First Full Moon* to his two-year-old niece when the book was first published. I'm told that the little girl loves the book so much that, over time, she's licked a hole in the page that shows a triumphant Kitten lapping up milk after her journey.

I've rarely been paid so high a compliment. Except for tonight—another first for me, to have a book of mine honored with the Caldecott Medal. I feel as if I've come home to a bowl of milk as big as the moon.

And there really is only one thing more to say: "What a night!"

ILLUSTRATOR PROFILE BY SUSAN HIRSCHMAN

Kevin Henkes ────

TWENTY-FIVE YEARS

I AM LUCKY. Over the past twenty-five years, I have known Kevin Henkes as a very young author, a new husband, a brand-new father, a newly successful author-artist, an experienced father, an extremely successful author and supremely successful author-artist, a nontemperamental star on business trips, a joyous companion on holidays, and, always, a much-loved and loving friend.

It all started when Kevin was nineteen and came to New York with his portfolio and the dummy for his first picture book. He had made a list, in order of preference, of his choices of publishers. Greenwillow was number one. I remember looking up and seeing this apparent child walk into my office. I said something like, "What did your mother say when you told her you were coming to New York?" He looked slightly embarrassed and said, "Well, she cried." Then I looked at his portfolio. It was the work of a young man, but it was the work of someone who knew what he was doing and where he wanted to go. There was nothing tentative or out of place. And the dummy—a completely finished dummy of his first book, *All Alone*—showed that he knew what a picture book was, and that it was an art form in which he was completely at home.

I remember thinking that talent like this did not stay undiscovered for long. "Where is your next appointment?" I asked. And when he said "Harper," I accepted the dummy on the spot. Then I went to the telephone to call his mother.

A few weeks later, Kevin called to tell me he planned to drop out of college and devote himself to working on his book. "You can't," I said. I predicted every doom I could think of. A college degree was obligatory. How could he support himself? It was a precipitate and crazy decision. He was polite—and adamant. And as on so many other occasions over the years, he knew what he was doing.

In those early years, Kevin came to New York once or twice a year. We would give him an empty office, and he would write. By the end of the visit, his next book would be well under way. He would also help my assistant with the mail, read and report (brilliantly) on the unsolicited manuscripts (years later, he was the first reader of Suzanne Freeman's *The Cuckoo's Child,* and I will always remember his excitement when he told me about it), go out to get coffee for anyone who would let him, read every Greenwillow F&G and bound galley, and lunch with the younger members of the department, all of whom were his friends. He found Manhattan stimulating and wonderful. He went to the theater, he walked all over, he conquered the subway, and he stayed in a hostel run by nuns and paid $8.50 a night for his room.

I remember when he first showed that he could be funny in his books—when the little boy in *Clean Enough* iced the soap with his father's shaving cream. I remember when he enlarged *Margaret and Taylor* from a brief picture book to an early chapter book—presaging the novels to come. I remember when he changed his human characters to his signature mice—which allowed them the freedom to act in ways that are acceptable for mice but questionable for humans. And I remember when he wrote *Words of Stone.*

It was the winter of 1991. I read it, Elizabeth Shub read it, and oh, we talked. It needed work. Lots of work. But Kevin was becoming known for his mice, had written several very interesting shorter novels, and his popularity was growing. Would he listen to us, or would he want to show the novel to another publisher? And would they publish it as it stood, in order to have him on their list? It is a perennial problem for publishers, and in this case the ending was a happy one for Greenwillow. I did not know then what a perfectionist Kevin is. I did not know that there is no limit to the amount of work he will do to make something right. But I learned. And I think he learned. He never again showed us anything until he felt that each word, each sentence, each punctuation mark was exactly as he wanted it. I have known him to go over a picture-book manuscript for weeks and even months, refining, perfecting, honing, reading it aloud, listening, and listening some more. He is always open to suggestion, but he trusts himself, and certainly that trust has proved to be merited.

One of the things that distinguished Kevin as a young author, and has continued and grown as the years have passed, is his love and respect for the children's books that came before. When I first knew him, he was a regular at the Cooperative Children's Book Center in Madison. He was a passionate admirer of Crockett Johnson, Ruth Krauss, Margaret Wise Brown, Marvin Bileck, James Marshall, and many other authors and artists from the forties, fifties, and sixties. Of course that thrilled me, having grown up at Harper and learned almost everything I knew from Ursula Nordstrom. Kevin was always willing to listen to a "When I Was Young at Harper" story. And his was not an academic love. Recently he and his children, now aged ten and seven, made a list of the books he had read aloud to the two of them in the last couple of years. There were fifty-four novels on the list, including *Mr. Popper's Penguins, Freddy the Detective,* all the Ramona books, *The Moffats, Gone-Away Lake,* and *The Twenty-one Balloons.* Both kids are avid readers on their own, and both kids have always been read to separately as well as together.

Kevin and his wife, Laura Dronzek, live in a big house at the end of their street. The large yard is a gathering place for the neighborhood children. Laura is a superb painter as well as a children's book artist. She is talented, generous, wise, funny, loving, unflappable—and the best cook I know. When *Olive's Ocean* was named a Newbery Honor Book, she picked up the phone, and every friend and neighbor arrived at the house that evening to celebrate. Laura bakes with the ease of someone opening a jar of peanut butter, and there was a huge cake with a facsimile of the Newbery Honor medal, cookies, and champagne. I think the neighborhood was as excited and as happy as the Henkes family. And I understand that this year the celebration was even bigger and better. A friend of theirs recently wrote me, "Sometimes I just can't believe the amount of artistic talent, grace, and friendliness that dwells in that house." Anyone who has read his novels or his picture books knows how important family is to Kevin. Parents are three-dimensional and interesting. Children are respected and thoughtful. They enjoy each other, and they listen, eat, laugh, work, and play—together. Lilly, Julius, and their parents; Fanny and her father; Owen and his parents; Martha Boyle and her mother, father, grandmother, and siblings; Spoon, Joanie, and the other Gilmores; Sheila Rae and Louise—families all. Just like Kevin, Laura, Will, and Clara.

Kevin is almost as old now as I was when we first met. And his son, Will, is just nine years younger than Kevin was on his first trip to New York. Time is a funny thing. But what has not changed in all these twenty-five years is Kevin's

KITTEN'S FIRST FULL MOON 105

joy in his work, his appreciation of what preceded him, and his excitement at the possibilities of perfecting his craft. At any signing, people tell him about their daughter Lilly or their son Owen. And in the last few years they have begun telling him that *they* grew up on his books. They tell him what his books have meant to them and to their children. The emotion in the air is love. But then, that is the emotion that surrounds Kevin—from family, friends, readers, librarians, colleagues, teachers, and booksellers.

Someone once asked me, years ago, if I knew from the very beginning where Kevin was going and what he would do in the future. I said I had always known he was bursting with talent but no, I had had no idea of what the future would hold. That is equally true today. But I knew then, and I know now, that whatever it is, it will be worth the wait. And for now, all I can say is, "WOW."

Criss Cross

written by
Lynne Rae Perkins

published by
Greenwillow, 2005

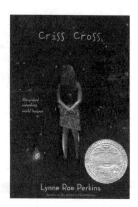

HORN BOOK REVIEW

Catching fireflies in a jar, fourteen-year-old Debbie (first met in Perkins's spectacular debut novel *All Alone in the Universe,* rev. 9/99) watches the bugs' "glow parts go on and off," appeasing her guilt over capturing them by convincing herself that "once they were free, their small, basic brains would . . . have no memory of being imprisoned." Perkins's wonderfully contemplative and relaxed yet captivating second novel, again illustrated with her own perfectly idiosyncratic spot art, is a collection of fleeting images and sensations—some pleasurable, some painful, some a mix of both—from her ensemble cast's lives. Like *All Alone in the Universe,* the story is set in a 1970s small town, but teen readers won't have to be aware of the time period to feel connected to Debbie, Hector, Lenny, and the rest as the third-person narrative floats back and forth between their often humorous, gradually evolving perspectives. The book's title refers to a radio show that the neighborhood teens listen to on Saturday evenings; on a thematic level, it also refers to those barely perceptible moments of missed communication between a boy and a girl, a parent and a child, when "something might have happened" but didn't. In keeping with Perkins's almost Zen-like tone, such flubbed opportunities are viewed as unfortunate but not tragic. "Maybe it was another time that their moments would meet." Like a lazy summer day, the novel induces that exhilarating feeling that one has all the time in the world.—*Christine M. Heppermann*

2006 NEWBERY ACCEPTANCE SPEECH

Lynne Rae Perkins

I'd like to read you a poem. It was written by Denise Levertov; a friend of mine copied it out and gave it to me for Valentine's Day one year, and I keep it, framed, in my studio.

It's called "The Secret."

Two girls discover
the secret of life
in a sudden line of
poetry.

I who don't know the
secret wrote
the line. They
told me

(through a third person)
they had found it
but not what it was
not even

what line it was. No doubt
by now, more than a week
later, they have forgotten
the secret,

the line, the name of
the poem. I love them
for finding what
I can't find,

and for loving me
for the line I wrote,
and for forgetting it
so that

a thousand times, till death
finds them, they may
discover it again, in other
lines

*in other
happenings. And for
wanting to know it,
for*

*assuming there is
such a secret, yes,
for that
most of all.*

In Michigan, where I live, there are mushrooms called morels that pop up through the earth for a few unpredictable weeks in the spring, sometime after the snow has turned to rain and the sun has started to warm up the soil. They're a delicacy; all the local restaurants have ads in the newspaper offering to buy morels, and they feature dishes made with them.

Morels are a democratic delicacy, because they are free if you can learn how to find them.

Even people who don't especially like to eat morels like to hunt for them. When you see a car parked on the side of the road in the springtime, with nothing nearby but a tree-covered hill, you know that the driver of the car is in those woods looking for morels. People have secret spots they return to every year, and while they may be only too happy to hand you a grocery bag filled with morels, they will never tell you where they found them.

There is an art to finding morels, which are brown and wrinkled and blend in with the rippled bark and the fallen twigs and the dried-up leaves and the mottled lumps of dirt. They are nearly impossible to see. Until you see them. There are people who say they can find them anywhere, and other people (including me) who almost never find them.

It's an art most often described in mystical terms:

"You look for them by not looking for them."

"You have to unfocus your eyes."

Even resolute Polish Catholics become Zen masters when it's time to hunt mushrooms in Michigan. As for me, I tromp, focusing and unfocusing, looking and not looking, through last autumn's leaves flattened by the winter's snow, and I find myself thinking of the line from Dylan Thomas's *Under Milk Wood* about Bessie Bighead watching for Gomer Owen, "who kissed her once by the pig-sty when she wasn't looking and never kissed her again although she was looking all the time."

I think the secret of life does that. It hides, brown and wrinkled, among the dead leaves and broken twigs and the lumps of dirt. It kisses you when you aren't looking.

Okay, not always—sometimes it hits you over the head. With a baseball bat.

But I think a lot of us—most of us, maybe—are looking. Even if we're looking by not looking. Looking all the time. Believing there is such a thing.

We come across little pieces of it, all six-and-a-half billion of us blind people coming across gray and wrinkled pieces of the elephant in the room that is life, that is the world.

When we arrive here, as babies, we come into such very particular situations, which can be so very different from each other. But we don't know how particular our situations are because we don't have anything to compare them to. Our world is the whole world; it's all that we know. We are pretty busy just figuring out how it all works and how we fit into it: what pleasures are there for us, what we will try to steer clear of. For a long time, our world grows larger as our parents, or those who are standing in for them, allow it to. We depend on them to help us understand it.

But all along, bit by bit, we begin to meet the world that is beyond our parents' explanations. We encounter people with ideas that contradict what we have been taught; we get new information that doesn't seem to dovetail with what we already know. We begin to try to understand the world for ourselves. And we begin to be aware that we have our own ideas that are in some way separate and different from the ideas of those around us.

The extreme example of this, of course, is if you are one of those children raised by wolves, but it happens to most of us, I think. We realize that the world is larger than anyone told us. We find out that our parents are human beings, with strengths and limitations, that they don't know everything.

Some of them are aware of this even before we tell them. Others are harder to convince.

Either way, we head out on the road that is our own life.

So, what is it like out there?

It's scary and exciting, lonely and crowded. Noisy. Boring, sometimes. It's heart-stoppingly beautiful, with unexplainable ugliness. There is kindness, cruelty, and indifference, there is serendipity, and there is being in the wrong place at the wrong time. I could go on.

It's a lot to try to make sense of, and often the tools we have seem so inadequate. If we are lucky, we might find at times that someone is walking along next to us, and they say, "You're not crazy; I see it, too." Or they say, "Did you ever notice how . . ." and for a moment the discombobulated mechanics of the world organize themselves according to some principle we hadn't perceived before, and we even see that we are a part of it, we are connected.

We pocket these moments and string them up like beads on a rosary. Like clues to a mystery. They are gifts, given freely to us by our fellow travelers, and they come in many forms. A conversation. A meeting of glances. An embrace. A song on the radio. A story.

Stories entered my life early on—stories that were told on the porch or at the kitchen table. I heard the events of our family's life reshaped creatively to make them more interesting or to support a point of view.

In what seemed to be a completely unrelated development, reading also entered my life early on. My sister Cathie taught me to read when I was four and she was six. She had learned to sound out words, and she showed me how to do it, too. I don't remember this myself; it was one of the stories I heard.

I do remember finding both the drawings and the poetry of *Go, Dog. Go!* to be deeply compelling.

The stories and the reading seemed separate because the stories were so social, while reading was, on the surface, a solitary pleasure. My parents read newspapers and magazines; they only occasionally read books. I think my attraction to reading books was seen as a harmless eccentricity, good in the sense that it was related to doing well in school. I was largely unguided, free to float down the stream of whatever reading materials came my way. I read *TV Guide* and *Little House on the Prairie* and the Childcraft encyclopedia with equal involvement.

I also watched TV and movies, and listened to music and rode my bike and had friends and stayed awake all night at sleepovers. Our family went on vacations to the seashore.

But books had a special place, an important place. I don't think I could have said why.

In junior high, when I went to the bookmobile I would pick out the thickest books I could find; if they had small, dense type and a lot of unfamiliar words, all the better. I can still picture my copy of *David Copperfield*. (This is because I still have it.) I'm sure a lot of what I read went over my head. When I reread these books now, I can hardly believe they are the same books I read then.

When I think about junior high, I think about it as the time when the rules I had been taught no longer seemed to apply. There was a new social order, and I didn't like it or my place in it. I felt suddenly insufficient, and the advice I received on this topic, while given with love and the intent to reassure, did not often seem to help me find a satisfying way to be in the world I actually lived in. This, of course, was something I had to learn for myself over a long time.

Books, though, acknowledged that life was complex. They offered up the possibility that other things besides what was happening, could happen. And I think now that though I didn't fully understand it at the time, they showed me that whatever you encounter, if you can meet it with honesty, intelligence, compassion, and humor, on some level you win. To tell the truth in an interesting way, a way that allows for real sorrow, a way that allows for real laughter, is to open a door where there had seemed to be only a wall. This is the opposite of spin, which paints a picture of a door and hangs it on the wall in a gilded frame.

I was looking for doors. Sometimes I found them. They appeared in different forms: a conversation with my dad. A song on the radio. A feeling of familiarity with someone I had only just met. A story that offered possibility. The secret of life in a sudden line of poetry.

I remember being smitten with the novels of Kurt Vonnegut, with sentences such as, "Her smile was glassy, and she was ransacking her mind for something to say, finding nothing in it but used Kleenex and costume jewelry." Or, "Her face . . . was a one-of-a-kind, a surprising variation on a familiar theme—a variation that made observers think, *Yes—that would be another nice way for people to look.*" I remember being struck by these sentences, these thoughts, these stories about the imaginary island of San Lorenzo and one of the moons of the planet Saturn and feeling that they had something to do with my life, the life I was actually living.

All of these ideas, songs, and stories helped me to meet the world that was larger than, while also contained in, the specific little town where I grew up.

They were gifts from fellow travelers. But if we only receive gifts, if we keep them all to ourselves, life dries up. If we share what we receive or give a gift of our own, however poor we think it is, life grows.

We learn this in fairy tales. The two brothers who refuse to share their "beautiful" pancakes and wine with the gray old man have incapacitating woodcutting accidents. The youngest brother, who is considered a fool, offers to share his cake made with water and baked in ashes and his bottle of sour beer, and he finds that they have been transformed into fine cakes and wine—and the gray old man also directs him to the golden goose. If you share what you have, the roles of giver and receiver reverse themselves, like alternating current. There is a connection and electricity.

Writing and drawing are two of the ways I respond to the world. There are so many ways, so many wonderful ways, but words and pictures have always been important to me, so that's what I do. A lot of what I write and draw will never see the light of day, and that is fine; it's as it should be.

But as I go along, I find that there are stories and pictures and ideas I want to share, and so—at the risk of adding one more metaphor to this whole heap that is about to topple over—I put my pancake baked in the ashes into a bottle called a book and toss it into the ocean. Actually, since I live in the Midwest, I have to send it to Virginia Duncan in New York City, who tosses it into the ocean for me.

And then I steel myself for the very real possibility that it will get lost out there. It's a big ocean, I say to myself. And such a little bottle. The important thing, I say, is to do it, whether anyone sees it or not.

But writers write because they want to connect. The agenda of a writer is simple. It is "I want to tell you something." Maybe it's a joke. Maybe a story. Maybe the secret of life. Or all three. So, try as I might to pretend it doesn't matter, I toss my bottle out there with the hope that it will be found, and even more, that someone who finds it will care about it. I have asked myself sometimes, how many people do I need to find it and care about it? And the answer I have come up with, in my moments of lowest expectations, is five or six. I've thought, if you really, really connect with five or six people, what more can you want?

And then in January of this year, I got kissed when I wasn't looking. In one short phone call, I learned that my five-person quota had been exceeded by two hundred percent, to fifteen people. And not just any fifteen people, but fifteen librarians—who in my experience are among the top one percent of humans on the earth in terms of being smart, funny, thoughtful, and principled.

That would have been enough.

But what this phone call also meant was that in a very concrete way, I get to be a fellow traveler. I get to share my pancake. I get to say to someone who may be feeling as out of sorts as I did, as I still sometimes do, "It's okay. You're not crazy. I see it, too. But have you ever noticed . . . ?"

It takes two people to make a book—a writer and a reader—and it's not clear-cut who is doing the giving and who is receiving. The roles of giver and receiver go back and forth like alternating current, when there is a connection.

I'd like to thank the American Library Association, ALSC, and Barbara Barstow and the Newbery committee from the bottom of my heart for giving me this immense opportunity to make that connection.

And because what I just said about it taking two people to make a book was a patent understatement of the truth, I also thank Virginia Duncan, my editor; Sylvie Le Floc'h, my designer, who made my book beautiful; and every wonderful person at Greenwillow Books and HarperCollins Children's Books.

I thank Bill and Lucy and Frank.

And I thank those of every persuasion, from Polish Catholic to Zen master, who have shown me doors when I couldn't see them.

Thank you all.

Lynne Rae Perkins

"I AM ALWAYS surprised at what she sees looking at a view," says Lynne Rae's husband, Bill. "I see this and that, and Lynne starts to go on about, maybe, the power line towers, which I didn't even register as being in the picture." *Surprised at what she sees looking at a view.* That may be the essence of it. Lynne Rae Perkins has the gift of surprising—and, once she's caught you and often delighted you, of shifting your point of view, or showing you something new, or getting you to think about something you hadn't thought about before, at least in quite that way.

Lynne Rae Perkins was born in 1956 in Pittsburgh, Pennsylvania, and she grew up in Cheswick, a small town along the Allegheny River. She received her B.F.A. degree in printmaking from Pennsylvania State University and her M.F.A. degree from the University of Wisconsin–Milwaukee. Lynne Rae and her husband, Bill, have two children—Lucy, fourteen, and Frank, twelve—a cat named Goldentree, and a dog named Lucky. Lucky has a wire or two loose and an insurmountable inability to come when called, a trait celebrated in *Snow Music*. Bill Perkins is a furniture maker; he builds graceful rustic pieces from branches, twigs, and bark.

After a courtship that involved Bill wooing Lynne Rae back to the Midwest from Boston, where she was working as a graphic designer, the Perkinses moved to the north woods of Michigan. They planted evergreens and rented a bit of a parking lot in St. Louis, and they would drive down to Missouri with thousands of Christmas trees, sleep in a little trailer, shower in the health club next door, and make enough to live on for a good part of the year. Until recently, the Perkins family lived in a magical "Dr. Seuss" house on top of a very steep hill—initially it was a sixteen-by-twenty-foot shack built by Bill. This house inspired Janet's house in *Clouds for Dinner,* and it was reachable only by climbing 104 steps. When Bill and Lynne Rae first moved in, they had no electricity or telephone service or running water; they got their water from a park down the road and carried it up the hill in five-gallon buckets. A friend carved a yoke for them, and that was a huge improvement over carrying the buckets by hand, especially when there were babies and toddlers in tow. A propane-powered refrigerator came next, and a light that was about as bright as a twenty-five-watt bulb but was a big step up over oil lamps, which, according to Bill, "left our eyes as red as maraschino cherries." They got a phone and electricity—but only in the workshop at the bottom of the hill, at first, so they'd run down and make toast and then run back up with it, hot in their hands. Toast was the thing they missed most during those first years on the hill. It snows and snows and snows in northern Michigan, and the Perkins house and workshop were always heated by woodstoves. Bill would get up early to light the stove for Lynne Rae, who begins work in her studio before dawn. Lynne Rae and Bill added to the house over time, gradually turning it into a home.

Lynne Rae, Bill, Lucy, Frank, Goldentree, and Lucky still live in northern Michigan, but they've moved into town and into a brand-new house designed by Lynne Rae and mostly built by Bill. Bill and Lynne Rae did the finish carpentry on the house, and it is, like their first home, constructed mainly out of reclaimed materials.

In 1993, Lynne Rae heard through a friend that Ava Weiss—the art director for Greenwillow Books from 1974 until her retirement in 2002—was going to be at the Society of Children's Book Writers and Illustrators conference in Pittsburgh, evaluating portfolios. Ava had agreed to look at ten portfolios, and she was just finishing up when a very tall and very upset woman came running in a bit late. "Of course it was Lynne Rae," remembers Ava, "and she had driven six hundred miles while six months pregnant to have her work looked at, and since I am a softie at heart, I said, 'Well, okay, let's see what you've got' . . . and after two or three minutes I realized there was a rather special talent in front of me." Ava encouraged Lynne Rae to consider writing her own material, since it is often so hard to find good manuscripts that need illustrators. They talked about format and how to present an idea, and after a short period Lynne Rae sent a very good book dummy to Ava. She showed it to Susan Hirschman (Greenwillow's founder, and its publisher until her retirement in 2001), who accepted it for publication. Greenwillow Books published *Home Lovely* in 1995. Lynne Rae Perkins has written four picture books in all: *Home Lovely, Clouds for Dinner, Snow Music,* and *The Broken Cat.* She has written two novels about Debbie Pelbry, *All Alone in the Universe* (originally, and for some of us always, known as *Debbie of Insulbrick*) and *Criss Cross* (originally, and always, *Criss Cross*).

Bill Perkins is famous for his fierce maintenance of what is affectionately (or not) known as "Bill's firewall." While she is working, Lynne Rae thrives on complete and uninterrupted quiet. From the time that Robin Roy (Lynne Rae's first editor at Greenwillow) called with the news that Greenwillow wanted to publish *Home Lovely,* Bill has allowed only editors—not friends, not relatives, not anyone, no matter how small the question—to get through. Since the announcement of the Newbery Medal, publicists have also been allowed to breach Bill's firewall, but Bill has hinted that their days are numbered, for Lynne Rae has a new picture book to finish and a new novel to begin.

Because Lynne Rae Perkins writes and illustrates picture books, and writes novels that she also illustrates and creates jacket art for, everyone at Greenwillow Books works intensively with her at one stage or another, from early drafts to finished manuscripts to thumbnails and sketches to type design and galleys to mechanicals to color proofs. Lynne Rae likes to say that she sends her manuscripts to us; we toss them out into the world for her. And we do. We toss them with love, a good deal of attention to detail, and great respect and admiration. And, of course, faith in the power and beauty of what she wants to share—faith and delight in what she sees.

The Hello, Goodbye Window

written by
Norton Juster

illustrated by
Chris Raschka

published by
Michael di Capua/Hyperion, 2005

HORN BOOK REVIEW

"Nanna and Poppy live in a big house in the middle of town." In Juster's paean to loving grandparents, the young narrator relates the small, comforting routines she shares with her grandparents when she visits, from coloring at the kitchen table to counting stars with Nanna to finding all the raisins Poppy hides in her breakfast oatmeal. The quiet, gently humorous first-person narrative presents a very young child's worldview ("when I get tired I . . . take my nap and nothing happens until I get up"); occasionally, an adult perspective intrudes ("You can be happy and sad at the same time, you know. It just happens that way sometimes"). The familial love that is Juster's subtext finds overt expression, spectacularly, in Raschka's illustrations—lush mixed-media creations saturated in watercolor and pastel crayon and set off perfectly by white space. In paintings that are freewheeling yet controlled, Raschka incorporates tight circular scribbles (for the little girl's and Nanna's hair, for bushes, for clouds); solid shapes (for furniture, for floors); thick strokes of watercolor (for trees, for the door that separates the little girl and her grandparents when her parents come to take her home); and a black line that outlines occasional objects—everything from Poppy's glasses to electrical outlets to a flower Nanna picks. A varied layout, balancing exterior and interior landscapes with smaller character vignettes, helps sustain the book's energy. Say hello to Raschka at the top of his form.—*Martha V. Parravano*

2006 CALDECOTT ACCEPTANCE SPEECH

Chris Raschka

Being thankful is easy, being happy is a little harder, but being useful is the hardest thing of all. Or so it seems to me.

In my life, the three are tied together in some way: one leads to the other or two stand together producing the last, or, simply, the third derives from the second, which derives from the first. I have never been exactly certain which stands where. Other problems I have solved by getting them down on paper.

For instance, in a large ledger book, I have charts of time spent on projects and time expected to be spent on projects; graphs tabulating projects completed satisfactorily, needing improvement, or failing; diagrams depicting the relationships between hours spent drawing, reading, painting, or writing; income from each book plotted carefully against its brothers; and comparisons of outflow of cash on paper versus tubes of paint versus Chinese ink and so forth. Perhaps my favorite tool is the x and y axis—let x equal my ability and y my desire. Once, even, I plotted the thematic movement of Wagner's *Parsifal*, where $-x$ equals the subconscious, $+x$ equals the conscious, $-y$ equals faith, and $+y$ equals reason. Dull work, but I have rarely enjoyed myself more. However, I have never managed to draw precisely the relationship of usefulness, happiness, and thankfulness.

When I left college, I spent a year in a little town in the province of Hessen, Germany, working in a home for children with physical disabilities. I joined the home as a volunteer, becoming one of four charged with the care of nine children ranging in age from twelve to seventeen. Our group, Gruppe Steppenwolf, had rooms on one half of one floor of a four-story dormitory. The coworkers were split into two pairs, alternating biweekly between the early and the late shift, the shifts overlapping in the afternoon. So you see that two workers were needed to get nine teenage children up, breakfasted, and out the door to school and, at the end of the day, dined, washed, and to bed. This was not impossible, as far as the physical care went, since only two children required complete help in rising, bathing, dressing, and so forth.

When I arrived, of these two I was given the responsibility for Jörn. My coworkers assured me that my job would not be difficult to learn as Jörn would tell me precisely—and they winked as they repeated "precisely"—what to do.

I saw Jörn on my first afternoon as he rolled down the wide tiled hallway in his electric wheelchair. He was a fourteen-year-old boy with dirty-blond hair, cut shaggily. He had clear blue eyes, an upturned nose, and a very sardonic mouth. In fact, he was much disliked by his dormmates for being a frequent taunter, dealing out wicked barbs to younger and older children alike. He was very round. He had a round head and a round torso. Each joint of each finger was round, and the small folds at the back of his neck were round. His toes were roundest of all, probably the result of never having been walked upon. Jörn saw to it that he was kept very clean and, as a result, he smelled good.

On my first morning rousing Jörn and his roommate Peter, I entered their room at 6:30. I gathered myself together and gently placed a hand first on Peter's and then Jörn's shoulder to wake them. Jörn groaned, and Peter slept on. Abruptly, Jörn called for his urine flask, which I stumblingly looked for in the half-light, then found. I stood expectantly beside his bed until Jörn said irritably, "Well, pull down my pants and stick it between my legs." "Okay," I said.

Then, following much precise instruction, I removed his pajama pants, *without* dropping his legs, pulled on his underpants, *carefully,* by gently rolling him toward me onto his right side, his great belly lolling, then to his left side, then back to his right side, tugging up his underpants as each side became free. Next I lifted him to a seated position *without* forgetting about his head, and pulled off his pajama top, then, selecting the correct pullover and T-shirt from his dresser, I pulled them down over his round head, *minding the ears.*

So the morning went, and all the while, after attentively receiving each instruction, I said, "Okay." At last Jörn turned his blue eyes upon me and said through the slit of his mouth, "You are getting on my nerves with all of your *okays.*" And I said, "Okay."

I determined then that the word I would use as a substitute anytime I felt the word *okay* bubbling up would be *mucus. Mucus. Mucus, mucus.* Jörn tried it. It sounded like *moi-kooss.* This was agreeable to Jörn. Indeed, when I explained to Jörn precisely what *moi-kooss* meant, we became friends.

I spent a year with Jörn. I dressed him in the mornings. I bathed him. I learned to anticipate his melodiously trilled "Pinkeln," which indicated a dash for the urine flask. I will never forget the special sound of the automated flask washers; I was so proud to know how to use them. By the second week I was lifting Jörn into and out of his electric wheelchair alone, Jörn in my arms like a great seventy-five-pound Jell-O mold. This was definitely against house rules and certainly dangerous to both of us, but we didn't care; we were too impatient to wait for the arrival of my coworker, too haughty to use the hydraulic lifter, and I never dropped him. In the afternoons, I sat with him and Peter, helping with their homework, doing my best to explain the proper use of negative numbers; supplying the answer to the question, What is the past participle of "to go," or indicating, as well as I could, the difference between a *Phylum* and an *Order*.

Often, when Jörn was sitting on the toilet or tormenting some child in the opposite wing, I sat and wondered about him, gazing at his collection of posters on the wall above his bed, mostly of the rock band KISS. An assortment of these arrived each month in his teen magazines, and when one was deemed worthy, we removed it, with infinite care, from its center staples. Then, taking off my shoes, I climbed onto his bed and stuck it with pink wall gum to a critically chosen spot.

One particular afternoon, sitting next to Jörn as he puzzled out some piece of homework, I realized that all my years of education had exactly prepared me to do this work; that at this moment in my life, I was perfectly useful. And I could not help noticing that I was profoundly happy, probably as happy as I have ever been.

A few years later I was very unhappy. I had just gotten married, but this was not the reason. Lydie and I were on our way to Liberia in the Peace Corps, but a number of complications, including an imminent civil war, detoured us to St. Croix in the Caribbean. We began a job there that made us both very unhappy. In fact, we felt less than useless.

Our job was a good job, a job of service, but a job also of extreme stress. To put it too briefly, we were responsible for nine orphaned or foster children, aged three to twelve—beautiful children, but children who had already endured more than we ever could. Perhaps our feelings of uselessness came from the knowledge of our own guilt and entanglement in New World history, the ills of slavery and its racism reaching across the generations to trip us. We, the descendants of the slave-owning race, fresh-faced, happy, healthy, well-fed, thrilled by an adventure in the islands; the children, the descendants of the enslaved race, dirty-faced, unhappy, unhealthy, unfed, caught already by the woundedness of the islands. We did what we could.

Thankfully, we were given some time off, seemingly scant, but in hours and minutes, one-third of our time was our own. The work schedule followed a three-week cycle: three days on, two days off, three days on, two days off, four days on, one day off, four days on, then two days off before beginning again. (We learned a couple of years ago that the Vista Volunteers who now form the staff changed this schedule to seven days on 8 a.m. to 8 p.m., then seven days on 8 p.m. to 8 a.m.—in other words, every day on for twelve hours—which they find much easier, which tells me that if that schedule is better than our old one, then my memory of grueling days must not be far wrong.)

A particularity of the old schedule was that the work shift began and ended at 2 p.m. with a briefing of the new workers. Thus, during the dreaded and so-called four-one-four, the offgoing workers had exactly from the end of the meeting, sometime after 2 p.m. on a Sunday afternoon, to 2 p.m. on the following Monday afternoon to do whatever was necessary to heal themselves from the past four days and prepare themselves for the next four.

But this leads me from my point. My point is that I was unhappy. And Lydie was unhappy. In an effort to find an antidote, we turned to what had brought us together in the first place—painting. I can remember my father saying to us as we left for Detroit and then the plane south to the Caribbean, "I'm sure you'll find a lot to paint." And we did.

As our turn on a Sunday afternoon came, and we faced our scant twenty-four hours to ourselves, we asked ourselves, Where to? We answered, Out, out—open spaces are needed, air, sun, breezes. So thinking, we climbed into one of the little cars kept for off-hour use and, quite literally, headed for the hills.

One afternoon, we found ourselves in the beautiful Danish colonial town of Christiansted on the other side of the island. We parked the car on a steep side street of charming, if dilapidated, Victorian gingerbread houses, tilting telephone poles, and much populated by great numbers of frightened stray dogs. We gathered up our big watercolor blocks, pencils, and X-Acto blades and simply walked out of town, uphill. Soon the red tin or tile roofs lay wrinkled below us, the overall yellow of the house walls peeking out between them and beneath the green of the palms, themselves revealed by the glory of the scarlet flamboyant trees in bloom. Should we stop here? No, a little further up; we wanted the island to ourselves. The air became clearer, the breeze stronger, and the whole of the town sat below us, cupped by the piercing blues of the Caribbean sky and sea.

We sat down on rocks among acacia trees, cooled by that perfumed breeze of mangos and rot, listening to and watching the life of the town, and drawing. The hours passed. At last, backs and knees creaking, we gathered our things, walked down the cooling hill and drove back to the west side of the island. There, from the brick steps of a tumble-down house not far from the apartment where we stayed, we again watched the life of a town, this time the poor town of Frederiksted, lit up by the horizontal rays of the setting sun in yellows and greens to stop all speech.

After the sun had plunged below the horizon, remarkably speedily, the way it does in the tropics, we turned the lights on, and the various chameleons and cockroaches watched us as we painted late into the night, painting the scenes we had observed in the afternoon—painting not, however, in the colors of the Caribbean, but in emulation of their glory, we used the purples and oranges and greens of the *fauves* we loved so much and for a time produced paintings remarkably alike.

Twenty-one years and six months have passed since we began painting pictures on St. Croix, and I sigh each time I think of that great joy we had. Painting was useless work, but, strangely enough, for those twenty-four hours, we were incredibly happy.

A year and a half later, I faced a decision. I perched on the proverbial horns of a dilemma. It was four in the morning. I sat in the family room of my in-laws' house in the town of the university where I was expected to attend the first day of orientation for that year's matriculating medical school students.

You see my dilemma. Was I to seek usefulness by becoming a doctor, looking for the happiness that I know comes with usefulness? Or should I continue to paint, happy now, though useless, knowing that uselessness might one day end my happiness, going beyond uselessness to become selfishness, pointlessness, good-for-nothingness?

As you know, I chose to paint.

Let me talk about thankfulness. I was extremely thankful to open this letter dated July 3, 1991.

> Dear Chris,
>
> Thank you for CHARLIE PARKER. I quite love it, but need to talk with you—or should I say: I quite love it and want to talk to you.
>
> Please call me (collect is okay) . . .
>
> Thanks.
>
> Sincerely,
>
> Richard W. Jackson, Editor

I remain ever thankful for Dick's wit, guidance, company, and wisdom.

Of course I am thankful that Norton Juster and Michael di Capua, our editor, together had the idea to invite me to illustrate Norton's wonderful text for *The Hello, Goodbye Window.* Their combined good humor, great experience, and will continue to delight me. Furthermore, I thank everyone at Hyperion, you who are here and you who stayed in New York; your expertise is everything this book required.

And I thank every editor I have worked with, every art director, every designer, in fact, everyone working in all of the several houses I have published with. I thank everyone, everyone, everyone, everyone. I thank you all.

Thank you.

But I say thank you a bit sheepishly. Why? Because I know that you do not really do the work you do for me, particularly. I know this. I am not dumb. If you are good at what you do, and I know you are, then you write, edit, and design books because it is what you like to do; you do it not for me but for yourselves.

I would feel equally foolish saying, "Thank you for eating that delicious oyster po' boy."

"Thank you for curling up with that Agatha Christie novel."

"Thank you for getting ten hours of sleep."

Or you to me, "Thank you for each day, nine to five, winter, spring, summer, and fall, fifty weeks of every year, day in and day out, painting hippos."

It just doesn't sound right.

No, I want to thank someone else.

I have in mind one person I would like to thank, and I hope she does not mind if I invest in her all the thanks I would express to all of you.

It was like this. You remember that lovely letter from Richard Jackson. *Charlie Parker Played Be Bop* was published a year later. It received mixed reviews; some glowing, some damning. Nevertheless, I was invited to read my book at a neighborhood bookstore (now driven out of business by the Barnes and Noble that opened a block away, prompting one friend to lament, "Now where will we go to be ridiculed and condescended to by the sales staff?" It was that kind of bookstore.) Still, someone there read my book, found me, and invited me to do a *story time.*

I had never done a *story time.*

I was willing, however, so at eleven o'clock on a Sunday morning in late fall, I wandered the nine blocks to the store. My audience consisted of a two- and four-year-old brother and sister, and another girl, also about four. My memory is a bit hazy, but certainly one of them toddled and mumbled, the other two spoke, and I remember leggings and a fair amount of stripes. I know the parents were not much in evidence, probably taking a breather in the self-help section. The toddler sat in my lap.

There was one more person in the audience, a rather taller person, but she only comes into focus later, as my attention was fixed, at that moment, at about knee level. As I had only one book to my name, I brought others along to read, including *Little Fur Family.*

I brought *Charlie Parker Played Be Bop*, of course, and its reading went very well. On the second time around the children "bopped" when I told them to "bop" and "boomba-ed" when I asked them to "boomba." The four-year-olds wanted to know about the cat. The toddler toddled.

So the morning went merrily.

After the appropriate half-hour spell, the parents returned to gather their children, giving me a passing smile as they rooted in their baby bags for bagels.

Someone approached me; an elegant woman in blue, silver-haired and bangled.

She spoke quickly and with a bit of a pleasant twang that I could not quite place. She said to me, "I can't believe you're here."

I smiled blankly.

"Why not?" I said.

She clarified. "I was in town last night to hear Wayne Shorter," or perhaps it was another jazz personage. She went on, "And I just saw this book, and I couldn't believe my eyes, and then I look in the paper, and I see you're going to be reading here, and I was going to go home last night but I just had to stay over to see you this morning. I can't believe you're here."

What could I say? Nothing.

She said, "How did you write that book?"

I still did not know what to say, but I know I said something, for we spoke several minutes, and then, with a rustle of coats and scarves and well-wishes, she left.

I gazed after her. I knew that she mentioned she used to live in the city, now lived on Long Island, shared a place on 90th Street (my own street), and came in for concerts. I believe her husband was a pilot. I think she worked with books. I guessed she was into bookstores, libraries, schools, and lots and lots of jazz.

But I did not catch her name.

Her name is Karen Breen.

I mention this story not because it might be amusing, but because it is essential. I know now from many sources that Karen spent the next few weeks describing my book, reading my book, presenting my book to whomever she could make stand still for it, regardless of age or desire. She pushed, she shoved, she cajoled on behalf of that book. I have heard many times of her remarkable persuasion at that year's Notables meeting.

I know that if Karen had not spoken then, there, I would not be speaking here, now. I have no doubt that one little thing has led to another thing and another thing until it is a big thing. I am sure it happens this way all the time—one person has an enthusiasm for one book, thereby creating success or failure.

You may say, "Well, someone else could have come along and discovered that book."

Yes, perhaps. But that is not what happened. What happened was that Karen Breen liked my first book, gave it a start in the world of librarians—the most important world for children's books—and made my career.

I know Karen is not the only person to do this. Of course not. You all have or you all will for my books and for many others. So I thank all of you. I thank all of you, with special thanks to all of the members of the Caldecott committee.

So now, finally, I must finish this discussion. It is inconclusive, as it is only anecdotal. Still, I can say that over the years my happiness levels for painting have remained steadily high. My usefulness levels go up and down but now, with this award, are at a peak. I assert, and I hope it is clear, that my thankfulness to all of you is off the charts.

I know I am happy. You are telling me I am useful. And for that I am very, very thankful.

Thank you.

....

Chris Raschka ————

THE GIFTS OF CHRIS RASCHKA

IN OUR LIVING room hangs a painting from *Mysterious Thelonious,* inscribed inventively to the editor. A woman at a local poster shop suggested we frame it in four different colors: violet, Chinese red, celery green, lemony yellow. The piece dances Klee-like on the wall—fine art as much as "illustration," and the essence of Chris Raschka. Like Monk's *Misterioso,* which inspired the book, the piece is joyous, joyful, joy-inducing.

Mysterious, to be sure.

And, as always with Chris's work, musical.

Also in my collection: a tetrahedron he made from cast-off paintings for *The Blushful Hippopotamus,* a cube constructed from outtakes of *John Coltrane's Giant Steps,* a kitten from *Like Likes Like,* a beautiful small watercolor of birches sent as a get-well message, a birthday greeting performed by the boys from *Yo! Yes?,* Chris's second book.

From his public beginnings, in the early nineties, it was clear to many that Chris would take children's literature to new places—in both words and pictures. It's about the books he's written as well as illustrated that I can speak. Look, for instance, at *Can't Sleep,* at those magical floating windows, at the way the words soothe and play simultaneously, or at his most recent work, *Five for a Little One,* for younger children than his earlier books, classically spare (whether he used Yukon golds or red russets for the potato-stamped illustrations has yet to be revealed), its language suffused with fatherly feeling. These books are of a piece, as if they'd been hummed into existence.

Now, I doubt that many people will have been treated to Chris's notebooks on Wagner, sketched during intermissions and subway rides uptown after the Metropolitan Opera's most recent performances of *Der Ring des Nibelungen* (for which he stood nineteen hours!). We never discussed publishing them, and most likely he never thought to ask. He's unassuming that way. . . . To understand something personally is his pleasure; to make art of the understanding is his work. The selling of either is never his goal.

Seeing these notebooks—as well as early dummies of many books (*Charlie Parker Played Be Bop* came unheralded in the mail for the price of a single first-class stamp; the dummy measured just two-and-a-half inches square)—seeing ideas spin free one from the other, seeing color palettes change and techniques evolve, has been an ongoing gift to me. The man behind them, gifted and gift-*ing*, is simply a genius. His book view is like no other's. His recognition this year delights me, not least because genius isn't easy. And is its own reward. Winning the Caldecott won't change him a jot.

When Chris and Lydie Raschka's son, Ingo, was ten, Chris devised a scavenger hunt for a birthday party (seven girls, three boys), the clues of which led them around and about Manhattan's Upper West Side, to the Soldiers' and Sailors' Monument, beneath Joan of Arc on her bronze horse, past the sign reading, "Babe lived here," and finally back to home base:

> Now you've seen the neighborhood,
> All the best of all the good.
> Seeing sights can be a hobby.
> Now find treasure in our lobby.

For many years I have worked in beyond-Manhattan buildings with no lobbies—from bedroom offices, actually—and have found treasure from Chris most often in my mailbox: out-of-the-blue book dummies like dress rehearsals, each nearly ready for opening night. Oh, we fiddle, play and replay, but the light-fingered and whimsical impromptu that is *Waffle,* the choral richness of *New York Is English, Chattanooga Is Creek,* were there for my hearing from the start. Lucky me, to unwrap such gifts.

I treasure them. Bravo to you, my friend, and thanks.

THE **NEWBERY MEDAL 2007**

The Higher Power of Lucky

written by
Susan Patron

illustrated by
Matt Phelan

published by
Richard Jackson/Atheneum, 2006

HORN BOOK REVIEW

Ten-year-old Lucky lives in Hard Pan, California, a tiny enclave on the out-skirts of the Mojave Desert. Her legal guardian is the beautiful, melancholy Frenchwoman Brigitte, the first wife of Lucky's absentee father. Lucky is one of few people in her community of forty-three to have a paying job in town, cleaning up after various "Anonymous" meetings held at the Found Object Wind Chime Museum and Visitor Center. As she eavesdrops on the participants' stories of redemption, she wonders how to find her own "higher power." When Lucky becomes convinced that Brigitte is planning to go back to France, her cathartic running-away into a desert windstorm allows her to come to terms with her mother's death, as well as prove to herself a compassion she's afraid she lacks. Author Patron's tale of a grieving, insecure little girl is never heavy-handed or maudlin, due in part to quiet bursts of humor. Quirky supporting characters include future presidential hopeful and knot artist Lincoln Clinton Carter Kennedy, Lucky's best friend; and recovering alcoholic/hippie/cowboy Short Sammy. The book's brief chapters reflect the cyclical, episodic nature of life in Hard Pan, while meandering yet meticu-lously crafted sentences illustrate Lucky's natural curiosity and the impor-tance of storytelling in her life. Patron's sensory descriptions of Hard Pan and the surrounding desert, supported by Phelan's gentle spot art, animate this unique community.—*Elissa R. Gershowitz*

2007 NEWBERY ACCEPTANCE SPEECH

Susan Patron

When my sister Georgia assured me that I really didn't need to recount my entire life history in this speech, I was relieved, as I'm sure you are, too. But I should touch on some highlights that led me to write the book I am so honored you are honoring.

My older sister Patricia hacked a path through the dense, impenetrable underbrush of childhood, so my own way was greatly eased as long as I stayed close behind her on the trail. My skirmishes off to the sides brought trouble. Patricia had a quality of empathy and generosity in childhood and adolescence that has become legendary in adulthood. She taught me how to read, for instance, when she was six and I was a four-year-old yearning to know the words that explained the pictures in the *Los Angeles Times* comics page.

On the first day of instruction, she made me find the word "a" each time it appeared in every strip. I already knew "A" was a letter, the first letter, but I hadn't figured out it was also a word.

On day two, I was told to find every "the." So far, reading was easy, and I knew two different important words on sight. This went on for a while, and I remembered thinking I would be old, like around six, before I learned each word in the English language, one by one. But somehow eventually I was just reading, as Patricia had told me I would.

As we grew up, she continued to give me important life skills: she taught me, for example, the all-but-impossible skill of not caring if you were cool in junior high, and she taught me to play chess.

I was, and am, a crazed collector of objects most people throw away. I'm drawn to the idea of amassing a huge quantity of some unlikely thing, as prison inmates of the 1920s and 1930s did, making beautiful, functional lamps out of Popsicle sticks and fashioning picture frames and purses out of intricately folded, gluelessly connected cigarette packages.

Sometimes my collecting is seriously misguided, as in the 1990s, when I hoarded fabric-covered, foam-stuffed shoulder pads with the intention of sewing them into a quilt. The fact that by its nature a shoulder pad will not lie flat and is defined by rounded borders did not deter me.

Writers present may recognize here the sick and insidious signs of writer's block. Patricia saved me from wasting hours of time on this project. "The foam inside will deteriorate," she said in a way that made me pay attention. "It'll be an awful quilt and you will hate it." This was how she told me to get back to writing. I am still grateful.

I began making up stories in third grade to entertain my then-four-year-old sister Georgia. My job was to give her a bath. The rule was that she couldn't get out of the tub until she was clean, which I determined by the degree of wrinkledness of her fingertips. Patient waiting on both our parts was required, so I sat on the lid of the toilet, inventing stories to pass the time. She sat unmoving in the tepid water, sucking a corner of the washcloth, forgetting, perhaps deliberately, to keep her hands in the water so they'd wrinkle. I loved to watch her eyes turn inward as she immersed herself in the story. Mesmerizing this little-sister listener, then and now a first audience for a new story, became a powerful stimulant and reward for me. (Georgia reported this experience to Richard Jackson at an ALA Conference; he urged me to write about it, and then published the result at Orchard as a chapter book called *Maybe Yes, Maybe No, Maybe Maybe.*)

During the ten years it took me to write *The Higher Power of Lucky,* Georgia often told me she needed a new story from me, even offering to get in the bathtub (metaphorically, of course) if I needed her to.

Another lifeline during the long period of doomed attempts and writer's block was the faith of my editor, Richard Jackson. Dick doesn't measure time in the usual way. His form of encouragement is to make it known that he will wait as long as it takes. He is kind. He is ferociously protective of his authors. Compliments are rare from Dick Jackson because the shining force of his faith in the work, the great gift of that faith, constitutes the true compliment and requires no further embellishment.

Wanting to become a writer from the time of the bathtub stories, I constructed elaborate romantic fantasies of my adult writer persona. In junior high and high school, I studied French for the sole purpose of assuming a French identity when I finished school and would be living in the maid's room on the top floor of an apartment in Paris. There I would write novels anonymously, so as not to get in trouble with my parents, that probed and clarified all aspects of the human soul. I would live on wine, coffee, and baguettes, wear white lipstick, and suffer willingly for my art. Three years of Mr. Gottlieb for French at Hollywood High School reinforced this notion: he played Edith Piaf records to give us an authentic flavor of the language. I would be tragic, like Piaf, only taller.

Coincidentally, at about this time, when I was sixteen, a young Frenchman came to Los Angeles for an extended visit, staying with my sister Patricia and her then-husband. One evening they were to attend a Ravi Shankar concert with some other friends, and Pat had asked me to babysit her two-year-old. When I arrived, there was a fire in the fireplace, lighting the rich wood paneling and Oriental rugs; Erik Satie's *Trois Gymnopédies* was playing on the turntable. The shy foreign guest, whose name was René Patron, wore a three-piece suit, looked like an actor in a François Truffaut movie, and smelled interesting and very French.

I was horrified and embarrassed not to be grown up yet, which didn't seem fair because I'd been working at it all my life. It was unbearable to be the babysitter, outside of the sophisticated, intellectual group who were all in their twenties, or at least nineteen. As everyone was leaving, my sister and René had a murmured conversation in French, which I tried mightily (but failed) to overhear and understand. Patricia shrugged and turned to me. "René's not going to the concert," she said. "He'd rather stay home with the babysitter."

Finding ourselves alone (with my niece tucked away in bed), neither of us able to converse in the other's language, we sipped wine by the fire, and I studied the Erik Satie album jacket intently, as though there would be an exam on it later. It felt as if we were suspended in time. So we did the one thing we could do to connect in a nonverbal but thrilling way. I am sure you have guessed what that was because you remember that Patricia had long before taught me all the life skills. We played chess. He won, but only because I wasn't feeling competitive.

Sometime after this, René rented a room from my mom's best friend, Helen Trimble, who lived across the street. He had brought only a small suitcase, not much bigger than a laptop. Helen Trimble became his surrogate American mother. Her son, Jimmy, took René on his motorcycle to Pink's, Barney's Beanery, and the best jazz dives in L.A.

Several years later, after René and I were married, I'd become a children's librarian at the Los Angeles Public Library [LAPL], and he had established his rare book restoration business. Jimmy Trimble began imploring us to visit his cabin in a hardscrabble town in the high desert of the Eastern Sierras. René was for it; I, not. For one thing, Jimmy was a larger-than-life kind of guy, a handsome, romantic outlaw, third-generation Irish; and who knew what kind of wild adventure he would launch us into? For another, the tiny town he described sounded strange, excessively remote, depressed, and depressing. The idea of going there frightened me.

Then it was discovered that I had a serious illness, and mortality got up into my face, clamped my head in its vise, and blew its cold breath into my mouth. This changed me. When it was over, I was twenty-seven years old and had not died, which filled me with gratitude, recklessness, and the urge to experience everything. On our next vacation we crammed the trunk of the car with what I imagined were desert-survival necessities and went to visit Jimmy Trimble at a place similar to the fictional Hard Pan.

We were entranced by the landscapes and the exotic inhabitants—human, animal, and plant. Eventually the region became the first "character" in *The Higher Power of Lucky*. Jimmy Trimble played hard and died in his forties, and I gave his name, and his mother Helen's, to Lucky.

Lucky and I have had a pretty exciting ride, beginning with my prepublication realization that illustrations had not been discussed, yet to me they were important for a nine- or ten-year-old's understanding of some of the book's particular details, such as cholla burrs and parsley grinders.

An illustrator hadn't been budgeted and it was late, but Dick Jackson is an editor who listens to cries from the heart. He pulled out all the stops, asking me if I had someone in mind, and I leapt at the chance to suggest an artist whose only work I'd seen was a jacket reproduced in a Simon and Schuster catalog. It was a line drawing of a boy, sweet and vulnerable, surrounded by white space. That tiny picture was filled with emotion. The artist was Matt Phelan, who agreed to illustrate Lucky. To Matt, I give profound thanks for expanding access to the story through his thoughtful, tender, and delicate pictures.

The next part of the story of Lucky involved my waiting for some stranger's fingertips to wrinkle and eyes to turn inward, thrilled from being immersed in the book. Advance reader copies were sent to reviewers and given away at the ALA Conference a year ago. I waited eagerly for reviews. Being in collection development, I knew where to check—databases, websites, blogs, print media. A Fuse #8 Production published the first review. With publication in November, I figured there would be more response. In fact, there was very little, except a beautiful star in Kirkus, a light in the darkness. By December, a few lukewarm reviews. Best-of-the-year lists came out; Lucky appeared only on NYPL's. Mock Newbery award contests were held, but The Higher Power of Lucky wasn't selected as a contender for children to read.

By the third week in January, people close to me knew I was seriously and uncharacteristically depressed. On the Sunday before the day of the Newbery announcement, I thought hard about the children's literature community's reception of this book that, in Katherine Paterson's phrase, I'd given myself to. Then I played computer solitaire for three or maybe four hours straight. René checked on me periodically, pretending to adjust the Venetian blinds. "André Gide only sold twelve copies of his first book," he mentioned, almost casually.

Eleven years earlier, Maybe Yes, Maybe No, Maybe Maybe had received starred reviews, was selected as an ALA Notable Book, and appeared on several best-of-the-year lists. I thought I had grown since then as a writer, and that Lucky was a deeper, richer book. I'd learned a lot and worked hard on getting better at the craft. It seemed I'd instead become a whole lot worse as a writer. "I'm going to give back the advance for Lincoln's Knot," I told René, referring to the companion book that I'd almost completed and that was, with Dick Jackson's retirement, to be in the hands of the brilliant Ginee Seo at Atheneum.

To paraphrase Donald Westlake, I'd decided to take myself out of the game and warm the bench of despair.

Having given up my writing career on Sunday night, I woke up Monday not as an author but as a librarian. My writer persona had thrown in the towel, but my LAPL juvenile materials collection development manager side was filled with excitement and anticipation and looked forward to going to work to hear the podcast of the award announcements live from Seattle.

When the phone rang at 6:30 a.m., I assumed it was a colleague; something to do with work. The person calling said she was Jeri Kladder, chair of the Newbery committee. OK, I thought, but why call me? Maybe they needed some last-minute bibliographic information and had heard what a hotshot I was in those matters. She said I'd won the Newbery Award. This struck me as very weird and probably a mistake.

"Are you sure?" I asked. "Maybe you mean a Newbery Honor?" I heard a bunch of people in the background laughing—I was on speakerphone.

"Did we wake you?" asked Jeri Kladder. Synapses in my brain were sparking and snapping but not connecting. "No, I got up early to watch the podcast," I explained conversationally; just a little chat between colleagues.

I had made a chicken sandwich to take to work, and Gandalf, our 130-pound Rhodesian Ridgeback, was waiting impatiently for his rightful piece of chicken skin. He was agitating for it. Dogs are the most ritualistic species on earth, and if you gave yours a piece of chicken skin in 2002 when you made yourself a sandwich from last night's roast, that dog will expect, and lobby heavily and relentlessly for, his piece of chicken skin forever afterward.

The people in the background on the phone were cheering as Gandalf and I danced around the kitchen. Jeri told me not to tell anyone until after the podcast at 8 a.m. That made me remember when the Caldecott and the Laura Ingalls Wilder committees I'd been on years before called our award recipients. You love your winner and you have worked very hard, and very honorably, to arrive at your decision.

So I cried and said, like someone on *The Sopranos,* because I was now in a completely surreal world, "I love you guys," something I would probably not say to a group of fifteen strangers in real life, and hung up. Then I gave Gandalf his piece of skin and went upstairs to tell René that I was going to be a writer again.

Jeri Kladder and the 2007 Newbery committee, I thank you deeply.

Then the story of the book gets a little bizarre. When some school librarians discovered that the first page contains the word "scrotum," an enormous national discussion ensued. Blogs and websites asked, "Shall we buy this book? What if parents object?"

Publishers Weekly interviewed me and ran a piece on the controversy, followed by a front-page article in the *New York Times,* in which I said that the word "scrotum" is delicious. I meant: the sound of it! To Lucky! This didn't help things. Then there were interviews on *Talk of the Nation* and other radio shows; Barbara Walters defended the book; and Roger Sutton of the *Horn Book* pointed out the insidious dangers of a subtle form of censorship that involves simply not buying a book that has won a major award.

I was trying to keep a copy of everything being said, published, blogged, and podcast about the controversy. In a librarianesque way, I set up a folder: "SCROTUM." Soon that folder was inadequate. I needed subheadings such as "popular culture" for online scrotum-inspired products: T-shirts, mouse pads, coffee cups, tote bags, and thongs. Subheading "wikipedia," where *The Higher Power of Lucky* has the dubious distinction of being referenced in the entry under "scrotum." Subheading "nasty e-mails." Subheading "endorsements from organizations and colleagues." This included online support from PEN, SCBWI, ALSC, the National Coalition against Censorship, and a beautiful affirmative statement posted on the websites of my distinguished co-honorees Jennifer Holm, Kirby Larson, and Cynthia Lord.

All this was, by turns, disturbing, ominous, reassuring, and exciting in its own strange way, but I began to long for someone, a child, to read past the first page. For weeks, the discussion went on and adults talked passionately about it. In France, our Patron relatives Googled their American aunt and found more discussions on French-language *blogues*. Finally, a teacher from Oakland wrote that her fourth-grade class, to whom she had read the book, could not guess what the controversy was about, though they thought it might be because I'd introduced the idea of cremation. When she told them it was over the word, they went to the dictionary and looked it up. They concluded that if the book were banned because of that word, then the dictionary should be banned, too.

And then a letter came from a young reader, which I'll share with you:

> Dear Susan. My name is Leah. I am eight years old—I live in Creston Iowa. I read your Book Higher Power of Lucky. I really enjoyed it. Here are some things that I enjoyed. Lucky was brave to get that bug out of her ear. It was great that she found her higher power. I liked how Brigget spoke French. Oh, La vache! [smiley face drawing] I liked when Brigget adopted Lucky, just like when my mom adopted me. Also I liked how the numbers are on the side of the pages. Love, Leah.
>
> PS tell me when you write another book.

That's a promise, Leah.

The question every reporter asked was, "If you were to write the book again, would you use a different word?" Would another word, or another body part, have done? Did I throw that scrotum in gratuitously for shock value?

My answer is that I chose the word very carefully and deliberately. But neither intellectual freedom and related issues nor shock value was in my mind at the time of writing. What I wanted was to tell a story that would be compelling to kids. I was interested in relating to readers on a deeply emotional level, in a way that could help them figure out a little about how the world works.

I needed a sensitive word and subject, something a little bit taboo, in order for one of the final scenes to have impact and power. In that scene, enough trust has been engendered between Lucky and her guardian, Brigitte, that now, at last, Lucky can ask her question straightforwardly. It's very significant that Lucky finally has enough trust that she can go to Brigitte with her questions, because she is trying hard, throughout the book, to prepare herself for growing up. Lucky is teetering on the brink of womanhood, and she swipes Brigitte's red silk dress as a metaphor of this.

Brigitte's answer, explaining the meaning of scrotum, is equally important. It shows Lucky, and the reader, that Brigitte deeply loves her ward. If the question had been less intimate, the scene wouldn't have had the same impact.

Many thanks to my agent Susan Cohen of Writers House, and to everyone at Simon and Schuster/Atheneum for supporting *The Higher Power of Lucky,* especially Emma Dryden, Rubin Pfeffer, Rick Richter, Ann Bobco, Ginee Seo, Paul Crichton, Michelle Fadlalla, Lila Haber, Carol Chou, Mary McAveney, Mara Anastas, Jodie Cohen, Kim Lauber, and Richard Jackson.

Thanks to all my LAPL buds, Eva Cox in particular.

With the firestorm and controversy out of which *The Higher Power of Lucky* has emerged unscathed, I am more than ever confirmed in my belief that librarianship is a noble profession, essential to free speech and free access for children. It is crucial to children's ability to make sense of this fragile, battered world—the world we're handing over to them. I'm grateful to have spent thirty-five years promoting children's books. It's work you can look back on and know you made a difference in people's lives, and as clichéd as that sounds, I believe it profoundly.

To teachers and librarians who take risks using books that may occasion objections or challenges, bravo. To publishers and editors who stand behind authors as they work to make a story true to its characters, and as they try to write in a way that respects the intelligence of readers, bravo. Bravo and thank you.

Susan Patron

BEFORE I KNEW Susan Patron the Famous Author, I knew Susan Patron the Librarian. It began more than thirty years ago, when we were both radical young employees of the Los Angeles Public Library. A small cohort of like-minded colleagues started an underground newsletter called *Giraffe: We Stick Our Necks Out.* This newsletter, which had a mercifully short run, took on such issues as administrative pig-headedness and customer advocacy. Susan and I were working on layout, no small task in those days before computers. At the time, I was a young adult librarian in the West Valley region, about to be promoted to branch manager; Susan was a children's librarian in the East Valley. Our paths might not have crossed without that odd (and oddly seventies) experience.

I suspected that she was a fine children's librarian, but it was more than twenty years before I had direct evidence of this. I was teaching library science at UCLA and invited Susan to visit my children's literature class. One of my students went into paroxysms of delight when she heard the name. "Mrs. Patron?" she exclaimed. "Mrs. Patron was *my* children's librarian!" Lynn Lampert talked with me recently about Mrs. Patron, *her* children's librarian. She told me how, as a four- and five-year-old, she felt overshadowed by an older sister who was skilled at so many things, especially reading. It was Mrs. Patron, so young and pretty and enthusiastic, who made Lynn feel respected for who she was. Mrs. Patron never let her leave the library until she had just the right books. She also guided Lynn's older sister, a voracious reader, through the children's collection and over to the adult side when the situation called for it. When Mrs. Patron left the Studio City branch to work downtown, Lynn was devastated. She cried and cried until her parents took her to the Central Library to visit her children's librarian. You will not be surprised to learn that Lynn is now the chair of reference and instructional services at the California State University, Northridge, library, and her sister, Dr. Lisa Lampert-Weissig, is a professor in the department of literature at the University of California, San Diego.

As a senior librarian in the children's literature department and then in children's services at LAPL, Susan no longer served children directly, but her influence was still strong. She trained hundreds of new children's librarians and guided collection development for the entire city. When I became children's services coordinator in 1987, I had the privilege of working with her on a daily basis and came to admire her organizational skills, her vast knowledge of children's literature, and her commitment to children. She is truly a librarian's librarian, at the peak of her powers and the top of her field.

Susan had started to write and to work with editor Dick Jackson by the time I left LAPL to teach at UCLA in 1990. She reveled in the experience of seeing her words visualized by gifted artists such as Mike Shenon in *Burgoo Stew* and its companion volumes and Peter Catalanotto in *Dark Cloud Strong Breeze*. She dug into her own childhood for the story of three sisters in *Maybe Yes, Maybe No, Maybe Maybe*. And then she dried up. She still had stories to tell, but the right words wouldn't come. It was agony for her. Her editor and her friends had faith that she would find her voice again, however; and when she did, it was with the book that we are honoring this year, *The Higher Power of Lucky*.

No longer my work colleague, Susan Patron is now my treasured friend. We have nurtured our relationship over many meals, at her home and mine, and at countless restaurants. We have rejoiced over the addition of Theresa Nelson, another of Dick's authors, to our circle. Theresa and I believed in *Lucky* long before the Newbery committee validated our judgment.

Here are a few things you should know about Susan Patron:

She is earthy, in a delicate kind of way. It makes perfect sense that she would find a place for the word *scrotum* in a book for nine- to twelve-year-olds.

She is possessed of unnerving curiosity about almost everything, but especially language. She probably collects other less delicate words for *scrotum*, but she would not use them in a book for children.

She is intensely practical and has many versions of Lucky's survival backpack at the ready. When we worked together at LAPL, she was the only person in our office who took any interest in the barrel that arrived one day with the label "earthquake kit."

Her adult worldview is informed in part by her long marriage to a droll Frenchman who enables her to see American society through fresh, affectionate eyes.

She is equally at home in her quintessentially Southern California Spanish-style home in the Hollywood hills and in her cabin in the high desert, where there is no telephone, no Internet, no television, and little in the way of government structure. That is where she does most of her writing, far away from the distractions of city life.

If you want to know more about Susan Patron, read the two novels she has published so far. Imagine that the eight-year-old PK who discovers stories in the family's dirty clothes hamper grew up to write a novel that won the Newbery Medal. Imagine that ten-year-old Lucky grew up to be a great cook, an exemplary librarian, and a witty, caring, generous friend who long ago managed to cut off her meanness gland using nonsurgical techniques. My friend, Susan Patron.

TEN

Think 1993. Rabbit (in the tub, waiting) and her older sister PK (on the toilet lid, toes curled up in readiness) contemplate the room's built-in laundry hamper. Earlier, on her own, Rabbit has searched the hamper for the bath-time stories PK always finds in it.

> "Did you smell anything?" [PK asked.]
> "Yes," said Rabbit. "I did."
> "It was stories you smelled. They rub off people's skin. Those stories rub off onto sheets and shirts and jeans. So stories smell like people. And that's the proof that they are in the hamper."

PK, the center sister of Susan Patron's first middle-grade novel, *Maybe Yes, Maybe No, Maybe Maybe,* shares an interest in stories with Lucky Trimble, heroine of *The Higher Power of Lucky.* PK makes them up, Lucky lives them.

Published thirteen years later, Lucky's own story began flickering on the horizon several months after PK appeared. It had cropped up in conversation, or even early chapter form, only to slip away like a desert mirage, until a dinner in 2004 at the San Diego midwinter ALA conference. Ginny Walter, Amy Kellman, and I heard that Lucky lately had been up to some eavesdropping. We loved her thenceforth.

The tales she heard—about real, imperfect adults, and one dog—certainly sound like the truth. They are told in first person. Lucky's story is told in what I think of as "intimate third." Try it yourself; it's a tricky point of view to pull off, but it is crucial to *The Higher Power of Lucky.*

Editors know their books well—and long for acknowledgment of each book's higher qualities. The highest in this case is Susan's purity of voice on behalf of a specific ten-year-old. Look on page 2 of the book, at how the girl's perceptions of the world dramatize (without a whisper of telling from "an author") her need for parents and love and some reassurance that the vicissitudes of life can be survived.

Look at pages 14–15 for how Lucky appreciates her father. I cannot see any literary convenience to his absence, but rather see the hard fact of it for his daughter—who is, after all, only trying to understand why her dad has abandoned her. Hence Lucky's presentation of him as mostly mysterious, even mythic. The mother's death has in it an element of scold. Psychologically apt, and funny, too. The writer does not instruct us about how to feel toward these parents, their natures or fates, but leaves it to Lucky to puzzle them out.

Take Brigitte. It's Lucky's discovery of a passport and misreading of phone calls from France that lead the girl to panic. An adult voice, narrating from aloft, could have straightened that out in a sentence, but then Lucky would not have run away, stumbled across Miles, been found by Lincoln, or discovered, at last, the perfect resolution for that urn of ashes. Lucky, then, is responsible for her own plot. To the newspaper that sniped at the happy ending with a parenthetical "(naturally)"—intending to skewer a whole string of Newbery Medal winners, I suppose—I'll snipe back on Lucky's behalf: "Is that too much to ask for a kid you love?" Brigitte loves Lucky, yes, like the daughter she never had, and isn't it fine? When Lucky's illustrator Matt Phelan was reading the manuscript—at Susan's request, for she'd seen his jacket art for Betty G. Birney's *The Seven Wonders of Sassafras Springs* and knew as a librarian the value of illustrations in books for middle readers—he came to Brigitte's fiercely loving "You know if anyone ever hurt you I would rip their heart out" and called me excitedly with "Yes!"

I want to say a word about Miles, the betrayed, from whose sorrow Lucky learns so much about herself, and about Lincoln, that desert Galahad. When Lincoln comes around the side of the hill on page 125, I always weep with relief for Lucky and cheer with pride for young American manhood. The people of Hard Pan, California, are fortunate to have Susan Patron's deft touch on their shoulders. Like E. M. Forster in his essay, "What I Believe," I am with the old Scotsman who wanted "less chastity and more delicacy." An editorial mantra, I guess, as well as a hallmark for the writing here, which I am happy to hold up in awe. I know of only one other book, Paula Fox's *How Many Miles to Babylon?* that portrays so surely a ten-year-old's sensibility. It's the surety of the point of view that appeals to me foremost in *The Higher Power of Lucky*—but then it's also the book's humor, its ultimate optimism, its truthfulness. All these are qualities of the woman who wrote it without intruding herself upon a single word.

Finally, a mention of dogs. HMS Beagle's original name, well into page-proof stage, was Rachel Carson. I agreed to changing it with some misgivings, because I feared errors would creep into the text and not be caught, despite the best of human efforts. Instead, a deeper connection emerged between Lucky and the concept of adaptation, Darwin, and her own "highly evolved" being. The now notorious Roy the Dog—bless him—was so named from the beginning.

There is another book on the schedule about Lucky, her pals, and a newcomer to Hard Pan, a girl from Hollywood who is just Lucky's age. Susan and Atheneum's exceptional Ginee Seo will be contemplating that story together.

May the hamper overflow.

THE CALDECOTT MEDAL 2007

Flotsam

written and illustrated by
David Wiesner

published by
Clarion, 2006

HORN BOOK REVIEW

With its careful array of beach-combed items, the title page spread of Wiesner's latest picture book makes it look like one of those Eyewitness books, but the following wordless story is far stranger than fact. In clue- and fancy-strewn full-page paintings and panels, a boy at the beach closely examines items and animals washed in from the sea; when a wave deposits an old camera on the shore, his viewing takes a radical shift. He gets the camera's film developed at a nearby shop, allowing Wiesner's bountiful imagination great play in the series of photos the boy then examines: a robot fish, an octopus reading aloud to its offspring, giant starfish with islands on their backs. And: a seaside photo of a girl holding a seaside photo of a boy, holding a seaside photo of another child, ad infinitum. The inquisitive boy's ready magnifying glass and microscope allow him to see further and further into the photo, and further back in time, as revealed by the increasingly old-fashioned clothes worn by the children pictured. What to do but add himself to the sequence? The meticulous and rich detail of Wiesner's watercolors makes the fantasy involving and convincing; children who enjoyed scoping out Banyai's *Zoom* books and Lehman's *The Red Book* will keep a keen eye on this book about a picture of a picture of a picture of a . . .—*Roger Sutton*

2007 CALDECOTT ACCEPTANCE SPEECH

David Wiesner

Got some flotsam?
Yeah, I've got some.
Got some jetsam?
No, but I can get some.

When I was in the fourth grade, my teacher read a poem by Ogden Nash to the class. I've never forgotten it. From that point on, the words *flotsam* and *jetsam* were part of my vocabulary. They were funny-sounding and interesting in meaning. While flotsam technically refers specifically to maritime debris, I like the more colloquial definition referring to odds and ends that can turn up anywhere—on the beach, on land, even in your mind.

Flotsam on a cosmic scale—images, ideas, and memories floating through time and space—appeals to me now.

As a kid, though, I only knew the down-to-earth kind. The most remarkable piece of flotsam I ever found was buried in a brook that ran through the woods at one end of my neighborhood. The woods seemed huge back then, but they were really just an undeveloped acre of land. It was an exciting and mysterious place to play, and, despite repeated severe cases of poison ivy, I couldn't keep away.

One day when I was eight or nine years old, my friend Brian Wilbur and I were digging around in the brook, as we often did. We were probably trying to build a dam, one of our favorite activities. We were soaked. Suddenly, we saw something poking out of the mud under the water. It appeared to be a face. And a leg. And they weren't human.

I dug my hand into the mud and pulled the object out—it was very heavy—and rinsed it off in the flowing water. It was a black metal figure of a bull, about six inches long. At one time it had had ivory horns, but they had been broken off and only stumps remained. Its posture was wonderfully contorted, with the head lowered and twisting to look up. The face was an intense grimace, and the features and musculature were rendered in minute detail.

We were stunned. This wasn't a toy. It was a grown-up thing. How could it have gotten here, in our brook, in our woods? I was fascinated by the idea that this object had a whole unknown history. I'm sure that my imaginings were far more exotic than reality—but who knows?

I kept that bull on my drawing table for years, right up until 1983, when the apartment building my wife, Kim, and I were living in burned down and took everything we owned with it. Fortunately, we didn't have much at the time.

There were a few very hard losses, like Kim's cello and my college sketchbooks. But in the days after the fire, as I mentally went over the contents of the apartment, I can recall the pang I felt when I realized that the bull was gone. It was like losing a little piece of my childhood.

After a long time, my friend Brian and I got together. We hadn't seen each other for at least twenty years, but it took him less than five minutes to ask, "Do you still have that bull we found in the brook?" I was amazed! He hadn't seen this thing since he was a kid, and yet it was still lodged in his mind as firmly as it had been in mine. It was maybe even more remarkable because he hadn't set eyes on the object in nearly thirty years, since I was the one who kept the bull after we found it. How did that come about? Well, it's funny, but my memory gets a little hazy about this part of the story. There seemed to be some dispute over who really discovered it. Let's just say that at the time I was a year older and a lot bigger than he was.

Anyway, Brian proposed that since I had had it all that time, maybe he could have a turn keeping it. Which would have been a great ending to this story, except that I had to tell him about the fire. We were both pretty bummed about losing the bull, but we liked the idea that it was out there somewhere. Maybe it had fallen off the dumpster as the building debris was being carted away. Maybe it was poking through the ground in a landfill that was being developed. And maybe, hopefully, another kid found it.

As a story idea, a kid stumbling across something extraordinary, something with secrets to reveal, had been floating around my mind for some time when I started working on this book. I am not consciously aware that my childhood flotsam story played a part in this, but I think it had to have been some kind of motivation. Visually, though, this story about finding something has always taken place on the beach. Or, as we say in New Jersey, down the shore.

From before I was born until I was fourteen, my family spent the last two weeks of August on Long Beach Island, New Jersey. Squeezed into the back of our station wagon, I always felt that the trip there took days.

Crossing the causeway to get to the island was like arriving in another world. When we got to the house, I would immediately run down to the beach. Coming up over the crest of the sand dune and experiencing the sight and smell and sound of the ocean was always overwhelming to my senses. The island seemed to me like an enchanted land. It was a shock to learn that people actually lived there year-round. I saw evidence of that enchantment in the permanent residents from whom we rented a house—the Segals. As a kid, I thought, Wow, they live at the beach and they're named the Seagulls!

Sometimes the ocean water would collect in a tide pool high up on the beach. One day I saw a group of people gathered around, pointing at something. I approached and saw a fish trapped in the pool. Actually, I wasn't really sure if it was a fish at all. It was yellow with black spots. It was blown up round, like a balloon. It was covered with spikes. It had a beak. It looked like an alien! It elicited from me the simultaneous reactions of "Ewww!" and "Coool!" And then I realized that this thing, this puffer fish, had been out there in the water where I had just been swimming. So, there might be more of them. And there might be . . . well, who knew what else might be out there?

After I won a second Caldecott, for *The Three Pigs,* people kept saying such helpful things as, "Gee, how are you going to top that?" Hmm. I hadn't been thinking about topping anything. Maybe, I thought, it would be a good idea to step out of the limelight for a bit. I began to think that I should do a smaller-scaled, quieter book. And, for a change of pace, one with a text. My previous two books were forty-eight and forty pages and had taken ages to complete. I was determined not to go over thirty-two pages this time, and I wasn't going to let three or four years go by between books again. So, five years later, I came out with a wordless, forty-page book.

The creative process can be such a pain in the neck. It's not like I didn't really try to make that quieter thirty-two-page book with a text. I was concurrently working on three different story ideas. The first, which is the one my contract was for, was about aliens landing in a backyard. It had a great beginning, but nothing as good to follow it. The second idea was about fish living in a house. It had lots and lots of great imagery, but no plot to speak of.

The third idea was *Flotsam.* I knew from the start that *Flotsam* would be the title of whatever my kid-on-the-beach story turned out to be. At first I had no idea what the kid would find. I started by making it a small crystalline sphere. How this object would reveal any hidden secrets, I had no idea. It was really just a placeholder until I figured out what that object actually was.

In its first incarnation, the story spanned from the dawn of time to the present. It then developed two parallel story lines with two different, tightly formatted design layouts that would merge at the end—a visual device that I really liked. Eventually, I decided that a camera would be a great way to show the secrets beneath the waves. In one version it was a talking camera. I then introduced a text. My main character was a girl. For a time the story was about sibling rivalry. For a long time the story focused too closely on the journey the camera made. At some point my main character became a boy.

All the elements of a story seemed to be scattered throughout the many book dummies that I had made, but I hadn't yet had the "Aha" moment. The story was pushing in new directions, but I was still clinging to a strict design template that wouldn't let the pictures evolve as well. I realized that I had to put aside all my preconceptions and start over. This time I should just tell the kid's story.

The pictures flowed out, the text disappeared, and the parallel stories became one.

As I was working my way through the fantastical undersea photos that the camera would reveal, the final piece of the story fell into place. The camera had shown octopi reading in a makeshift living room, sea turtles with cities on their backs, a puffer fish hot-air balloon, starfish islands, and aliens on vacation. I needed one more extraordinary photo, and suddenly, surprisingly, I saw it—an image of another kid looking directly out at the viewer. And that kid in the photo was holding a photo of another kid, who was holding a photo of another kid, who was holding a photo of another kid, back through all the kids who had had the camera before, finally reaching the child who had started it all.

Aha! At last, this was what my character was meant to find on the beach—another kid. That connection was what I had wanted to achieve all along.

Relinquishing my original, tightly structured, parallel page designs allowed a single, more organic design to develop. Despite my intention to stick to thirty-two pages, I found that I really needed more room to give the book a greater visual variety. At thirty-two pages, the book would have had too many dense multipaneled pages. Forty pages let me alternate these multipaneled pages with single full-page images and double-page spreads to give a visually interesting rhythm to the flow of the pictures. The eye scans the multipanel page quickly. The detail-rich double-page spread is a place where the eye can linger and spend time slowly exploring. Especially in a wordless book, this kind of visual variety makes for a far more exciting reading experience.

I draw and revise compulsively until each composition is exactly as it will appear in the final painting. The one place I don't plan ahead is in the color palette. Not until I begin to paint the first piece of a book do I truly know what the color concept for that book will be. *Tuesday* was about intense nighttime blues and indigos. *The Three Pigs* was all about white space.

With *Flotsam,* the first piece I painted was the first double-page spread of the boy on the beach looking through the magnifying glass. It's a clear, sunny day. His beachcombing equipment, much of which is made out of primary-colored plastic, surrounds him. He is lying on a patterned beach towel. Uh-oh, I thought, this book is going to be about bright colors.

I've spent most of my life running away from bright colors, but there was no escape, so I dove into the bathing suits, T-shirts, buckets, shovels, and beach towels. The culmination of this cavalcade of color was the decision to fill the cover of the book with a close-up of a red snapper. There is more cadmium red in that one painting than in all the other art I have ever produced.

Deliberately leaving part of the process open to spontaneity can be scary. But to grow as an artist, I have to be willing to move into unfamiliar territory. It is there that I learn new things and keep my creative process from becoming routine.

It can also get scary when one idea doesn't work out, and then another doesn't, and time drags on. Panic can set in. But I've been through this before. Only two of my contracts have on them the name of the book that I eventually produced. It would be nice if the path were always straightforward, but, in the end, I simply trust that if I focus on the process, something valuable will result.

There are many people who help me achieve that result. They are the same people I have mentioned previously, when I have addressed this gathering. I like that. I like that a lot.

Dinah Stevenson, Carol Goldenberg, and Donna McCarthy are, respectively, my editor, art director, and director of production. Those titles superficially describe our relationship. They are, truly, my collaborators.

Dinah Stevenson had great patience and great wisdom throughout the *Flotsam* saga. Her input during my creative meandering was thoughtful and subtly delivered—particularly during the cheese incident. At one point in the process I had the idea of making the camera talk. The Chatti-cam, as I called it, would say, "Cheese!" Not, "Say cheese!"—I thought just "Cheese" would be funnier. So funny, in fact, that I decided I should retitle the book *Cheese*. While her words argued politely, yet firmly, against this, her eyes were saying, "Not in a million years!" Thank you for that, Dinah.

Incredibly, Carol Goldenberg is even more compulsive than I. Who knew simple black lines around pictures could lead to so many sleepless nights? Putting Flotsam together was exciting and challenging, and we continually found solutions that added even more to the book.

All this work might be wasted if the book were not printed with such attentiveness and skill. I never lose sleep over this, knowing that Donna McCarthy is overseeing the production of my books. Her care and meticulousness are a joy to behold.

And, once again, to everyone at Clarion Books, especially Marjorie Naughton and Joann Hill, thank you for all you do for me.

For the past twenty-eight years, Dilys Evans has been my agent. Again, that is a term that only superficially describes our relationship. Throughout our many adventures together, she has been first and foremost my good friend.

When I was growing up, artistic insecurity never had a chance to take hold at home. My mother and my father and my sisters and my brother always supported and encouraged my art, unconditionally. It was a wonderful environment in which to create. Likewise, where I work now is all I could ever ask for. I have a studio at home with my family around me. Kim, Kevin, and Jaime are the audience I want to please most. This is the best environment in which to create.

One of the top ten questions that kids ask is, "Which one of your books is your favorite?" They really seem to want me to pick one, but I can't. Each of my books has been a distinct creative experience, with its own struggles and insights. Each is unique to me.

When the phone rang that Monday morning in January, I looked at the caller ID, saw "Washington State Convention Center," and thought, "No way." But when I picked up the phone, Janice Del Negro informed me that, indeed, *way*. It is hard to describe my reactions. Elation over the fact that *Flotsam* had been chosen for the Caldecott collided with the overwhelming realization that I was receiving the award for a third time. Three times is a lot to absorb, and I'm still working on it. For now, I am enjoying the recognition that *Flotsam* is receiving. To be singled out by fifteen people who have devoted an entire year to the jury process is a very special thing. Thank you, Janice, and all the members of the 2007 Caldecott committee, for this incredible honor.

What will I say when people ask me, "How are you going to top this?" Well, I'm thinking about a smaller, quieter book. But you never know.

Thank you.

ILLUSTRATOR PROFILE BY DINAH STEVENSON

David Wiesner

PEOPLE ASK ME how I edit David Wiesner's books, the ones that don't have any words. An editor is usually a person who gets a manuscript, offers comments, and suggests revisions. A wordless book has no manuscript. Therefore, I don't edit David's work.

True enough. What I do, for the most part, is wait for it.

Flotsam was seven years in the making. David was already playing with ideas for it while creating *The Three Pigs,* which was published in spring 2001. That fall, David and his family moved from Milwaukee to Philadelphia and lived for almost a year in a rented apartment, which didn't include an art studio, until their new house was ready. David's wife left her surgery practice. In June 2002, David received the Caldecott Medal for *The Three Pigs*. Five days later, his father died, leaving an estate to be settled. Following this period of upheaval and uncertainty, it's not surprising that the next picture book wasn't completed till four years later. It's amazing that a book emerged at all—and a brilliant book at that.

All, or almost all, of the picture-book ideas he was considering turned out to be *Flotsam*.

Fortunately, David doesn't throw anything away. He keeps his sketchbooks, thumbnails, line drawings, dummies, revised dummies, and jacket sketches—a complete paper trail. This makes it easy to trace the evolution of *Flotsam*, element by element, in hindsight. At the time, though, David's progress seemed almost random. Every few months, he would appear in my office with a sketch dummy, and sit with me while I turned the pages. (For sheer self-consciousness, looking at artwork in the artist's presence is even worse than eating a three-course dinner on a dais in front of two thousand people.) We'd have a brief conversation, in which I'd allude to what I felt was or wasn't working. Then there would be a period of silence, sometimes several months. I would wait. And then David would appear with another sketch dummy—which might or might not be for the same story.

With the exception of *Tuesday*, which resulted from a single burst of creativity, David's stories have come together one piece at a time. His sketchbooks are full of isolated images and sequences of panels and scribbled lists of words and ideas, some of which move in one direction, some in another, some apparently in no direction at all. Each turn of the kaleidoscope yields a new design. With *Flotsam*, a key piece was the insight that it wasn't a story about fish; it was about a boy. Now it had focus. Another was the realization that a camera could provide a link between one kid and another, across time and space. Now it had a plot.

The fact that nothing gets thrown away—consciously or unconsciously— is a valuable resource. Long before *Flotsam* took shape, David drew in his sketchbook a boy scrutinizing a cereal box, on which there is a picture of a boy scrutinizing a cereal box, on which there is a picture of a boy . . . a short step from the photographs of photographs in *Flotsam*. And it wasn't until David had (after several false starts) created the jacket for *Flotsam* that he rediscovered, in a sketchbook, the image of a jacket centered on a fish's large, round eye, which he had drawn months earlier for some other reason and forgotten entirely.

David trusts his creative process, even when he doesn't know where it's taking him. He doesn't make these connections happen; he waits for them. And then he draws all the pictures, because otherwise he doesn't know whether they tell a real story. This step is labor-intensive for him, but I'm glad he takes it. Otherwise I might be called upon to respond to a wordless book that I couldn't see.

I trust David's process, too. As one book idea morphs into another and another and recovers and recombines elements of what has gone before, it can seem directionless, and is definitely indirect. I have learned from experience, though, that while David Wiesner's creative journey may not be a straight path, it invariably takes him to the right place—this time, to the marvelous creation that is *Flotsam*. I'm lucky to be along for the ride.

Good Masters! Sweet Ladies! Voices from a Medieval Village

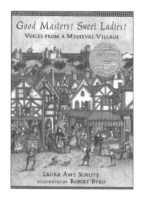

written by
Laura Amy Schlitz

illustrated by
Robert Byrd

published by
Candlewick, 2007

HORN BOOK REVIEW

Schlitz gives teachers a refreshing option for enhancing the study of the European Middle Ages: here are seventeen monologues and two dialogues that collectively create a portrait of life on an English manor in 1255. A plowboy, a knight's son, and a sniggler (eel-catcher), among other boys and girls ages ten to fifteen, say their pieces. Rhythm and style vary to suit each role, from breathless, thrusting phrases as a knight's son describes a boar hunt to the lighthearted rhyming of a shamelessly dishonest miller boy. Schlitz conveys information about class, attitudes, and social practices through the monologues, footnote-like sidebars, and six spreads titled "A Little Background" that offer fuller explanations of farming practices, the Crusades, falconry, and more. Schlitz acknowledges some of the nastier aspects of this oft-romanticized period (such as its persecution of Jews), but in gentle, moderate language. Byrd's pristine, elegant pen-and-ink illustrations in opulent colors make the book almost too visually appealing, belying the realistically dirty, stinky conditions described in the text.—*Deirdre F. Baker*

2008 NEWBERY ACCEPTANCE SPEECH ———————

Laura Amy Schlitz

Dear friends, a cadre of perceptive and passionate readers has decided that my book is good. This is earthshaking. As a writer, there is nothing in the world I want more than this: that my work should be good. And now, in my joy, I am supposed to speak to you, and this is dangerous, because I am apt to be both maudlin and grandiose. I must remind myself that good is an approximate term. A second grader once asked me for "a really, really good book," and I asked him, as librarians do, what he considered a good book. He eyed me with thinly veiled impatience and replied, "Medium-long with poisonous snakes." By his standards, *Good Masters! Sweet Ladies!* falls short. It is medium-long, but there is only a glancing reference to poisonous snakes.

So I must catch hold of myself and try not to be vainglorious. I must remind myself that the Newbery Medal comes with strings attached. The biggest string—a rope thick enough to hang a writer—is the speech. Whenever I've dreamed, as writers do, of winning the Newbery, my dream has always ended with the sad conclusion that I never would. And then I've comforted myself: "Well, all right, I'll never win the Newbery, but at least I won't have to give one of those speeches."

Thus the whirligig of time brings in his revenges.

My friends, you deserve a good speech: something coherent and profound. But even if I trusted myself to be profound, being coherent poses a problem. I have a storyteller's mind—a deranged junk drawer, clogged with memories and metaphors. I deal in mental pictures: a carousel horse, a devil in a green coat, a girl balancing a basketful of eels on her hip. I brood over these images until I divine their stories.

When I first conceived of my Newbery speech, I found myself haunted by three anecdotes. These stories have something to do with what I want to tell you. So—sweet ladies, good gentlemen—let me begin there. Let me tell you about playground duty, a kite, and having moles removed.

We'll start with playground duty, and Tessa. At the time of my story, Tessa was in second grade. She was an appealing child, with brown eyes and a round sweet face. I was on playground duty when Tessa's friends flocked up to me, telling me that Tessa was stuck on the playhouse roof and afraid to come down.

So I went to help. The playhouse had a peaked roof eight feet high, and the edge of the roof was five feet off the ground. Tessa perched on the ridgepole, not crying. I suggested that she hold onto the ridgepole, turn around backward, and let her feet dangle, so that I could grab her legs. She looked dubious. I couldn't blame her: Coming down backward means coming down blind. So at last I held out my arms. "Just pretend it's a sliding board and come on down. I'll catch you."

For some reason, this solution struck Tessa as workable. She grimaced, let go of the rooftop, and slid.

I caught her. But I had neglected to take into account the fact that the average second grader weighs fifty-five pounds, and a fifty-five-pound weight gathers momentum on an inclined plane. That small, soft-limbed child hit me like a cannonball. My knees gave way and I staggered, wondering what irreparable damage I had done to my spine. I fell—hard—onto my well-upholstered rear end.

But I didn't drop Tessa. And since I am well-upholstered in front as well as in back, she fell softly and scrambled to her feet as nimbly as a little squirrel. We asked each other if we were hurt. Neither of us was. Then Tessa met my eyes and said, "Thank you," with a purity and grace I have never forgotten.

Why does this memory come back to me? I think it has something to do with the fact that winning the Newbery was like catching that fifty-five-pound, entirely lovable child. The stars danced. My knees buckled. I wasn't sure what had happened to me.

I also think this story has something to say about the way librarians feel toward children. We do our best for them. We try to help them when they're stuck and catch them when they fall—even if we never have quite enough books about poisonous snakes.

Now for the moles.

Several summers ago, I had moles cut out of my forehead. I ended up with an intriguing scar, a red-stitched crescent like a third eyebrow. My schoolchildren demanded, "What happened to your face?"

I was ready for them. One must be truthful with children, but a good scar warrants a story. "Do you want the true story or the interesting story?" I asked.

Bless them; they wanted both. "Here's the true story," I said. "I had moles removed. Moles are like pimples, but sometimes they turn into little cancers, so the doctor cut them off."

The children were unimpressed. "What's the interesting story?"

"Oh, well, the interesting story is this," I answered.

I DO NOT go camping. I like my comforts—indoor plumbing and air-conditioning and locks on the door. But my friend Faith is wild about camping, and last summer she talked me into an overnight camping trip.

We went to West Virginia. There were signs on the campground warning us about bears, which excited me, because I have a great yearning for bears. When Faith and I went walking, we saw the claw marks on the trees. Black bears of both sexes mark trees by rubbing and clawing them—scientists don't know why.

One of the marked trees held a few black hairs. I pried them out of the bark and twined them around my finger like a ring.

Night fell. Faith slept beneath the stars, but I zipped myself into the tent and fell asleep.

In my dream, I walked through the woods. I was searching for something—I don't know what. I came to a clearing that was almost a perfect circle. Moonlight poured into the clearing like milk in a bowl. At the edge of the clearing, there was a moving shadow: someone's dog, I thought at first, a Labrador or a Newfoundland. Then the bear smelled me. She lumbered forward, meeting me in the center of the clearing.

I say she, because she was a female. When she rose on her haunches, she was exactly my height. We stood face to face, so close that I could smell her. It was a rank and powerful odor. I could see into her eyes, and they were bloodshot, furious.

"Give me back my hair," she said to me. She made no sound. Nevertheless, I knew what she meant. I had stolen her hair, and I had no right to it. I held up my hand with the ring on my finger.

"Give me my hair," she said again.

I stood my ground. You must recall that this was a dream. "I want to be bear," I said. And that is true. I am an ordinary woman, a tame woman, but there is a part of me that longs to be as wild and unaccountable as a bear.

The bear didn't answer. It's always hard to know what a bear is feeling, because their facial muscles are rigid. "I want to be bear," I said again. I tried to say it in a way that would tell her that I respected her, loved her. But bears don't care about respect. She growled. I knew that if I defied her, she would tear off my face.

So I began to unwind the hair from my finger. But I went on begging. "Give me something else," I entreated her, "so I can be bear."

She raised her left paw—bears are left-pawed. The tip of one claw raked my face, slicing open my flesh. The blood began to trickle down my cheek. That's when I woke up.

I was safe. The tent was sealed. But when I put my fingers to my forehead, I found that my skin was wet with blood—and the ring was gone from my finger.

I TOLD THE story many times, and the children always said: "Is that true?"

"No," I said, "I had moles removed." And they said, "Oh."

But here's the real point: the children passed the story on. Not the true story—which every child forgot—but the bear story. I overheard two children talking when I was in the stacks. "She didn't really see a bear," one child said skeptically, and the second said, "Yes, she did. She said it was a true story."

Thus the surreal holds sway over the real. Fiction trumps fact. The true story was pointless, so the children forgot it. But the bear story was mysterious, numinous, and it stayed with them. Dramatic narrative creates meaning, and what is meaningful takes root in memory. That's why, when I decided to write about the Middle Ages, I chose to teach history through story. It's also why—like most librarians—I secretly favor fiction over nonfiction. Facts are necessary, facts are useful, facts are fascinating. But stories enlarge our lives. They awaken us to color and depth and pattern. They help us make sense of a random world. And the imaginary bears—which are endangered, make no mistake about that—dig their dens in the fiction section. They like the wilderness.

Last story. I have never been able to get a kite in the air. Lithe, active people get kites in the air, and if I am present, and if they are kind, they let me hold the string. I love the feeling of a kite, but I've never been able to fly one. They won't go up. I run as fast as I can, but the kite drags behind me like the broken muffler of a car.

When I turned fifty, I made up my mind that I was going to fly a kite. I went to the kite store and bought a purple and scarlet parafoil. The clerk in the kite store assured me that all I needed was a wind; small children, he promised me, could fly this kite. I cross-examined him, flattening him against the cash register. "You really think," I said sternly, "that I can get this kite in the air?" "Lady," he said to me, "you're gonna come back here; you're gonna be screaming at me because I didn't let you buy two of 'em."

I liked his panache. I believed him. But he was wrong, because I couldn't get the kite up. I tried—twice. Bystanders averted their eyes in pity.

Two years later, I won the Newbery Medal. I decided to go to the ocean to write my speech. The ocean, I believed, would help. So I packed my suitcase: fountain pens, ink, thesaurus, wrist splints . . . At the last moment, I tossed in the kite. After all, my life had changed. I was living in a world where anything was possible.

I worked on Monday. On Tuesday, I awoke to the keening of the wind. I hurried through breakfast and headed for the shore with the kite. It was chilly, a gray morning. The ocean was greenish and savage, with the waves breathing hoarsely against the shore. Even the seagulls looked cold. I took the kite out of my pocket. As I unfolded it, the ribbons of the tail began to flutter. I could feel the kite straining to be free. I let go of her, and she soared into the air. Once she was aloft, she ceased to be a kite and became a creature: a nylon falcon, willful and capricious.

It was a miracle. She rose above my head. I gave her a little more string, and she lashed her tail like a tiger. She pirouetted, and I unwound the string. I was flying a kite. I stumbled along the shore, bemused, enchanted, disbelieving. She was smaller than a postage stamp—a motley speck in a furrowed sky.

My hand was cold. I fumbled in my pocket for a glove, and all at once I dropped the spool. It was then that I made a discovery—quite an obvious one, really, but to me it was startling and wondrous. As the spool of string rolled over the sand, the kite faltered and plummeted. Without me, she couldn't soar. She needed the tension of my hand on the string.

I am not built for speed. But I clumped over the sand as fast as I could, trying to catch the uncoiling reel. A tuft of dune-grass snagged it, buying me time. I snatched the spool and yanked the string. The kite began to recover. She went on rising until there was no more thread.

I flew her for an hour before I brought her in. By now I was feeling superstitious about her, and I thought it would be good luck if I could lure her to my glove like a falcon. It was a bit like Tessa, come to think of it—I wanted to catch her before she hit the ground.

And I did. I pulled her within three feet of me, leaped skyward, and plucked her out of the air.

Why am I telling you this? Oh, because this story makes sense. First of all, the thrill of getting the kite in the air—of doing what could not be done—was like winning the Newbery. Unclouded joy, soaring disbelief. I was holding the wind in my hands.

And also, because flying a kite is a bit like being a writer. Most of the time, the words aren't right, and the prose drags on the ground. We don't know how to get the kite into the air. Flying defies gravity. If there are rules and laws that govern this flight, we don't know what they are. We only know that we have to go to the shore with the kite in our hands, in case the wind is there. When the wind comes—those are the extraordinary, the surreal times. They are worth all the other times.

Can you tolerate one more metaphor? Because I should like to draw your attention to the invisible presence, the secret protagonist of the kite story: the string. I tell the story as if it's about me—I flew the kite. Then I personify the kite, and it's a falcon. And then I wax rhapsodic about the wind. But the real hero of the story is the string—which stands for the connection between things. Without the string, I have no hold on the wind, and the kite falls to earth.

And this is the final, the most potent reason for telling you this story. Because the Newbery Medal isn't about my book, or any book. It's about the invisible fellowship of librarians, publishers, parents, teachers, and writers who want to give their best to children. The Newbery Medal is a symbol of our communion. We are threaded together by our commitment to children and the life of the mind. We dance together on one string.

And now it is time to say thank you, and to try to say it simply, purely, as Tessa did. Thank you for coming here tonight—for being readers, for knowing that children and books matter. Thank you, my parents, for opening the world of books to me. Thank you, my friends from the Park School, for helping me write and for helping me rejoice. Thank you, Robert Byrd, for your irresistible artwork—and thank you, Chris Paul, for your stunning sense of design. Thank you, goddesses of the Candlewick pantheon—but especially Danielle Sadler, who dredged this manuscript out of the slush pile, and Mary Lee Donovan, whose faith and compassion are heroic. And last of all, thank you, members of the Newbery committee, for feeding my bears, and granting me my heart's desire.

....

AUTHOR PROFILE BY MARY LEE DONOVAN, THE MIDDLE-AGED CHILDREN'S BOOK EDITOR

Laura Amy Schlitz

THE SUCCESSFUL WRITER

for two actors

LAURA	MARY LEE
A million years[1] it seems since I sent the damned manuscript.	A million years it seems since I've seen something this fresh, unique, exciting.
	This is brilliant. Who is this woman?

LAURA	MARY LEE
Why did I listen to those people who said, "You should get these published"? Five rejections I've had already![2]	
	Who is this woman?[3] Where did she come from?[4] This is brilliant.[5]
Why did I do it?[6]	
	But what in the world are we going to do with it?[7]
She said she loved it.[8] What's taking so long?	
	Whatever in the world are we going to do with it? What in the world . . . ?[9]
Finally, a contract!	Finally, I asked[10] and they said Yes!
I'm exhausted.	I'm exhausted.
Now what?	Now what?
Now what?	Now what?
Now what?	Now what?
"Are you still publishing my book?"[11]	
	"Yes!"
"Have you changed your mind?"[12]	
	"No!"

LAURA	MARY LEE
She has no idea. The insecurity[13]	
	The insecurity,[14]
the doubts,	
	the doubts,
the anxieties,[15]	
	the anxieties,[16]
the fearing-the-worst,	the fearing-the-worst. She has no idea.
the blood, the toil, the tears, the sweat, the fussing over every single word.	
	If only we could drink during office hours. "Does anyone have any chocolate?"[17]
Will she see the Real Story, the big picture, the heart of the matter?[18]	Will I see the Real Story, the big picture, the heart
	of the author?[19]
	Will she trust me?[20] Why should she trust me?
Trust.	Trust.
Trust.	Trust.
[*time passes*]	

LAURA	MARY LEE
	"Do you think you could create more of a narrative thread for the book, establish more connections between characters?"
Trussed.	
"Do you remember when you asked me to do that, and I couldn't stand it?"[21]	
	Vaguely.
"As if it would be an easy thing to pull off."[22]	
	Rings faint bells.
"Hello?"	"Hello?"
"It's me."	"It's you!"
"I think I have the solution."	
	Homicide?
"It was easier for me to write several new monologues instead of trying to jam the existing ones all together into one story."[23]	
	Easier? *She thinks that was easier?*
"Do you want to see them?"	
	"Of course!"

LAURA	MARY LEE
And then everything went terribly smoothly and happily after that. The end.	
	The story does have a happy ending, but like a poorly edited novel, it took far too long to get there.
But we did. Get *There*, I mean. *There* is great! I'll take *There*, any day.	
"I wouldn't say no to more *Theres*."	"I am certain of more *Theres*." But while we're getting to more Theres, let's agree to:
The finest chocolate, the best champagne, the most beautiful flowers.	the finest chocolate, the best champagne, the most beautiful flowers.
	More exquisite letters, please, and witty e-mails, and stories! More stories! Never enough stories! As many stories as possible, please.[24]
What else can I tell you about myself? Tufts of bear fur make me happy. Anything bear-related, actually. I have a thing for bears, you know.	I know.

LAURA	MARY LEE
I sometimes disagree with Candlewick about book covers and punctuation.	
	I do, too.
You know that I swear?	
	I do, too.
Even on holidays.	
	Cussing was invented for holidays.
Did I mention the champagne?	
	Several times. In fact, alcoholic themes crop up with surprising frequency in your correspondence.[25]
But it has to be good champagne.	
	Of course.
Chocolate, too. Must be quality chocolate.	
	Whenever possible.

LAURA	MARY LEE
"I trust you, in your profile of me, not to let slip how vain and obstinate and anxious I am[26] because that kind of thing really doesn't make interesting reading. It's much easier to read about entirely admirable people.	Interesting reading. Extraordinarily talented woman.
And you are not, of course, obliged to be entirely truthful."	Entirely truthful.

NOTES

1. Laura Amy Schlitz submitted her manuscript—at that time called *A Clamor of Children*—to Candlewick Press in 2000. *Good Masters! Sweet Ladies!* was published in 2007.

2. The author submitted her manuscript to publishers alphabetically, opting not to use the Reverse Sort function on her computer.

3. LAS: "Always lived in Baltimore, Maryland. Librarian. Spinster. Bourgeoise. Enjoy reading. I wish I had some splendidly picturesque thing I could tell you, but even the things that are really important to me aren't very interesting. I've been to Venice four times—adore Venice, wrote an 800-page novel about Venice—but who doesn't adore Venice? I sang the *Sprechstimme* in *Pierrot Lunaire* when I was in college—I did it without a score, even—but nobody knows what that is." 3/12/08

4. Discovering a manuscript or an author is, more often than not, a combination of dumb luck and divine intervention, often having very little to do with an editor's genius and foresight (or lack thereof).

5. Whether the editor was the beneficiary of luck and divine intervention or was possessed of genius and foresight is still the subject of intense debate. These two things are certain: the author is brilliant 100 percent of the time, and anyone would have to be asleep not to notice; the editor is a genius 99.99 percent of the time but in this case was merely divinely lucky to be conscious.

6. LAS: "The writer is at all times haunted by the twin demons of shame and fear." 10/13/05

7. An editor is at all times hounded by the often-opposing considerations of critical and commercial success.

8. MLD: "Every time I read this, I get a thrill." 2/21/01

9. Regarding the lack of commercial prospects for the book, the editor wrote to a colleague: "There is nothing like this on the market, and it is always an uphill battle to help folks

understand something new and unusual. But once people open this up and hear these voices, I'm certain that it will stir excitement precisely because it is so unique and because it is so much fun!" 6/11/01

10. MLD: "The things that fuel my conviction are the quality of the material, the sharp wit and keen mind of the author, and a pioneering spirit!" 10/18/01

11. LAS's exact words: "I haven't heard from you in such a long time, am I to assume you no longer wish to publish my book?" (date withheld)

12. LAS's words, paraphrased: "My mother wishes to know if she can expect to see my name on the cover of a book before she is dead." (date withheld)

13. LAS: "Intelligent flattery is very good for artists; they metabolize it like turtles make sunshine into calcium for their shells; everyone knows that." 5/30/01

14. One of an editor's greatest fears is that she will, by her clumsy and misguided direction, disfigure what was already a thing of beauty.

15. LAS: "For me the work of writing is so grueling that judgmental criticisms cut like a whip. I can feel myself shrivel and flinch and grow small." 10/13/05

16. Another of an editor's greatest fears is that she will inadvertently crush the creator's spirit and paralyze the pen.

17. A fixture of any serious writer's desk or respectable children's book publishing department is the candy bowl. Fine European chocolate is the preferred choice, but American chocolate made with real cocoa and real butter is also acceptable. In the absence of those, artificially flavored petroleum byproducts of unknown origin may suffice.

18. LAS: "For every book there's the Real Story, and the writer is in love with the Real Story, and in pursuit of it. Lots of times the Real Story comes shrouded in a sort of fog, and the writer only catches glimpses of it—a hoof here, a pair of ears there—and has to piece it together as best she can. The Real Story is always more glorious, more fascinating, more radiant than what ends up on the page, and the writer knows this and is frustrated by it. But the writer wants to grapple with the Real Story anyway, and tell it to the Ideal Reader in the hopes that the Ideal Reader will love it, too. . . . The first task of the editor is to be clairvoyant enough to see the Real Story." 10/13/05

19. An editor's greatest hope is to live up to the task of being the writer's Ideal Reader.

20. LAS: "The second task of the editor is to tell the writer truths that may be helpful without making the author want to curl up in a fetal position and die." 10/13/05

21. LAS's exact words: "It feels completely false to me and would entail disemboweling each of the individual monologues in order to insert something extraneous, something that doesn't belong. I can't do this." 7/23/01

22. LAS: "I'd end up with something like a cockatrice. Medieval cooks actually did take the trouble to sew a chicken to a pig and stuff it, but I don't think anybody believed in the result . . . I haven't spent the advance. I am willing to send it back to you." 7/23/01

23. LAS: "Sometimes the editor honestly can't see the Real Story, and then the editor has to trust that the writer does." 10/13/05

24. Not just about Heinrich and Maud and Pask and the pantheon of memorable characters yet to be born of your imagination, but about your visit to Venice or to the home of Charles Dickens; about sorting pictures of pain relievers for a lady with a clipboard at the mall; about burying the garden shears when you were ten so that you wouldn't have to trim the garden; about what life has been like ATN (After the Newbery). . . .

25. LAS: "Thank you for the kind words—they are even better than the champagne I drank Friday night." 10/2/00

"As one who is still eating birthday cake, I can testify that champagne and chocolate go awfully well together." 5/31/01

"I think you should edit my book at home. With a pair of really comfortable shoes (or maybe just socks) and the smell of coffee and breakfast toast in the air, you're bound to be more broad-minded about tiny little errors in taste, grammar, et cetera. If you like, I'll send you a bottle of something alcoholic, just to hone your editorial judgment to the utmost. Bourbon? Anise? Fra Angelico? Let me know." 9/28/01

"Do you ever drink Spanish coffee? A good, hot strong cup of coffee, with generous shots of Grand Marnier and Kahlua, plus lashings of sweetened (but not too much) whipped cream, with freshly ground nutmeg on the top . . . they say it's just the thing to drink while reading a manuscript. It provides editorial insights like nobody's business." 10/3/01

26. "I realized there's a lot you don't know about me. You know a lot about my insecurities and obstinacy and testiness, but you're probably not going to put that in the profile (though you can if you want to; tell the truth and shame the devil) and the lot of my life is dull, dull, dull." 3/12/08

The Invention of Hugo Cabret

written and illustrated by
Brian Selznick

published by
Scholastic, 2007

HORN BOOK REVIEW

Here's a dilemma for the Newbery committee . . . and the Caldecott: what do you do with an illustrated novel in which neither text nor pictures can tell the story alone? Not to mention the drama to be found in the page turns themselves. A brief introduction sets the time (1931) and place (Paris) and invites readers to imagine they're at the movies. And with a turn of the page, they are, as, over a sequence of twenty-one double-page wordless spreads, a story begins. A picture of the moon gives way to an aerial shot of Paris; day breaks as the "camera" moves into a shot of a train station, where a boy makes his way to a secret passage from which, through a peephole, he watches an old man sitting at a stall selling toys. Finally, the text begins: "From his perch behind the clock, Hugo could see everything." The story that follows in breathtaking counterpoint is a lively one, involving the dogged Hugo, his tough little ally Isabelle, an automaton that can draw pictures, and a stage magician turned filmmaker, the real-life Georges Méliès, most famously the director of *A Trip to the Moon* (1902). There is a bounty of mystery and incident here, along with several excellent chase scenes expertly rendered in the atmospheric, dramatically crosshatched black-and-white (naturally) pencil drawings that make up at least a third of the book. (According to the final chapter, and putting a metafictional spin on things, there are 158 pictures and 26,159 words in the book.) The interplay between the illustrations (including several stills from Méliès's frequently surreal films and others from the era) and text is complete genius, especially in the way Selznick moves from one to the other, depending on whether words or images are the better choice for the moment.

And as in silent films, it's always just one or the other, wordless double-spread pictures or unillustrated text, both framed in the enticing black of the silent screen. While the bookmaking is spectacular, and the binding secure but generous enough to allow the pictures to flow easily across the gutter, *The Invention of Hugo Cabret* is foremost good storytelling, with a sincerity and verbal ease reminiscent of Andrew Clements (a frequent Selznick collaborator) and themes of secrets, dreams, and invention that play lightly but resonantly throughout. At one point, Hugo watches in awe as Isabelle blithely picks the lock on a door. "How did you learn to do that?" he asks. "Books," she answers. Exactly so.—*Roger Sutton*

2008 CALDECOTT ACCEPTANCE SPEECH

Brian Selznick

The speech I am about to deliver takes place in 2008, under the roofs of Anaheim. It concerns a young boy named Hugo Cabret, who once, not that long ago, starred in a book that changed his life forever.

But before we turn the page, I want you to picture yourself sitting in the darkness, like the beginning of a movie. You'll remember how you zoomed toward a hotel in the middle of the city, rushing through the halls into a crowded ballroom. On screen, you will eventually spot a boy, asleep in his secret apartment. Watch out for him, because this is Hugo Cabret. He's unaware that in a city he's never heard of, a man he doesn't know has taken the stage, and a speech all about him has just begun.

Which brings us to tonight.

The Caldecott Medal was first presented in 1938, having been established the year before by a man named Frederic G. Melcher, who in 1921 had also created the Newbery Medal. For the Caldecott, his intention was to honor the work done in picture books by American illustrators. But right from the start, there was a question of what exactly defined a picture book. In her *History of the Newbery and Caldecott Medals,* Irene Smith states that Melcher believed that the "dominant feature must be the work of the artist."

When I began work on *The Invention of Hugo Cabret,* I had no idea that the "dominant feature" would be the work of the artist; that the story would be told so prominently through images. So tonight, members of the Caldecott committee, esteemed colleagues, fellow honorees, friends, and family, I'd like to talk a little bit about how I came to make a 550-page picture book.

The story begins, as everything does, with childhood. I grew up drawing, reading books, and watching movies. I had my favorites, and among them were the artist Leonardo da Vinci, the hilarious picture book *Fortunately* by Remy

Charlip, and the movie *King Kong,* produced by my grandfather's first cousin David O. Selznick. I eventually grew up and became a writer and illustrator of children's books, a job that combines all my childhood loves. But about five years ago I came to an impasse. I needed some kind of change, even though I didn't know what, exactly. Something about my work wasn't satisfying me. I stopped illustrating. Everything came to a standstill. I grew quite depressed.

This lasted for six months.

During this time, there was one thing that graced my life and saved me from going completely crazy. I met Maurice Sendak.

He talked to me about my work, which he said showed great promise, but he steadfastly maintained that I hadn't come close to reaching my full potential yet. These words resonated with me very strongly. I think I had secretly felt the same way. I talked to him about how lost I felt, about how I didn't know what I should do next. His words were simple but powerful: "Make the book you want to make."

I didn't know what that meant at the time. I had no new ideas.

So, with nothing else to do, I decided to turn this period of my life into a sort of apprenticeship to Sendak, even if he didn't fully know it. I surrounded myself with the things he loved, like *Moby-Dick,* Mozart, and the paintings of Vincent van Gogh, and I studied Sendak's own work even more closely. I read, and I tried to leave myself open for things to come. But as for my own work, I created nothing.

The Invention of Hugo Cabret grew out of this period in my life. I came across a book called *Edison's Eve* by Gaby Wood, where I learned that Georges Méliès, the man who made the first science-fiction movie, *A Trip to the Moon,* in 1902, had owned a collection of automata, and at the end of his life they'd been destroyed and thrown away. I had seen *A Trip to the Moon* long ago and loved it. As soon as I learned about Méliès's lost automata, I suddenly, mysteriously, imagined a boy climbing through the garbage and finding one of those broken machines. It was almost like a flash of light had gone off in my head. Here was the beginning of a story.

Perhaps this was the book that Sendak was talking about.

I was both greatly relieved and terrified, because it quickly became clear that this book would incorporate everything I'd learned about bookmaking up to this point, while at the same time it would be unlike anything I'd made before. I wanted to create a novel that read like a movie. What if this book, which is all about the history of cinema, somehow used the *language* of cinema to tell its story? How could I do this?

I looked to picture books for the answer.

And the secret was in the page turns.

Think about the wild rumpus in *Where the Wild Things Are.* The pictures grow until they take over the entire book and there is no more room for words. Only the reader turning the page can move the story forward. We are put in charge at the exact moment Max himself takes charge. We become Max, all because of the page turns.

Think about my favorite childhood book, *Fortunately,* by Remy Charlip, which employs page turns so brilliantly to tell its story. We watch what happens as Ned, page by page, tries to get from New York to a surprise party in Florida. Having *fortunately* borrowed a friend's airplane, which has *unfortunately* exploded, he *fortunately* finds himself with a parachute that *unfortunately* has a hole in it, and so on. The story moves forward after each line of text, always bringing a surprise when we turn the pages.

Through my friend Dan Hurlin, I met Remy Charlip a few years ago, and we became friends. This friendship is one of the great joys of my life. I was so excited to meet the creator of *Fortunately* and to really get to know him. While I was working on *Hugo,* I tried to explain to him what my book was going to be about and how I wanted to use page turns. He said, "Oh, I wrote something about that a while ago. I'll send it to you." This brilliant little essay, called "A Page Is a Door," ends with this paragraph:

> A book is a series of pages held together at one edge, and these pages can be moved on their hinges like a swinging door. . . . Of course if a door has something completely different behind it, it is much more exciting. The element of delight and surprise is helped by the physical power we feel in our own hands when we move that page or door to reveal a change in everything that has gone before, in time, place, or character. A thrilling picture book not only makes beautiful single images or sequential images, but also allows us to become aware of a book's unique physical structure by bringing our attention, once again, to that momentous moment: the turning of the page.

In the end, Remy posed for me as Georges Méliès because of his uncanny resemblance to the filmmaker, and I'm extremely proud that he is one of the stars of *The Invention of Hugo Cabret.* Amazingly, Remy told me that he's long loved Méliès and that he even used drawings by Méliès as inspiration for pictures in one of his books. It is beautiful little coincidences like this, which occur again and again while I work, that convince me I must be on the right path.

I SHOULD MENTION here that *The Invention of Hugo Cabret* would not exist at all without my editor at Scholastic, Tracy Mack. The first book we did together, in 1995, was Pam Conrad's *Our House,* and since then Tracy has pushed me to be a better artist and writer than I ever could have been without her. From the moment I told her I wanted to write about a boy who meets a famous French filmmaker, she and editor Leslie Budnick embraced the story and the format and helped me craft every line, every word, every image. I share this award with them and will forever be grateful for their guidance and friendship. Thank you, Tracy and Leslie.

And I must extend these thoughts to art director David Saylor, who, along with his partner Charles Kreloff, made the book more beautiful than I could have imagined. I must also thank Scholastic Press for publishing *Hugo* so exquisitely. Everyone understood that even though *The Invention of Hugo Cabret* is a book about movies, and it's told *like* a movie, the main concern was still *the book*. We wanted readers to be aware of the object in their hands, to fall in love not just with Hugo but with the book itself, the thing with covers and pages and pictures and words.

While I was making *Hugo*, I also shared early drafts with friends who helped me with the story. I have to especially thank Pam Muñoz Ryan and Sarah Weeks for their insights and comments. You helped make Hugo the man he is today.

THIS SPEECH PROBABLY should have begun slightly differently. It should have begun with the door opening into Eeyore's Books for Children in 1989, because this is where my life in children's books really started.

The manager of the store took me under his wing, and I learned what it meant to truly be a bookseller . . . getting the right book into the right child's hand, something everyone in this room has in common in one way or another. I also learned how difficult this could be. I remember the time a customer, an elderly woman, wanted a book for her grandchild. Nothing I recommended was right: one book was too long, one too short; the pictures were not good enough, or bright enough, or engaging enough. Finally, in desperation, I said, "Here, this book is a classic. Your grandchild will love it. It's Dr. Seuss's *Green Eggs and Ham*." She looked at it and said, "They're Jewish. Do you have it without the ham?"

When I was finally ready to start making my own book, it was the manager at Eeyore's and his girlfriend who helped me first get published. The manager soon left the store and eventually became a wonderful editor himself. Steve Geck, now at Greenwillow, married his then-girlfriend Diana Blough, now at Bloomsbury, and I must say a profound "thank you" to you both. In so many ways, I'm here tonight because of you.

Noel Silverman has been my lawyer, advisor, and very close friend since my first book was published, and I have to thank you for all your guidance and wisdom.

Thank you especially to my parents, Lynn and Roger Selznick, who have been endlessly supportive. My mom traveled with my first book in a Ziploc baggie in the trunk of her car in case she ran into anyone who hadn't seen it.

My dad, an accountant who had wanted to be an archaeologist, never liked his job, and because of this, both my parents made sure their three kids followed their dreams. As a kid, I wanted to be an artist, my sister wanted to be a kindergarten teacher, and my brother wanted to be a brain surgeon, and that's what we're each doing today.

My dad died just before I began work on *Hugo,* and for a long time while I was writing the story I didn't know what was going to happen to Hugo's father. I didn't want Hugo's father to die, so I kept him alive. But there were huge holes in the story—the plot simply wasn't working. I still remember the moment when I realized what needed to happen. It was a profound and complicated moment. I was sad, but also uplifted. Hugo's father's death gave reason to the entire story. It meant everything that happens to Hugo would be conected to *his* father. I discovered, a year into writing the book, that it was his love for his father that gives the plot power and meaning and makes the story matter, for Hugo himself, for me as the creator, and hopefully, by extension, for the reader.

I certainly don't have the words to thank my boyfriend, David Serlin. I think I can only be described as *unbearable to be around* while I'm working. If he says, "Your drawings look good," I get angry because he obviously knows nothing about art and can't see all the flaws that I'm trying to fix. And if he says nothing, then I get mad at him for being unsupportive. He's really in a no-win situation, yet he manages to handle me with patience and understanding and love. He's a brilliant thinker, a respectful listener, and, well, I'll say it again, a very, very patient man. I know that I wouldn't be here tonight without you, D. Thank you.

And finally, to Karen Breen and the Caldecott committee, thank you for this great honor. Tonight's banquet marks the seventieth anniversary of the Caldecott Medal, Frederic G. Melcher's brainchild. Melcher wanted to define what exactly picture books were and how best to honor them. I think he would be proud to see that his intentions are still being discussed so seriously, and that we are still passionately debating what exactly a picture book *is.*

But however we choose to define or label them, I think the most important thing to remember is that kids want good books, with good stories. That's what we're here to provide—books that are serious, or funny, or true, or made up. We need to give children the books they want, and the books that they don't yet know they want. And sometimes, we have to remember, the one thing a child *really* wants in their book is a little bit of ham.

Brian Selznick

THE AMAZING BRIAN SELZNICK:
A PROFILE IN THREE ACTS

Any proper introduction to Brian Selznick should open with red velvet curtains.

Close your eyes and imagine said curtains draped elegantly across a grand stage. Now picture the curtains parting to reveal an elaborately designed set. Dramatic music rises. Our star steps into the spotlight. He is tall, lean, bespectacled, and, most notably, poised. In his finely tailored suit, he is classically handsome, with dark, wavy hair; dancing brown eyes; and a beguiling, ready laugh. Even from your seat in the audience, you can feel his warmth, his coltish energy, his passion and charisma. And suddenly you know you would travel anywhere with him—London, Paris, Washington, D.C., the moon!

Now you have a sense of how it feels to work with Brian.

ACT I: ARTIST

Each time art director David Saylor and I begin a new book with Brian, it is like setting out on a bold adventure. There is a tremendous spirit of collaboration, dedication, trust, respect, and fun. Those qualities have accompanied all eight books we have worked on together.

When Brian and I first met in 1995, I was a fledgling associate editor apprenticing with the legendary Jean Feiwel, and he was a fledgling artist who had recently left his job at Eeyore's Books for Children in Manhattan to work full-time as a freelance illustrator. Jean and I were looking for the right illustrator for Pam Conrad's *Our House: The Stories of Levittown*. As a huge fan of *The Houdini Box*, I suggested Brian, and was thrilled when Jean agreed.

Browsing through the *Our House* file recently, I was appalled to discover that I had written a detailed illustration list for Brian, suggesting *exactly* what he should draw. (Clearly, I had a lot to learn.) Luckily for me, Brian didn't balk or back out. In fact, he dove in with fervor. He made a trip to Levittown, toured the town and surrounding areas with Pam, met with the local librarian, dug around in the library's archives, took tons of photos, read tons of books, and followed his immense curiosity wherever it led him. He then created fourteen beautiful little pen-and-ink drawings, each one filled with detail and feeling.

Tireless and meticulous, he poured his whole heart into the project, giving it as much attention, respect, and care as if it were his own.

From the very beginning, Brian has shown a kind of reverence for creativity. And his studio is a sanctuary for it. Books, toys, handmade sculptures that serve as models for his characters, paintings, props, and miscellaneous collections surround his work in progress, laid out on his drafting table and pinned to the walls. In someone else's space it might look cluttered, but in Brian's it is harmoniously arranged and inviting, as though you have stepped into a mini-museum of the artist's mind.

Every time I visit, I am amazed to see how Brian weaves his vast and wide-ranging interests (from Houdini to robots to movies) into his work in a way that is both fascinating and accessible. Everything flows together seamlessly. The seeds of an idea he used in one book might flower in another. It is all part of a beautiful continuum.

When a new book is in progress, Brian frequently comes in to Scholastic to talk to us about his broad vision as well as details he might have uncovered in his research and is eager to include. Nearly always, he brings pint-sized sketch dummies. Rather than having us review thumbnail sketches on a single flat page, he wants us to hold these three-dimensional mini-books, turn the pages, and feel the story's visual flow and dramatic build. The dummies are always enormously helpful. They allow us to see exactly how the book will unfold—no surprises at a stage too late to fix. They also give us the time to be creative with other aspects of the bookmaking, from the jacket design to the endpapers.

Then there are the times we don't hear from Brian for weeks. After one of his vanishing acts, invariably, he shows up in our offices—looking a little tired, a little thinner, but somehow still radiating that quintessential Brian energy—and delivers all of his final artwork *early.*

Brian's attentiveness to the page turn and his love of the book as an object began early on and has culminated in *The Invention of Hugo Cabret,* for which he created numerous half-pint-sized dummies, detailing all of the 284 drawings that would ultimately appear in the book. His vision for how the pictures would unfold and advance the plot was so strong that, while the text underwent several rounds of revision, only a handful of the illustrations that appeared in those early sketch dummies were changed or dropped.

Brian has lots more ideas for how to experiment with the page turn and the book as an object, and this is one of the things I find most exciting about working with him: he continues to challenge himself, push the boundaries of what's been done before, and surprise us with his inventions. My job is to trust his vision, encourage him to follow his instincts, ask questions, and occasionally nudge him in one direction or another. I don't tell him what to draw anymore.

After *Hugo Cabret* came out, people asked me if it was scary to publish such a risk-taking book. To me, it never felt risky. Innovative, groundbreaking, and different, to be sure, but there was nothing uncertain about it. It was a big leap in Brian's evolution as an artist—but still part of that beautiful continuum.

ACT II: SHOWMAN

Some of you know that Brian is also a puppeteer. He has worked with the world-renowned puppet master Basil Twist and has created three productions of his own. Performing Twist's "Symphonie Fantastique," Brian made me feel joy and sadness simply by manipulating strips of colored cloth. In his own "The Dinosaurs of Waterhouse Hawkins" (adapted from his and Barbara Kerley's book of the same title), a little dinosaur bone inspired awe as it "narrated" the story, floating around an antique desk (piled with dirt to resemble an archaeological dig) and over boxes, books, and cabinets—which opened to reveal miniature dioramas! Brian's imagination, much like a film or theater director's, works as well in three dimensions as in two.

Like all good showmen, Brian is spontaneous. He can speak thoughtfully and articulately without notes. He is quick-witted. He can find humor in just about anything, including himself. And he has a big imagination. This quality revealed itself to me early on when Brian invented a parade.

Three months after *Our House* was published, Pam Conrad died from an illness she'd been bravely fighting for years. Even though we had known her only a short time, Brian and I were deeply affected by her death and wanted to find a way to honor her life. So, in the fall of 1996, when the Levittown children's librarian, Mary Ann Donato, called Brian to let him know about a parade the town was hosting to commemorate its fiftieth anniversary, we were excited. Of course we would come, Brian told her. We would march in Pam's honor.

We'll have to dress up, Brian told me. Everyone will be in costume. Really? I asked. Oh, yes, he assured me. We would dress as the first citizens of Levittown, from the 1940s. And I was not to worry—Brian had a friend who was a costume designer for the theater, and she would lend us what we needed. He came to my apartment a few weeks later with bags of clothing and accessories. Like a child eagerly anticipating his first school play, he couldn't wait for the big day. He'd even made a beautiful sign with the book jacket on one side and the words "In memory of Pam Conrad, who loved Levittown" on the other.

As it turned out, we were the only ones in costume. Brian just chuckled, and for several hours we proudly carried our sign alongside cheerleaders, police officers, and marching band members. From the sidewalk, kids called out, "Look, it's grandma and grandpa!"

I've been carried along by Brian's imagination ever since.

ACT III: FRIEND

Not only are Brian's artistic talents limitless and his showmanship heartfelt, but his spirit is large and generous. Even after completing a project, he doesn't feel finished until he personally thanks all the people who helped him along the way.

In 2006, after we sent *Hugo Cabret* off to the printer, Brian made the whole team handcrafted antique clockworks, each one mounted on a little red velvet bed and tucked inside a glass case. I know that Brian had very little time to come up for air between finishing the book and embarking on a demanding book tour, and this is how he chose to spend it—saying thank you.

Though Brian gives many handmade gifts, he does not sell his artwork, or even part with it. Most of it is tucked safely in flat files in his studio. A few pieces hang on the walls of his mother's house. So it was especially touching when he gave me the jacket painting for *The Dinosaurs of Waterhouse Hawkins,* elegantly framed, for a wedding present. Every time I look at it, I feel Brian's love and friendship.

Brian's travels to promote *The Invention of Hugo Cabret* have taken him all over the United States and, several times, to Europe. I asked him how he was managing the busyness, and he confessed that he was having a little trouble keeping up with his e-mails. I suggested he hire someone to help him respond to the less personal ones. He paused and then said that he would have some difficulty weeding them out. If he were contacted by someone at a school he'd spoken at five years ago, for example, he couldn't imagine letting someone else answer on his behalf. For him, this was still a personal relationship.

When I look back at the extraordinary books Brian has created over his seventeen-year career and recall the many adventures we have had together, I am inspired by his work as an artist, delighted by his showmanship, and, most of all, honored to call him my friend.

THE **NEWBERY MEDAL 2009**

The Graveyard Book

written by
Neil Gaiman

illustrated by
Dave McKean

published by
HarperCollins, 2008

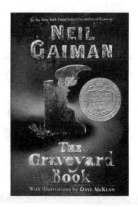

HORN BOOK REVIEW

When a toddler fortuitously escapes the murder of his family by "the man Jack," he is taken in by the ghostly denizens of a local graveyard, renamed Nobody Owens, and ushered through childhood by the kindly Mr. and Mrs. Owens and the enigmatic Silas. (As "Bod" soon learns, there are more kinds of people than just the living and the dead, and Silas falls outside those categories.) Growing up in this strange setting entails many adventures, from getting kidnapped by ghouls, to procuring a headstone for a shunned young woman who was "drownded and burnded" as a witch, to, most dangerous of all, attending school with other living children—all of which prepare Bod for a final showdown with the man Jack, who has never stopped hunting him. Lucid, evocative prose ("'Look at him smile!' said Mrs. Owens . . . and with one insubstantial hand she stroked the child's sparse blond hair") and dark fairy-tale motifs imbue the story with a dreamlike quality. Warmly rendered by the author, Bod's ghostly extended family is lovably anachronistic; their mundane, old-fashioned quirks add cheerful color to a genuinely creepy backdrop. McKean's occasional pages and spots of art enhance the otherworldly atmosphere with a flowing line, slightly skewed figures, and plenty of deep grays and blacks. Gaiman's assured plotting is as bittersweet as it is action-filled—the ending, which is also a beginning, is an unexpected tearjerker—and makes this ghost-story-cum-coming-of-age-novel as readable as it is accomplished.—*Claire E. Gross*

2009 NEWBERY ACCEPTANCE SPEECH

Neil Gaiman

In case you were wondering what I'm doing up here—and I think it's a safe bet that right now *I* am, so that makes at least two of us—I'm here because I wrote a book, called *The Graveyard Book,* that was awarded the 2009 Newbery Medal.

This means that I have impressed my daughters by having been awarded the Newbery Medal, and I impressed my son even more by defending the fact that I had won the Newbery Medal from the hilarious attacks of Stephen Colbert on *The Colbert Report,* so the Newbery Medal made me cool to my children. This is as good as it gets.

You are almost never cool to your children.

When I was a boy, from the ages of about eight to fourteen, during my school holidays, I used to haunt my local library. It was a mile and a half from my house, so I would get my parents to drop me off there on their way to work, and when the library closed I would walk home. I was an awkward child, ill-fitting, uncertain, and I loved my local library with a passion. I loved the card catalog, particularly the children's library card catalog: it had subjects, not just titles and authors, which allowed me to pick subjects I thought were likely to give me books I liked—subjects like magic or ghosts or witches or space—and then I would find the books, and I would read.

But I read indiscriminately, delightedly, hungrily. Literally hungrily, although my father would sometimes remember to pack me sandwiches, which I would take reluctantly (you are never cool to your children, and I regarded his insistence that I should take sandwiches as an insidious plot to embarrass me), and when I got too hungry I would gulp my sandwiches as quickly as possible in the library car-park before diving back into the world of books and shelves.

I read fine books in there by brilliant and smart authors—many of them now forgotten or unfashionable, like J. P. Martin and Margaret Storey and Nicholas Stuart Gray. I read Victorian authors and Edwardian authors. I discovered books that now I would reread with delight and devoured books that I would probably now find unreadable if I tried to return to them—*Alfred Hitchcock and the Three Investigators* and the like.

I wanted books and made no distinction between good books or bad, only between the ones I loved, the ones that spoke to my soul, and the ones I merely liked. I did not care how a story was written. There were no bad stories: every story was new and glorious. And I sat there, in my school holidays, and I read the children's library, and when I was done, and had read the children's library, I walked out into the dangerous vastness of the adult section.

The librarians responded to my enthusiasm. They found me books. They taught me about interlibrary loans and ordered books for me from all across southern England. They sighed and were implacable about collecting their fines once school started and my borrowed books were inevitably overdue.

I should mention here that librarians tell me never to tell this story, and especially never to paint myself as a feral child who was raised in libraries by patient librarians; they tell me they are worried that people will misinterpret my story and use it as an excuse to use their libraries as free daycare for their children.

So. I WROTE *The Graveyard Book,* starting in December 2005 and all through 2006 and 2007, and I finished it in February 2008.

And then it's January 2009, and I am in a hotel in Santa Monica. I am out there to promote the film of my book *Coraline.* I had spent two long days talking to journalists, and I was glad when that was done. At midnight I climbed into a bubble bath and started to read the *New Yorker.* I talked to a friend in a different time zone. I finished the *New Yorker.* It was 3 a.m. I set the alarm for 11, hung up a "Do Not Disturb" sign on the door. *For the next two days,* I told myself as I drifted off to sleep, *I would do nothing but catch up on my sleep and write.*

Two hours later I realized the phone was ringing. Actually, I realized, it had been ringing for some time. In fact, I thought as I surfaced, it had already rung and then stopped ringing several times, which meant someone was calling to tell me something. Either the hotel was burning down or someone had died. I picked up the phone. It was my assistant, Lorraine, sleeping over at my place with a convalescent dog.

"Your agent Merrilee called, and she thinks someone is trying to get hold of you," she told me. I told her what time it was (*viz and to wit,* five-thirty in the bloody morning is she out of her mind some of us are trying to sleep here you know). She said she knew what time it was in L.A., and that Merrilee, who is my literary agent and the wisest woman I know, sounded really definite that this was important.

I got out of bed. Checked voice mail. No, no one was trying to get hold of me. I called home, to tell Lorraine that it was all bosh. "It's okay," she said. "They called here. They're on the other line right now. I'm giving them your cell phone number."

I was not yet sure what was going on or who was trying to do what. It was 5:45 in the morning. No one had died, though, I was fairly certain of that. My cell phone rang.

"Hello. This is Rose Treviño. I'm chair of the ALA Newbery committee . . ." Oh, I thought, blearily. Newbery. Right. Cool. I may be an Honor Book or something. That would be nice. "And I have the voting members of the Newbery committee here, and we want to tell you that your book . . ."

"THE GRAVEYARD BOOK," said fourteen loud voices, and I thought, I may be still asleep right now, but they probably don't do this, probably don't call people and sound so amazingly excited, for Honor Books. . . .

". . . just won . . ."

"THE NEWBERY MEDAL," they chorused. They sounded really happy. I checked the hotel room because it seemed very likely that I was still fast asleep. It all looked reassuringly solid.

You are on a speakerphone with at least fifteen teachers and librarians and suchlike great, wise, and good people, I thought. *Do not start swearing like you did when you got the Hugo Award.* This was a wise thing to think because otherwise huge, mighty, and four-letter swears were gathering. I mean, that's what they're for. I think I said, *You mean it's Monday?* And I fumfed and mumbled and said something of a *thankyouthankyouthankyouokaythiswasworthbeingwokenupfor* nature.

And then the world went mad. Long before my bedside alarm went off I was in a car on my way to the airport, being interviewed by a succession of journalists. "How does it feel to win the Newbery?" they asked me.

Good, I told them. *It felt good.*

I had loved *A Wrinkle in Time* when I was a boy, even if they had messed up the first sentence in the Puffin edition, and it was a Newbery Medal winner, and even though I was English, the medal had been important to me.

And then they asked if I was familiar with the controversy about popular books and Newbery winners, and how did I think I fitted into it? I admitted I was familiar with the discussion.

If you aren't, there had been some online brouhaha about what kinds of books had been winning the Newbery recently, and about what kind of book should win the Newbery in the future, and whether awards like the Newbery were for children or for adults. I admitted to one interviewer that *The Graveyard Book* winning had been a surprise to me, that I had assumed that awards like the Newbery tend to be used to shine a light onto books that needed help, and that *The Graveyard Book* had not needed help.

I had unwittingly placed myself on the side of populism, and realized afterward that that was not what I had meant at all.

It was as if some people believed there was a divide between the books that you were permitted to enjoy and the books that were good for you, and I was expected to choose sides. We were all expected to choose sides. And I didn't believe it, and I still don't.

I was, and still am, on the side of books you love.

I AM WRITING this speech two months before I will deliver it. My father died about a month ago. It was a surprise. He was in good health, happy, fitter than I am, and his heart ruptured without warning. So, numb and heartsick, I crossed the Atlantic, gave my eulogies, was told by relations I had not seen in a decade just how much I resembled my father, and did what had to be done. And I never cried.

It was not that I did not want to cry. It was more that it seemed there was never any time in the maelstrom of events to just stop and touch the grief, to let whatever was inside me escape. That never happened.

Yesterday morning a friend sent me a script to read. It was the story of somebody's lifetime. A fictional person. Three quarters of the way through the script, the fictional character's fictional wife died, and I sat on the sofa and cried like an adult, huge wrenching sobs, my face running with tears. All the unwept tears for my father came out, leaving me exhausted and, like the world after a storm, cleansed and ready to begin anew.

I'm telling you this because it's something that I forget and need to be reminded of. . . . And this was a sharp and salutary reminder.

I've been writing now for a quarter of a century.

When people tell me that my stories helped them through the death of a loved one—a child, perhaps, or a parent—or helped them cope with a disease, or a personal tragedy; or when they tell me that my tales made them become readers, or gave them a career; when they show me images or words from my books tattooed on their skin as monuments or memorials to moments that were so important to them they needed to take them with them every-where. . . . When these things have happened, as they have, over and over, my tendency is to be polite and grateful, but ultimately to dismiss them as irrelevant.

I did not write the stories to get people through the hard places and the dif-ficult times. I didn't write them to make readers of nonreaders. I wrote them because I was interested in the stories, because there was a maggot in my head, a small squirming idea I needed to pin to the paper and inspect, in order to find out what I thought and felt about it. I wrote them because I wanted to find out what happened next to people I had made up. I wrote them to feed my family.

So I felt almost dishonorable accepting people's thanks. I had forgotten what fiction was to me as a boy, forgotten what it was like in the library: fiction was an escape from the intolerable, a doorway into impossibly hospitable worlds where things had rules and could be understood; stories had been a way of learning about life without experiencing it, or perhaps of experiencing it as an eighteenth-century poisoner dealt with poisons, taken them in tiny doses, such that the poisoner could cope with ingesting things that would kill someone who was not inured to them. Sometimes fiction is a way of coping with the poison of the world in a way that lets us survive it.

And I remembered. I would not be the person I am without the authors who made me what I am—the special ones, the wise ones, sometimes just the ones who got there first.

It's not irrelevant, those moments of connection, those places where fiction saves your life. It's the most important thing there is.

So I WROTE a book about the inhabitants of a graveyard. I was the kind of boy who loved graveyards as much as he feared them. The best thing—the very best, most wonderful possible thing—about the graveyard in the Sussex town in which I grew up is that there was a witch buried in it, who had been burned in the High Street.

My disappointment on reaching teenagehood and realizing, on rereading the inscription, that the witch was nothing of the sort (it was the grave of three stake-burned Protestant Martyrs, burned by order of a Catholic Queen) stayed with me. It would become the starting place, along with a Kipling story about a jeweled elephant goad, for my story "The Witch's Headstone." Although it's chapter 4, it was the first chapter I wrote of *The Graveyard Book,* a book I had wanted to write for over twenty years.

The idea had been so simple, to tell the story of a boy raised in a graveyard, inspired by one image, my infant son, Michael—who was two, and is now twenty-five, the age I was then, and is now taller than I am—on his tricycle, pedaling through the graveyard across the road in the sunshine, past the grave I once thought had belonged to a witch.

I was, as I said, twenty-five years old, and I had an idea for a book and I knew it was a real one.

I tried writing it, and realized that it was a better idea than I was a writer. So I kept writing, but I wrote other things, learning my craft. I wrote for twenty years until I thought that I could write *The Graveyard Book*—or at least, that I was getting no better.

I wanted the book to be composed of short stories, because *The Jungle Book* was short stories. And I wanted it to be a novel, because it was a novel in my head. The tension between those two things was both a delight and a heartache to me as a writer.

I wrote it as best I could. That's the only way I know how to write something. It doesn't mean it's going to be any good. It just means you try. And, most of all, I wrote the story that I wanted to read.

It took me too long to begin, and it took me too long to finish. And then, one night in February, I was writing the last two pages.

In the first chapter, I had written a doggerel poem and left the last two lines unfinished. Now it was time to finish it, to write the last two lines. So I did. The poem, I learned, ended:

Face your life
Its pain, its pleasure,
Leave no path untaken.

And my eyes stung, momentarily. It was then, and only then, that I saw clearly for the first time what I was writing. I had set out to write a book about a childhood—it was Bod's childhood, and it was in a graveyard, but still, it was a childhood like any other; I was now writing about being a parent, and the fundamental most comical tragedy of parenthood: that if you do your job properly, if you, as a parent, raise your children well, they won't need you anymore. If you do it properly, they go away. And they have lives and they have families and they have futures.

I sat at the bottom of the garden, and I wrote the last page of my book, and I knew that I had written a book that was better than the one I had set out to write. Possibly a book better than I am.

You cannot plan for that. Sometimes you work as hard as you can on something, and still the cake does not rise. Sometimes the cake is better than you had ever dreamed.

And then, whether the work was good or bad, whether it did what you hoped or it failed, as a writer you shrug, and you go on to the next thing, whatever the next thing is.

That's what we do.

IN A SPEECH, you are meant to say what you are going to say, and then say it, and then sum up what you have said.

I don't know what I actually said tonight. I know what I meant to say, though:

Reading is important.

Books are important.

Librarians are important. (Also, libraries are not childcare facilities, but sometimes feral children raise themselves among the stacks.)

It is a glorious and unlikely thing to be cool to your children.

Children's fiction is the most important fiction of all.

There.

We who make stories know that we tell lies for a living. But they are good lies that say true things, and we owe it to our readers to build them as best we can. Because somewhere out there is someone who needs that story. Someone who will grow up with a different landscape, who without that story will be a different person. And who *with* that story may have hope, or wisdom, or kindness, or comfort.

And that is why we write.

....

Neil Gaiman

IT'S FITTING THAT Neil Gaiman has become the first Newbery medalist to Tweet his good news, and perhaps equally fitting that his Newbery Tweet quickly became infamous not just for the fact of its existence but for its profane content as well. No doubt many a Newbery medalist has expressed him- or herself thusly on hearing the Newbery news, but Mr. Gaiman was the first to send it out unexpurgated to more than ten thousand Twitter followers. This isn't even counting the thousands more who later stopped by twitter.com/neilhimself to see what was on the author's mind that memorable day.

Neil is a trailblazer and an iconoclast, but not necessarily by design. Born in England, he pursued an early career as a journalist in London, but he quickly began creating comics, publishing into a genre small enough at the time that he in many ways helped to create its orthodoxy, with works like *The Sandman, The Books of Magic, Violent Cases, Signal to Noise,* and *Mr. Punch.*

In 1990, Neil published his first novel, collaborating with Terry Pratchett on *Good Omens.* By that time he was living in the United States, near Minneapolis, in a house that became the model for the one in which the eponymous heroine of *Coraline* lives. Since then, he has been prolific in a number of genres, producing novels, short-story collections, screenplays, picture books, and, occasionally, pieces that defy categorization. For those, Neil and his editor (me, in the lucky instance that the work in question is suited for young readers) tackle the question of how to shape them into book form. The picture book *The Dangerous Alphabet,* originally produced as a limited-edition broadsheet for friends at Christmas, was one of those works. *Stardust* was originally a series of comics, then a collected volume, a prose-only novel, and a film, which then created the opportunity for us to publish an edition for teen readers.

Neil's stories are often cited for their allusions—to literature, to mythology, to psychoanalytic thinking and writing. *The Graveyard Book,* of course, harks back to *The Jungle Book,* and all of the familiar Kipling characters have their counterparts among the denizens of the graveyard. But the tone of *Coraline, The Graveyard Book,* and Neil's other works written with young readers in mind is relaxed and intimate, almost confidential. That may have something to do with the English writers Neil often has cited as his influences, among them Tolkien, Lewis, and G. K. Chesterton, and perhaps with the habit more common among British writers of direct address of the reader (not a particular habit of Neil's but something suggested by his tone).

Or maybe his confidential tone has to do with his generosity as a writer, which extends very often to his three children, Mike, Holly, and Maddy, paired with a gift for turning the details of daily life into soaring fantasy. The dedication in *Coraline* notes, "I started this for Holly / I finished it for Maddy." Neil is happy to tell the story of *The Graveyard Book*'s origins, and it's been recounted in print a number of times: as a young family, Neil, his wife, and their firstborn, Mike, lived in a tall, narrow house with no yard and no place to ride a tricycle. So Mike rode his tricycle in the graveyard across the way, and that was when Neil first contemplated the story of a young boy raised within a cemetery's gates. He began the book then, but decided he might not yet be quite up to it and stopped working on it for nearly twenty years. When he picked it up again, he began with chapter 4, "The Witch's Headstone," which was only partially complete when Neil almost decided it was still not what he wanted it to be. But then Maddy asked him to read it to her and uttered the ultimate writer's charm: "What happens next?"

Neil has shared both of these stories with audiences and interviewers, but there is another *Graveyard Book* story you are not likely to have heard yet. Though not quite rivaling the book's gestation period, the novel's labor and delivery were also somewhat extended. After beginning with chapter 4, Neil returned to the beginning of the book and wrote the rest of it, more or less in the order that it appears. But at the same time that he was writing *The Graveyard Book,* he was occupied with the *MirrorMask* film and books, the *Beowulf* screenplay, the *Stardust* film, and a variety of comics projects, all of which seemed to involve a great deal of travel. When he could return to his desk and clear away other demands, Neil wrote and delivered *The Graveyard Book* a chapter at a time. Given the episodic nature of the book, it was quite satisfying to read the individual chapters, even if my preference after every one would have been to read the rest of them right away. The real issue was that chapter 4 had been such a charmer, sweet really (for all that the witch in question, Liza Hempstock, was a little bitter about her early demise and had something of an edge to her). Then arrived chapter 1: "There was a hand in the darkness, and it held a knife. The knife had a handle of polished black bone, and a blade finer and sharper than any razor. If it sliced you, you might not even know you had been cut, not immediately."

For weeks and months, as the chapters arrived one by one, I waited, wondered, and, I confess, fretted. (According to a blogger who has compiled a chronology of Neil's progress reports on the novel, that period actually lasted from 2005 to February 2008.) If there is one thing about editing that Neil Gaiman has taught me, it's the wisdom to stay out of the way of a writer clearly in full command of his material. And as I read what I had of *The Graveyard Book,* I knew that this was such a time. But I didn't know where this tale was heading or how it would get there. The book began with a full-blown crescendo of literary horror, then delivered a sweeter, softer melody. How would Neil reconcile this discordance? I held my breath. It wasn't until very near the end, between February and April 2008, when the final chapters began to arrive, that I breathed out again. What I saw was this: the story was briefly terrifying, till Bod entered the protection of the graveyard. But as he grew older and became more independent, the graveyard's protection no longer could hold him so safe. And as Bod begins to travel regularly into the land of the living, the volume begins to increase again, until it reaches another powerful crescendo. Like Beethoven's Fifth Symphony, it all made sense at last. Perhaps even before he did it, the writer had known exactly what he was doing, and it was my job as his editor to trust him.

That was not quite a year ago, and it's been quite a time since then: publication of *The Graveyard Book,* warm reviews, the Newbery Medal announcement coming serendipitously on the eve of the *Coraline* movie debut, which created more opportunities for the Newbery news to travel well beyond the usual borders.

It's just now begun to be a little bit quieter again. There's been talk of a prequel or a sequel, perhaps more among readers than by the author. What's the story of the man Jack? Or Silas, the vampire? What will happen to Bod? But first, for Neil Gaiman, there's the Batman publication, the children's novel *Odd and the Frost Giants* to come this fall, another movie project or two, and the nonfiction China book—or is it books, and might they include a fiction project or two? Like his readers, I'm willing to wait, and to trust Neil Gaiman.

The House in the Night

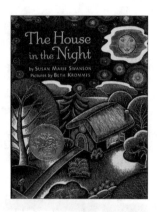

written by
Susan Marie Swanson

illustrated by
Beth Krommes

published by
Houghton Mifflin, 2008

HORN BOOK REVIEW

"Here is the key to the house. In the house burns a light." So begins a soothing bedtime verse that ends with a child tucked in bed, bathed by the light of the moon. The quiet patterned text is accompanied by dramatic black-and-white scratchboard illustrations with just enough gold touches to fill the pages with gentle light.—*Maeve Visser Knoth*

2009 CALDECOTT ACCEPTANCE SPEECH

Beth Krommes

Good evening. I'd like to begin by offering my heartfelt thanks to Nell Colburn and the members of the Caldecott committee. I am so grateful and amazed to receive this award. Thank you to the Association for Library Service to Children, the American Library Association, and librarians, teachers, and reviewers everywhere for bringing *The House in the Night* to the attention of so many people. I am most honored.

I would also like to congratulate the other honorees. You are my heroes, my role models, and my inspiration.

When asked what I was doing when I received The Call, I can honestly reply I was sitting at my drawing table preparing to work. Monday, January 26, 2009, was a teacher workshop day, and my girls were home from school. I was terribly aware it was Caldecott Day. I had heard that *The House in the Night* was being discussed as Caldecott-worthy, but I had convinced myself not to hope for it. I went to the gym early, came home, took a bath, ate breakfast, and sat down to work. And then, at 9:20 a.m., the phone rang.

It was a woman named Nell Colburn, who I assumed was a potential illustration client. I wrote down her name, and I started writing down "Association for Library Service to . . . ," and then thought, "Oh goodness." I could hear excited voices in the room with Nell, and though I was sitting down, my knees started shaking. As Nell told me the news, I kept repeating, "I can't believe it." My office is a little balcony overlooking the living room, so both my daughters, Olivia and Marguerite, heard my delighted reaction to the call.

Soon I was off the phone and we were all jumping around screaming. I immediately called my husband, Dave, at work, my dad, and the author, Susan Marie Swanson, who burst into tears when she heard the news.

The next few hours were chaotic. The phone started ringing, and every time I put it down, it rang again. The *New York Times* sent over a photographer. I learned, with an hour and a half's notice, that we needed to fly to New York so I could be on the *Today* show the next morning. I didn't have anything to wear. The girls and I drove downtown, found an outfit, stopped at the bank, and dashed back home. Dave walked home, and we all packed our suitcases and left for the airport. For days afterward, I kept asking my family, "Is this really happening?" I kept pinching myself.

ONE THING I know for sure is that I wouldn't be here tonight if it weren't for my children. So thank you to my wonderful husband, Dave, and to our beautiful daughters, Olivia and Marguerite. Having kids made me aware of the spectacular art in children's books and made me want to try my hand at it. But more important, the hours spent reading picture books to my girls were not only cozy but instructional. I saw the kinds of books my daughters enjoyed and which details in a picture captured their attention. Every day that I worked on *The House in the Night,* I thought about how it would feel to be lying next to a child and reading the book at bedtime. I tried to imagine what a parent and child would notice and talk about in my illustrations.

What all our favorite picture books had in common was that they were poetically written and artistically inventive. A parent would not get sick of reading them over and over. They included *Madeline*; *Millions of Cats*; *Bedtime for Frances*; *Little Fur Family*; *Lyle, Lyle, Crocodile*; *Miss Rumphius*; *Owl Moon*; *The Cat in the Hat*; and everything by James Marshall, especially *George and Martha* and *The Stupids*. My favorites of all were the books about Frog by the Dutch author and illustrator Max Velthuijs, especially *Frog and the Stranger,*

Frog in Winter, and *Frog in Love.* The goodnight books I loved most were *And If the Moon Could Talk* by Kate Banks, with pictures by Georg Hallensleben, and, of course, *Goodnight Moon.* All these books have an enormous amount of heart.

When the manuscript for *The House in the Night* was offered to me, I saw that this was also a story with heart. Ann Rider, my longtime editor at Houghton, knew I had always wanted to do a book in black and white, and Susan Marie Swanson's beautiful manuscript was right for me on so many levels. Not only was the text perfect for black-and-white art, as it was all about light and dark, but it was also lyrical, inspiring, and so open-ended that the story would be told primarily through the pictures. This is every illustrator's dream.

It took a while to figure out what the story within the pictures would be. I knew the main character would be a little girl. Authors are told to write what they know, and the rule remains the same for illustrators. Draw what you know. And I know girls. I have four sisters and no brothers, two daughters and no sons. I decided the girl would have to be me, as I couldn't choose one daughter over the other.

But what exactly would this child do that would take her from the key to the house, to the light, to the bed, to the book, to the bird, to the song, to the dark, to the moon, to the sun, and back again in reverse order? Somehow, she had to get out of the house, into the sky, return, and end up asleep in bed. The only way she could reach the sky would be on the back of the bird. I felt that this wasn't original, but hoped I could make it fresh.

I spent a year on the book. That year included six months on the design phase before starting the final art. Designing a book is my favorite part. It is like fitting together the pieces of a large puzzle. Because the text moves forward and then backward, I chose to echo the scenes from the first half of the book in the second half. I aimed for what I call *"pow* moments"—when one turns the page and is dazzled. I taped the pencil roughs in order on my studio wall so I could study the visual flow from page to page.

My scratchboard pictures begin totally black, and I draw by scratching white lines through the black ink surface. The more one scratches, the brighter a picture becomes. It was Ann's idea from the beginning to add the golden highlights. She had admired this effect in a book called *Goodnight, Goodnight* by Eve Rice, published in 1980, and she shared her copy with me. I thought maybe we should add another color or two in addition to the gold highlights, but Ann's brilliant instincts were right. She is always right, to tell the truth.

I knew immediately that the house in our story should look simple and timeless. This is the kind of house I would like to live in eventually, when the kids grow up and we can downsize. I knew that the household objects should be simple and humble, too: an umbrella, a coat rack, a rocking chair, a wooden dresser, a toy car, a basket, a cloth doll. I included many of my favorite things: the shell mobile we made after a vacation to the Jersey shore, Vincent van Gogh's *Starry Night,* my sister's teddy bear, and Marguerite's violin. The dog is my childhood dog, Scamp. I knew that the landscape would be the rolling farmland of my native Pennsylvania. I have also paid homage to Wanda Gág by including her house, Tumble Timbers, within the landscape on the second-to-last spread; and to Dr. Seuss's *The Cat in the Hat,* as we see just a glimpse of Mother's foot coming through the door.

I FEEL LUCKY to be an illustrator of children's books, and I have certainly been blessed in my life. I grew up in a wonderful family and had parents who supported my interest in art. They sent me to weekly art classes and encouraged me to attend art school. At Syracuse University, I majored in painting with a good dose of printmaking and spent my junior year abroad in London. I graduated with $60 in my bank account, worked as a secretary, and went on to graduate school for a master's degree in art education.

It was a long road for me to the world of children's books. I worked as a teacher, the managing director of a small arts center, the manager of a fine handcraft shop, and as an art director for a computer magazine, all before becoming an illustrator. For ten years, I illustrated mostly for magazines and cookbooks. Initially, my medium was wood engraving, but I soon switched to scratchboard, which has the same look but takes less time.

My college friend, the artist Salley Mavor, encouraged me to try illustrating for children. I joined the Society of Children's Book Writers and Illustrators and started attending conferences. A cover I did for the January 1998 issue of *Cricket* magazine caught Ann Rider's attention. Five of the six children's books I've illustrated to date have been in collaboration with Ann. Connecting with her was the greatest good fortune of my professional life.

WHEN PEOPLE ASK me what *The House in the Night* is about, I say art, music, books, imagination, family, home, and love. It is a comforting goodnight story that I hope will especially help children who fear the dark.

Our community was tested this past December when a severe ice storm hit much of New Hampshire and we were without power in our home for nine days. Some people on the outskirts of town had no electricity for as long as three weeks. I thought about light and dark often during those cold days as we hurried to get everything done during the daylight hours. I agreed with a few of the local elementary school children who quoted Dickens in their essays a month later, "It was the best of times, it was the worst of times." It was the best of times when we were all together in the same room every night: watching the fire, reading books, playing cards, or reading aloud. People were helping people at every turn. It was the worst of times when we never felt really warm, we were sleep-deprived from having to refuel the stove every two hours day and night, and we were running out of wood. I could feel my spirits slipping each night as the sun went down.

One night, I took the walk out to the garage to get a few more buckets of wood. The air was freezing and the icy ground treacherous underfoot. I looked around the neighborhood. The houses were all dark except for solitary rooms with flickering candles. I remember being stopped in my tracks as I glanced at the glorious night sky. It was the sky from *The House in the Night*! That light in the dark lifted my spirits more than I can say, and I suddenly felt a deep connection with the stars, the ice, and the night.

I HAVE SO many people to thank this evening. Thank you to Susan Marie Swanson for your lovely manuscript; to Ann Rider for your encouragement and guidance every step of the way, on this book and all the books we've done together; to Carol Rosenberg for your design expertise; to Donna McCarthy for your production genius; and to Sheila Smallwood, Lisa DiSarro, Karen Walsh, and the rest of the staff at Houghton Mifflin Harcourt for your help. I am so grateful to you all.

Thank you to my family and friends for your support: my husband, my daughters, my father and stepmother, my sisters and their families, my aunts, uncles, cousins. Thanks also to those departed: my mother, grandparents, and other family members and friends who cheer me on from above.

Lastly, I thank my little town of Peterborough, New Hampshire. Here the residents know that community matters, that the arts matter, and that books matter. In particular, thank you to my librarian friends at the Peterborough Town Library; the staff of the Toadstool Bookshop; and the Sharon Arts Center, where, years ago, I was first introduced to wood engraving. I have been overwhelmed by the excitement and good wishes of all. Friends tell me that all they heard for a week afterward was, "Did you hear about Beth Krommes?" The most amusing line relayed to me was when our friend Ray said, "Isn't it great! Beth Krommes has scratched her way to the top!"

As I SAT on the flight home from New York City after the *Today* show interview, I had a chance to reflect on all that had happened during the last day and a half. I felt like that little girl on the back of the bird in our story as we flew over the woodland and farmland of Connecticut, Massachusetts, and New Hampshire. The winter landscape was stunning. The sky turned rosy, then dark, and lights started to sparkle in the houses and buildings below. Soon I would be home and back to daily life, but for the moment I was filled only with wonder, gratitude, and great hope for the future. Thank you.

....

ILLUSTRATOR PROFILE BY ANN RIDER

Beth Krommes

SEVERAL YEARS AGO I was in a bookstore in Duluth, Minnesota, and the art on the cover of *Cricket* magazine caught my eye. It was of an Inuit woman—rounded, strong, striking—and though it reminded me of traditional Inuit soapstone carvings, it also felt wholly unique. Luckily, the inside cover of the magazine gave me the information I needed: Beth Krommes, Peterborough, New Hampshire. Not long afterward, I heard a woman answer her phone: "Hello, this is Beth."

That conversation led to Beth illustrating her first picture book, *Grandmother Winter,* by Phyllis Root. It also marked the beginning of our relationship and friendship. Four books and many good conversations later, I find myself more in awe than ever of Beth's craft. There's no denying the rare beauty of her accomplished scratchboard illustrations. But I continue to see more than beauty in her work. Beauty may draw us in, but it doesn't hold us. Beth creates alluring, comforting worlds, sure, but also worlds that feel unfamiliar, at least to me. Brave new worlds from which, we sense, we may not return entirely unchanged. There is a sweet utopian quality to her work, yet also a freeing and mysterious one.

Perhaps a look at Beth's books can best reveal this tension in her work. In *The Lamp, the Ice, and the Boat Called Fish* by Jacqueline Briggs Martin, Beth illustrates a secure world filled with cozy domestic details of sewing boots and cooking around stoves—but also one where the children's home floats on shifting ice and where at night they listen to the eerie sound of the ice cracking around them. In *The Hidden Folk* by Lise Lunge-Larsen, Beth brings to light benevolent creatures who live in and protect flowers—but also dangerous ones with dark holes in their backs who offer poison in golden cups. And in *Butterfly Eyes and Other Secrets of the Meadow* by Joyce Sidman, about the seemingly benign and familiar world of the meadow, she precisely observes a hawk that talks to its prey—before eating it. Her art invites, welcomes, says *please come in,* but also warns: *You may be a little surprised by what you find here.*

Her art for *The House in the Night* by Susan Marie Swanson asks us to make room for paradoxes, too. This spare manuscript—which began as a poem written for an exhibit with the theme of "home sweet home" for a nonprofit housing organization in the Twin Cities—offered great freedom and challenge for Beth, for she needed to construct the entire story line. Susan Marie wisely and graciously gave the artist free rein, and as Beth scratched away the dark on her black ink surfaces, she began to create a universe with pattern and order but also one that introduces the very young to seeming contradictions. Here is a universe where the sun is in the moon, where the child is both reading about and riding on the bird in the book, where the home at night, after all lights have gone off, is dark yet filled with light. This book reveals, as the *Kirkus* reviewer said, "that light and dark, like comfort and mystery, are not mutually exclusive, but integral parts of each other," and in doing so, it leaves the reader's world a little larger.

I happily concede that this is just one of many interpretations of this book. We have by now heard several fine ones, which I take as a healthy sign, for don't the best books invite us into worlds that we partly create?

Born in Emmaus, Pennsylvania, Beth now lives in a charming small town in southern New Hampshire with her husband, Dave, and her two girls, Olivia (16) and Marguerite (13), who remain her most trusted critics. Beth is a perfectionist and demands more of herself than perhaps any artist I know. At times it was a great relief to ask: "Well, what does Marguerite think? *She* likes it, doesn't she? She says it's wonderful, right?" Beth's family provides the sort of vital support and encouragement that is far beyond an editor's ability or reach. Beth's scratchboard technique is one of the most time-consuming and exacting of mediums (each book takes a year to complete), and the world of publishing is not always a nurturing one. Her family believes in her talents; they keep her going; and for that I am most thankful.

For most of our working relationship, Beth had only one car (her husband walked to work) and no cell phone. Until quite recently, she had no e-mail, a choice I both envy and admire. Though I've never visited Beth's house, I imagine it tall, like the New Hampshire pines that surround it, with a turret-like studio—because many times when we're talking on the phone, she'll say, "Wait a second, I have to run down five flights to get something." I also imagine it a home filled not only with art (including Beth's own beautiful casein meadow paintings) but with music, since her husband and girls play the violin and clarinet and French horn. And with dancing, since both of her girls dance. And probably with discussions of nature, since they live in rural New Hampshire, after all, and since Beth's husband has a Ph.D. in zoology, which I know because he was able to tell us about the eating habits of that red-tailed hawk in *Butterfly Eyes*. I also like to think of her home displaying beautiful fabrics and textiles, since Beth is inspired by textiles, from the bold Finnish textiles of Marimekko to the intricate medieval tapestries at the Cloisters in New York City, which she likes to visit with her girls.

And on that bright January morning, I like to imagine Beth in her tall house by the tall pines close to her family when she received the news. I like to think that she did not have to run up and down too many flights of stairs to answer the many other phone calls she received, though I suspect she did. I only know two things for certain: first, that her line was too busy for me to get through until I was at the Denver airport, hours after the committee had called; and second, that once I did get through, how good it was to hear that familiar voice—from this talented, hardworking, exacting, kind genius I have had the great honor to publish—tell me about her glorious morning, including this admission: "Ann, I'm still shaking."

When You Reach Me

written by
Rebecca Stead

published by
Wendy Lamb/Random House, 2009

HORN BOOK REVIEW

The first real indication that this book is going to get deeply, seductively weird is when broody classmate Marcus engages the heroine, Miranda, in a discussion about a flaw in the logic of *A Wrinkle in Time*: "So if they *had* gotten home five minutes before they left, like those ladies *promised* they would, then they would have seen themselves get back. Before they left." Miranda's life is an ordinary round of family and school, the first characterized by a pretty strong relationship with her mother and Mom's good-guy boyfriend, the second by ever-shifting (and perceptively limned) alliances in her sixth-grade class. But when her best friend is bizarrely punched by another boy on the street, and when she starts receiving anonymous notes that seem to foretell the future, it's clear that all is not as it seems. The mystery provides a thread that manages, just, to keep the plot's several elements together, and the closely observed relationships among the characters make the mystery matter. Closing revelations are startling and satisfying but quietly made, their reverberations giving plenty of impetus for the reader to go back to the beginning and catch what was missed.—*Roger Sutton*

2010 NEWBERY ACCEPTANCE SPEECH

Rebecca Stead

My favorite Newbery-speech advice came from a Texas librarian who told me to speak for the shortest time allowable and to remember that I am among friends. She's here tonight, and I have given her a flashlight, and when I have been talking for twelve minutes, she is going to give me a few blinks. And after fifteen minutes, she's just going to throw it at me. Because this is the kind of thing a real friend will do for you. Especially one from Texas.

I wanted to write a great speech. I wanted every person in this room to walk away knowing exactly what the Newbery Medal means to me, and how awed I am to have any kind of place in this room full of passion and talent. I wanted your knees to lock with the kind of happiness I felt on the morning of January 18th, and I wanted you to see the lightning bolts of joy that seemed to streak past my dark kitchen window.

But it turns out that it's really hard to write a great speech when I can still barely grasp that the book won the award in the first place. Whenever I think about it, my mind seems to go in four directions at once. And I want to say all of these four things, but I don't want to get hit by the flashlight. So instead of giving one long speech, I'm going to give four short speeches. And they are all mostly about the journey to this place where I am standing right now.

SPEECH #1

Philip Pullman has said that your life begins when you are born, and your *story* begins when you discover that you have been born into the wrong family by mistake.

But when does the life of a storyteller begin?

Mine began when I was about six. Up until then, I had half-believed that my mother could read my thoughts. But at some point during first grade, I realized that I was completely alone in my own consciousness. I used to regularly freak myself out by sitting still, closing my eyes, and asking myself the same question over and over until I was in a sort of trance. The question was, "How am I me?"

What I meant was, How did my particular self get in here? Again and again, I would close my eyes and plunge myself into this existential angst. Why did I do it?

I think that, like someone alone in a dark room, I was feeling around for a door. Because I really, really did not want to be alone in there.

And I did find a door, eventually. The door was books.

When I read books, I wasn't alone in the rooms of my own mind. I was running up and down other people's stairs and finding secret places behind their closets. The people on the other side of the door had things I couldn't have, like sisters, or dragons, and they shared those things with me. And they also had things I did have, like feelings of self-doubt and longing, and they named those things for me.

Take Meg, for example. In the first chapter of *A Wrinkle in Time,* she calls herself an oddball and a delinquent, makes a horrible face at herself in the mirror, and complains that she is "full of bad feeling." All of this was a revelation for me.

The people in books told me things that the real people in my life either wouldn't admit or didn't realize I needed to know in the first place. And the more I read, the more I thought about writing my own stories, with my own kinds of truth in them. By the time I was nine, I knew I wanted to write. But I didn't tell anyone, because it was too wild a dream. Instead, I told people I wanted to be an actress, which I thought was much more practical, and I waited. I waited about twenty years. Meanwhile, like a lot of people who secretly want to write, I became a lawyer.

Then one day it dawned on me that it's difficult to become a writer without ever writing anything. So I began to write short stories, and I worked on those stories for years until the universe intervened by telling my three-year-old son to push my laptop off the dining room table. No more stories. And suddenly the whole secret writing dream felt very worn-out. I asked myself why I had ever wanted to write in the first place.

And then I remembered that door, and what I had found on the other side of it, and I began writing again. But this time, I was writing for children.

SPEECH #2

I started writing *When You Reach Me* in 2007, after I read a *New York Times* article that brought two things to the front of my mind: the first was an idea for a book plot about a life-saving time-travel mission, and the second was the memory of a homeless man who stood on my corner a lot when I was growing up. We called him the laughing man.

And so the book took off on both of these tracks—an impossible mystery played out on the stage of my own New York City childhood. Here was my elementary school, my mom's apartment, and my lunchtime job at Subway Sandwiches on Broadway. But pretty soon, my younger self began to leak into the story in ways I'd never intended—memories of feeling mean and not being able to help it, of wanting things that I couldn't even begin to talk about, of that time in life when I started to see more, whether I wanted to or not. And as I wrote, the story became more and more about these ordinary mysteries of life, and less about the fantastic time-travel-y one.

I was halfway through the first draft of the book when I became afraid of it. There came a moment of doubt: was I really going to pour all of my inner weirdness into this book? Was I losing my story, or finding it? I wasn't sure. By the time my fortieth birthday rolled around in January 2008, I had stopped writing the book.

Even as a kid, I have always partly dreaded my own birthday parties, and this is because of the Happy Birthday song. I'd spend days thinking about streamers and little Dixie cups full of candy, but the Happy Birthday song hung like a funky black cloud over all of it. It was twenty seconds of torture. Everyone would be looking at me, and I had absolutely no idea what they expected from me, but whatever it was I was sure to let them down. It was only after a terrible period of anticipation, and then, of course, the singing itself, that I could really enjoy the party.

So for my fortieth birthday, I skipped the big celebration that a lot of our friends were having that year. Just dinner at a good Chinese restaurant, I told my husband. Maybe a little cake. But no singing.

The cake arrived quietly at our table at Shun Lee, and we ate it, and it was good. We were getting our coats on to go home when our waiter came out with the leftover cake in the cardboard box we'd brought it in. And on top of the box, someone in the kitchen had written my husband's instructions—my instructions—in pen:

"Table 16: One candle, no singing."

One candle, no singing: I stood there in my coat, looking at those words and wondering, for the first time, what it was that I was so afraid of.

A week later, I went to a writers' conference where Laurie Halse Anderson spoke about craft. Her talk was called: "Plot v. Character: Cage Match Smackdown."

It was a great talk, and at the end of it, Laurie spoke about fear. She told us that sometimes you just have to stop thinking and write.

"Don't think. Write." I drank these words down like an antidote. An antidote to the worry that my book was becoming too truthful or too strange. An antidote to the poisonous message written on that cardboard box: "One candle, no singing."

I walked out of the meeting room, opened my computer, and created a new folder, called "don't think." In that folder, I began writing my book again, and this time I managed to get to the end without worrying too much about exactly what kind of a book it was.

SPEECH #3

I recently sat next to my nine-year-old, Eli, on an airplane. He seemed to feel fine during takeoff, but as the plane began to climb, he looked more and more worried. I began to tell him about what keeps the plane up in the air, but he interrupted me.

"I'm not afraid it's going to fall," he said. "I'm afraid we're going to get sucked into orbit."

This is one of many examples of how adults assume they know what kids are thinking, and of how we are usually wrong. It's also a pretty good metaphor for how I felt as the morning of the Newbery announcements approached.

We have one phone in our apartment, and it's a finicky phone. It rings, or not. It'll take a message when it's in the mood. Occasionally it goes on what we writers like to call a retreat, and we can't find it for a day or two.

On the morning of January 18th, I woke up early (actually, I woke up earliest, and then earlier, and then just early), aimed myself toward the kitchen to make coffee, and noticed that the phone was not on its charger near our front door. I began to look for it.

I looked in all of the regular places—on the kitchen counter, and in the cracks between the couch cushions. I crawled around looking on the living room floor for a bit, and while I was down there, I began to wonder if I even wanted to find the phone.

The days leading up to that morning had been full of good wishes and mock-Newbery results, and now, despite my best efforts, I was nervous about something that I had always assumed would stay safely beyond my reach. To me, the Newbery Medal was an impossibility. But, like Eli, I was a little bit afraid that the impossible might actually happen. That the phone might ring. Because along with the wild happiness of that fantasy, there was also a fear that, like someone sucked into outer space, I wouldn't be able to breathe. I wouldn't know what to do. My head might explode.

It was 6:45 a.m. Maybe I didn't want to find the phone. Probably it was never meant to ring in the first place. I poured myself a cup of coffee.

And then the phone rang. My husband came flying out of the bedroom holding it as if it were something on fire. It turned out that he'd put it on my bedside table the night before. I had been too busy staring at the clock to notice.

And then Katie O'Dell was saying that she was about to tell me something that would change my life. A cheer went up—the whole Newbery committee, on speakerphone. I have a distinct memory of hearing it at the same time I looked down at my bare feet on the kitchen floor and realized I couldn't move my legs.

You know what it felt like? It felt like a lightning bolt of joy. It felt like knee-locking happiness. It felt like the longest, loudest round of Happy Birthday in the history of the world. And I loved every moment of it.

SPEECH #4

This last speech is about being grateful. The truth is that I could have written all four speeches about being grateful.

The first person I want to thank is a librarian whose name I don't remember. She worked at my elementary school library, where, about thirty years ago, someone left *James and the Giant Peach* out on a table. I picked it up and started reading. James's horrible aunts had just been squashed to death when the library period ended. Now I had a problem. I was in sixth grade. This book appeared to be for younger readers. How was I going to get it out of there while maintaining my dignity?

I lied to the librarian. For a good two minutes, I explained to her that I had a younger brother at home who might like the book. I have a vague memory of a complex story about why this brother did not attend school. It wasn't a good story, but she nodded at me a lot, and believed every word. Or so I thought.

And this is what I have come to love about librarians. In addition to being some of the smartest, funniest, most open-minded people I've ever met, librarians will do a lot to put a book into the hands of a kid, even if it means nodding enthusiastically in the face of a long and obvious lie. And I want to thank every librarian here for that, and for protecting and carrying the stories we all need.

I also want to thank the spectacular people at Random House, who gave this book absolutely everything they had to give, including Chip Gibson, Kate Gartner, Adrienne Waintraub, Tracy Lerner, Mary Beth Kilkelly, Barbara Perris, Colleen Fellingham, John Adamo, Rachel Feld, Alyssa Sheinmel, Judith Haut, Tamar Schwartz, Robert Passberger, Schuyler Hooke, and Joan DeMayo and her truly wonderful sales team.

Next, from the bottom of my heart, I want to express my gratitude to the following terrific people:

- Faye Bender, who is my advocate, my guide, and my friend;
- Caroline Meckler, gifted editor, who asked for more Julia;
- Emily Pourciau, a great publicist, who is also great company;
- and Sophie Blackall, for the gift of her gorgeous cover art.

I am grateful to my husband Sean, and my sons, Jack and Eli, for the joy that they bring me, and to my parents, who have made me feel loved every day of my life.

And of course, I am grateful to Wendy Lamb. I met Wendy thirteen years ago in a writing workshop at the 92nd Street Y, where she became the first person (other than my mother) who ever asked to keep something I had written. At the time, I was a lawyer daring myself to write, and I still remember how it felt.

Wendy is an enormously talented editor and a kind human being, and she is also a kind editor and a talented human being. She's the sort of person who brings you a brownie at the exact moment you most need one, and who hides nice notes in your desk drawer. I shudder to think that there might exist some alternate reality in which she and I have never crossed paths.

Finally, to Katie O'Dell and the members of the Newbery committee: thank you for the knee-locking happiness. Thank you for the lightning bolts of joy.

....

Rebecca Stead

A NEW YORK STORY

REBECCA STEAD IS a real New Yorker. Born in Manhattan. Grew up on the Upper West Side. She went to P.S. 75, where her first published story appeared in the school magazine, *The Spicy Meatball*. At Stuyvesant High School she studied creative writing with the writer Frank McCourt. She did go out of town for college at Vassar, but she came right back to law school at New York University, where she met her husband, Sean O'Brien. She then worked as a public defender on criminal cases in the Bronx.

She and Sean now have two sons, Jack and Eli. They live in the neighborhood where she grew up, and where *When You Reach Me* takes place. The family has moved a few times, but always to apartments close to Absolute Bagels. The bagels are too delicious to ever move away.

Rebecca and I met in 1997, as students in an adult short story workshop at the 92nd Street YMHA. She was a young lawyer and a fine writer. I was an editor at Delacorte, taking the class to get a break from children's books. After the workshop ended, a few of us, including Rebecca, formed a writers' group. But her job was very demanding; eventually she dropped out, and we lost touch. In 2003 I was delighted to hear from her. She was now taking time off between jobs to stay home with Jack and Eli, and to write. She brought me an early version of what became her first novel, *First Light*. *First Light* is set on, and within, Greenland's ice cap. In that book, Rebecca revealed an unusual talent: to examine the workings of the natural, daily world, while convincing us that astonishing things are possible.

Which brings me to *When You Reach Me*:

Rebecca was inspired by an article she read in the *Times* about a young man who appeared, wandering around with amnesia. Under hypnosis, he remembered that his wife Penny and children had been in a car accident, but could recall nothing else. His picture was broadcast all over the country, until he was finally identified by Penny herself. But it turned out that she was his fiancée, not his wife. And they had no kids yet.

Which made Rebecca think—what if? What if he had lost his wife and kids, in the future, and somehow found his way back to prevent it? But lost his mind in the process?

About that time, Rebecca and her family moved to an apartment near the building where she grew up. The move made her want to write about her memory of herself and her first independence (being on her own in her neighborhood for the first time, what she observed, what she thought about) and about her emotional landmarks. Back then, there was a scary man on her corner, and she tried to understand: who is he, why is he there? He was a mystery she was always trying to figure out. He became the anchor as she wrote *When You Reach Me,* although when she began, she had Miranda addressing "you" before Rebecca knew who that "you" was.

Rebecca sent me the first two-thirds of the book in December 2007, up to the line: "And then it was Christmas vacation."

I was hooked! I loved the tone, Miranda, the other characters, the way Rebecca had woven *A Wrinkle in Time* into the story, and how Miranda claimed the book for herself. It was fascinating to see the ominous, gritty Manhattan of 1979 through Miranda's eyes. I hadn't a clue who might be writing the letters. I wondered: where is this going? But I never doubted that she could pull it off.

The editing of this book was different from that of *First Light,* which went through several drafts, with line editing, rethinking, and reshaping. The language in *When You Reach Me* was always just right. Miranda's voice was natural and distinctly hers. I've worked on hundreds of books, and this is the only novel that I did not line edit. I don't believe that I changed a word in any draft.

Caroline Meckler, associate editor, had many valuable editorial suggestions. Revisions were subtle: refining, linking, adding clues, shading characters. When questions from readers came up (such as, Could Julia have more of a role? or, Why did the laughing man lie under the mailbox?), Rebecca quickly thought of inspired solutions that deepened the story immensely in a few lines.

We talked about *A Wrinkle in Time.* If the book was going to stay in, it had to play a significant part. Rebecca read and reread it from the perspectives of the different characters in *When You Reach Me,* and added scenes where the kids discussed *A Wrinkle in Time* and time travel. We hoped that L'Engle's iconic novel would help develop the characters and establish the possibility of time travel for readers who found that idea challenging.

Readers like me. Whenever I was actually talking to Rebecca, it all made beautiful sense. I felt so smart! A few hours later, I'd call her and say, "Wait! Wait a minute. *Why* did . . . ?" and I'd type madly as she explained, so I could hang onto it. Rebecca was endlessly patient. Though I was slow, I knew that young readers would understand. Children are open to big questions about the universe and can grasp all sorts of ideas that many adults cannot.

Rebecca was very careful about giving the reader enough clues to believe in the time travel and the logic, but not to get bogged down. We shared drafts with new readers, adults and children, to make sure that revisions hadn't created any holes or contradictions in the plot. All along, the goal was to be certain that the logic would stand up to the merciless scrutiny of a smart kid. Someone who would finish the book and then go right back and start again, reading so closely that she or he would spot any inconsistency. We didn't want to let that reader down.

Sometimes in the subway I see a sign:

Take a class! Improve yourself! Meet new people! Change your life!

That was some workshop at the Y in 1997. Who knew? Who knows? It's New York City. Anything is possible. But first, you have to lift the veil.

Rebecca Stead is a rare storyteller. In only two books, she has shown us a new way to look at the natural world, and to see it as more flexible, more responsive to human perseverance, faith, and genius, than we ever knew.

When You Reach Me begins with a quote from Einstein: "The most beautiful experience we can have is the mysterious."

There is still mystery at the heart of Rebecca's novel. There's plenty to wonder about after you finish the book. Just as we wonder why our feelings can change so suddenly, or why someone like the laughing man appears on the corner one day. Or whether something astonishing could ever happen one block from home.

When I walk by the corner Rebecca wrote about, I think of Miranda, and Sal, and Marcus, and Julia, and Annemarie. I think of twelve-year-old Rebecca, who inspired this story. I think of the children who now claim the book for themselves.

Such smart kids.

The Lion and the Mouse

illustrated by
Jerry Pinkney

published by
Little, Brown, 2009

HORN BOOK REVIEW

By retelling Aesop's fable entirely in his signature pencil and watercolor art, Pinkney encourages closer exploration of the pleasing detail with which he amplifies it. The mouse has just escaped an owl when she makes the mistake of running up the lion's back; his decision to let her go, over three full spreads, is all the more eloquent for being wordless. Her dauntless attack on the white hunters' densely knotted rope trap, in which the lion is caught, is related via numerous smaller frames; successful, the mouse takes one tough knot home to her young (as a toy? Or to tell them her story?). On every page, this beautiful book suggests even more than it tells about its real setting, and about that fabulous world where such bargains are made and such rescues may happen. It's a generous rendition: there are character-revealing portraits of the protagonists, unencumbered by text, on the jacket (a regal lion, sumptuous with golden mane, glances anxiously from the front; the doughty mouse, wide-eyed with intelligence, is on the back). On the front of the book itself is a second pair of telling portraits in lieu of a title; there's an African Peaceable Kingdom on the back. One endpaper celebrates the animal-crowded Serengeti setting; the second rounds out the story with the lion and mouse families on a shared outing. It will be a challenge for libraries to make every gorgeous surface available, but it's a challenge worth taking on. Artist's note appended.—*Joanna Rudge Long*

2010 CALDECOTT ACCEPTANCE SPEECH

Jerry Pinkney

In the weeks leading up to the ALA midwinter conference in Boston, there was little I could do to sidestep the active buzz surrounding *The Lion and the Mouse*. It bounced around in my head like a child on a brand-new trampoline. I understood that everyone meant well with their good wishes. However, as a five-time Caldecott Honor recipient, I couldn't entertain the popular talk of another ALA award. I tried to trick myself by not paying attention to the convention date or to the fact that my publishers would be in Boston.

On the Sunday morning before the press conference that would announce the Newbery and Caldecott awards, my wife, Gloria, and I were attending church services when I felt a gentle tap on my shoulder. A fellow member told me that she had given *The Lion and the Mouse* to her nephew and described with great excitement how he had read it by creating his own narrative. Then, when he read it a second time, he had a completely different interpretation of what he saw in the pictures. This is exactly what I had hoped for: a child claiming ownership of this much-beloved fable.

After the service, I was approached by another church member. With much warmth, she expressed how my depiction of the plains of the African Serengeti brought vividly back to mind her visit to that majestic slice of earth. It seemed remarkable to me that Sunday morning that even though *The Lion and the Mouse* had been published several months earlier, I now felt as if I were watching it embark on an entirely new voyage. I returned home with a deep feeling of satisfaction. I felt content that, even if my phone did *not* ring at all the next morning, *The Lion and the Mouse* was still a winner, to my mind, because of how it was inspiring the imaginations of children and adults.

Nevertheless, when Gloria and I turned in that evening, I brought a cordless phone up from my studio—just in case someone needed to reach me early in the morning. And, indeed, at 6:20 a.m. the phone rang. Both Gloria and I had been sound asleep, so neither of us was certain where the phone was. Gloria exclaimed, "My phone is ringing!"

"I think it's *mine!*" I responded, bouncing out of bed. The voice on the other end of the line was Rita Auerbach, chair of the 2010 Caldecott committee, informing me that I'd just received "the Caldecott . . ."

Time seemed to stand still as I waited for the word *honor*. And even after I heard her say *medal*, I was *still* somehow waiting for the word *honor* to sandwich itself between those two words. After the call ended, I kept wondering what the cheering librarians in the background must have thought when I took so long to respond. Gloria, who was standing close by, knew something special had occurred. "*The Lion and the Mouse* has just received the Caldecott Medal," I announced. Then, with much excitement, we held each other.

I am honored and humbled by this prestigious recognition. Many warm, heartfelt thanks to the Randolph Caldecott Award committee for your dedication and efforts. And congratulations to Rebecca Stead for her Newbery Medal.

Looking back over the years, at the age of seventy, I've found it interesting to trace how the early chapters of my life have knitted themselves into my art. As a young boy, my buddies and I were fascinated by all kinds of creatures and insects we found in our urban backyards and vacant lots in Philadelphia. On family trips to visit relatives in the country—back in the day, when New Jersey was "the country"—there were woods and streams filled with wildlife. Those were my first real experiences with nature. Even then I sensed that I was more centered, more balanced, when I was in touch with the natural world.

My first job after art school was delivering bouquets for a flower shop, where, later, I was promoted to floral designer. If you look at the body of my work, you'll find flowers embellishing many of my images. Sometimes they're used as a decorative device. Often they also lend a sense of harmony between humanity and nature. This interest in living, growing things, planted more than fifty years ago, blossomed in the illustrations for this adaptation of "The Lion and the Mouse."

Could my fascination for this tale have been fueled by field trips to the zoo when I was a child? In the late 1940s, zoos were not like the zoos of today. The animals were housed in dark, musty structures with just a little light trying to make its way through thick, humid air. The large cats were in rectangular cages, several feet off the ground, with guardrails in front. The animals paced back and forth with blank eyes staring into space, and I recall feeling that something was not right. I knew little of the big cats' natural habitats, but I still felt that animals should not be confined in such a way. I didn't want to be there and didn't want to return.

Many years later, I immersed myself in the natural habitat of animals, frequently enjoying walks in the woods surrounding our home in Croton-on-Hudson, New York, which is situated between a nature preserve and land governed by the Audubon Society. One day, I decided to break from the main path and hike up a hill to a favorite tree, when a plump, speckled grouse limped out of the tall grass in front of me. The grouse dragged its wing with great effort, as if it were broken. I veered out of its way, but slowly it worked its way in front of me again. This awkward dance went on for a minute or two.

Then I remembered I had learned that a mother bird, in order to protect her young from potential harm, might fake an injury. So I allowed her to guide me with her antics, and with deliberate calm, I looked back over my shoulder and saw movement in the grass. It was the grouse's little chicks. When the distance was great enough between her and her brood, the grouse's wing miraculously corrected itself. Then she lifted herself off the ground and flew back to her family.

I've remembered that experience so clearly because it was one of many moments when it seemed as if nature were speaking to me. And, from the very beginning, much of my art for children, at its core, was about nature speaking. *The Adventures of Spider* by Joyce Cooper Arkhurst, published by Little, Brown in 1964, was my first illustrated book, and I'm really pleased to say it's still in print.

But it wasn't until after illustrating over a hundred books for children that I decided to create my first nearly wordless picture book with *The Lion and the Mouse.* I'm not sure when I first heard this fable, but it's been coursing through my mind for years. I even gave its central characters a cameo appearance in an illustrated collection of Aesop's fables published in the year 2000. It seems fitting, somehow, that the book's only words are the sounds of animals, such as the owl's screech, the lion's roar, and the mouse's squeak. And so nature *still* has a voice in this book.

When beginning the thumbnail sketches for the fable, my intent was to add text after I had a clearer idea of the visual rhythm and pacing. But once I saw those sketches on paper, I wondered, Did this compact narrative really need words? The answer came back to me a tentative "no," which motivated me to think about expanding the tale in other ways. I knew of the fascination young children have with animal sounds and how captivated I am by the nature sounds that find their way to my ears when I'm at work in my studio. So I decided to experiment with incorporating sounds into *The Lion and the Mouse.*

I prepared a dummy purely as a visual exercise, and added sounds to the thumbnail sketches as well as animal action words, such as *scurry, flee,* and *scamper.* Another set of thumbnails was completely wordless. The two versions were sent to my editor, Andrea Spooner. She had been my editor on five previous books, and so I had great trust in her gifts and ability to listen and, most important, the clear space in her own head to see my vision. Andrea's skill in this collaboration of artist and editor is to sometimes push and sometimes pull in her own gentle manner, always bringing me closer to the fullest potential for each project. Her insightful response to the materials I sent was to keep the sounds, but drop the action words. She was right. Sometimes there can be too much of a good thing.

The next question to be answered was the story's setting. I chose the African Serengeti of Tanzania and Kenya in part because the lion was a central character in the story, and in part because of my fascination with Africa. The Serengeti provided me with an expansive backdrop that opened a host of visual possibilities. I began adding other creatures and vegetation of the Serengeti plains to provide a strong sense of place.

The lion and the mouse are two engaging characters, both heroes in this enthralling drama. I've always found it interesting that while the lion may be the majestic king of the jungle, if a gray or brown rodent were to scurry across a library floor, some of us would go running. The drawings of these two players were developed by sketching first in order to determine what I needed their body language to express, then research of the animals' anatomy using pictorial publications. Some days I would stand in front of a mirror and go through a series of expressions and body movements in order to incorporate what I'd learned into my drawings, and have them mimic the expressions of humans.

In my art you can find the influences of Beatrix Potter, Arthur Rackham, and A. B. Frost, all masters of personification. And if you remove the book jacket, you will find on its back case cover my homage to the artist Edward Hicks's painting *The Peaceable Kingdom*. While in my illustration I substituted the animals of the African Serengeti for Hicks's biblical animals, I believe ultimately the enduring strength of this tale is in its moral: no act of kindness goes unrewarded. Even the strongest can sometimes use the help of the smallest. To me the story represents a world of neighbors helping neighbors, unity and harmony, interdependence.

In fact, I learned from a librarian who had introduced the book to her students that the zebra, with its keen sense of smell, and the ostrich, with its sharp vision, sometimes warn other creatures of impending danger. The librarian pointed out to me that my art for the endpapers had both of these species depicted in the same scene with other animals who might depend on them for help. "Did you do that on purpose?" she asked me.

Here is the heart and soul of this book: it's about what *you* discover in the images, what someone other than the artist can bring to them. In many ways the journey each reader traverses parallels my creative process, that of discovery.

The journey of my own career has been deeply enriched by you, the librarians. With much gratitude, I thank all of you, for your continued friendship and support throughout my career.

The design, shape, paper, and printing of a good book all lend themselves to a quality reading experience. My thanks to Patti Ann Harris and Saho Fujii for their attention to every detail in the production of this book. Can you believe the jacket spine was scored from the inside?

Thanks also to Victoria Stapleton, Ames O'Neill, Megan Tingley, and all of my friends at Little, Brown and Company and Hachette Book Group for their support of this book, which is so important to me.

Thank you, Shelly Fogelman, my friend and agent of many years, for such strong support and wise guidance. I can still remember one of our early meetings when you said, "Be patient and wait for that right project that will be something that you're passionate about, but that also has the potential of reaching a large audience."

I can't help but also remember my mother's support when I, as a young boy, dreamed of becoming an artist. Her warm hand was always on my shoulder, encouraging me in her quiet way, saying, "You can do it, Jerry." That continuity of someone always being there for me was kept in place by my wife, Gloria Jean. By the way, in March we celebrated our fiftieth wedding anniversary. Gloria, this award is as much yours as it is mine. To our children, their spouses, our grandchildren, and our great-grandchild, thank you for your love, and for keeping me grounded.

At the end of my school presentations there is always a question-and-answer period where I get to ask the last question. The one I most often ask is, "Do you think I am just as excited today as I was some forty-six years ago when I illustrated my first book?" Tonight I am asking you. Do you think I am just as excited today as I was some forty-six years ago when illustrating my first book?

ILLUSTRATOR PROFILE BY ANDREA SPOONER

Jerry Pinkney

I'LL START BY stating this random fact: Jerry Pinkney gets stuck in a lot of airports.

Why would anyone begin a profile of arguably the most acclaimed children's book artist of our time with such a mundane observation?

Patience, dear reader . . . It's all about patience.

There are a few things everyone seems to know about Jerry Pinkney. First, of course, that his illustrated adaptation of the Aesop fable "The Lion and the Mouse" won the 2010 Caldecott Medal. Second, that he was awarded five Caldecott Honors prior to that landmark. And, last but not least, that he's the patriarch of a beloved family of talented children's book creators, including wife

Gloria Jean, son Brian, daughter-in-law Andrea, son Myles, and daughter-in-law Sandra. But many people don't know about the long, steady, determined journey he took to where he is today.

Jerry Pinkney was born in Philadelphia on December 22, 1939, a middle child in a family of six children. He shared a crowded bedroom with two brothers, and with no physical space to call his own, he created his own personal space with his drawing pad. His favorite refuge was hiding under the piano with paper and pencil. His work always had promise—at least from the point of view of his proud mother. When people asked why he was the only one of her children who didn't have a middle name, she would say, "'Jerry' is enough. He'll make something of that name, I just know it."

As a boy, Jerry sold newspapers at a stand across the street from a department store. Never missing an opportunity to draw, he frequently sketched the mannequins in the windows. A patron of the stand, John Liney, was a well-known cartoonist, and he noticed Jerry's talent and encouraged him. He opened Jerry's eyes to the fact that one could actually make a living as an artist. That's when the dream began.

But Jerry wasn't about to let it be just a dream.

Even though dyslexia caused him to struggle academically, his art skills gave him confidence, and he became a student of commercial art at Dobbins Vocational High School. His future wife, Gloria Jean, also a student there, remembers the first time she saw Jerry. "His sleeves were rolled up and he had a pencil behind his ear," she recalled. "He looked very busy!" And indeed he was. When he was a senior, one of his teachers told the art students about a scholarship—and then discouraged the African American students from applying since their chances of becoming professional artists were slim. Undeterred, Jerry marched down to the counselor's office and picked up applications not just for himself but for the other two black students in his class. Both Jerry and his best friend, also an African American, won a scholarship.

Not long after studying at the Philadelphia College of Art, he applied for an illustration job at the Rustcraft Greeting Card Company. He didn't have an illustration portfolio, so he set about creating one. In his and Gloria's cramped studio apartment, which they shared with their new baby, sometimes the only space to draw was in the bathroom. Jerry placed a drawing board on the tub, sat on the closed lid of the toilet, and made the drawings that won him this life-changing job.

Thus began Jerry's thriving career as a commercial artist. He produced work for advertising agencies, corporate annual reports, and even fashion and retail, including six-foot-tall paintings for Thom McAn shoe stores. Half a dozen years after starting his first job, he was already a founding member of an independent art studio, Kaleidoscope.

From the beginning, Jerry's singular work ethic was apparent: once, when he seriously injured his thumb and a doctor told him he might not be able to draw again, Jerry taught himself to draw with his left hand. His right hand healed eventually, but in the interim he was able to make a living. He didn't see it as a particularly remarkable act. "What else was I going to do? I had to work!"

Jerry's first children's book project was illustrating *The Adventures of Spider* (1964) by Joyce Cooper Arkhurst. His style then was so different that fans today would not recognize *Spider* as a Jerry Pinkney book. Angular, strong black lines, deceptively improvisational, created playful characters. Flat color washes characteristic of the pre-separated art of the day added punch, but it was Jerry's distinctive line work that brought these traditional tales to life.

Illustrating *The Patchwork Quilt* (1985) by Valerie Flournoy was a turning point. By that time, Jerry knew that creating art for young people was what he wanted to focus on. As years passed, he was frequently called upon to illustrate stories that demanded very specific characters, setting, costuming, or historical accuracy: *The Talking Eggs* (1989) by Robert D. San Souci or *Minty: A Story of a Young Harriet Tubman* (1996) by Alan Schroeder. But his collection of *Aesop's Fables* (2000) was a particularly eye-opening experience for him creatively: the animal tales allowed him to bring his own sense of humor and imagination to the table. It was a necessary prequel to *The Lion and the Mouse*.

Great artists make a name by finding a style they can truly call their own, and Jerry Pinkney is no exception. His intricate yet organic line work is deftly meshed with layers and layers of transparent color—some of which build to swaths of lush vibrancy—in a manner that is distinctly Jerry's. Some areas of each painting leave the under-drawing to shine through, so the piece never loses connection with that initial flow of pencil to paper. "I always considered myself a draftsman first, then a painter," he said to me once. While this seems startling, given his rich and intensive watercolor technique, it makes sense. His sketches are full of energy, and creating his final drawings is typically the most time-consuming stage of a project.

Every stage of a Pinkney book reveals much about how Jerry's philosophies and professionalism set him apart. First, he takes research very seriously: he's amassed an immense library of books and photo references in his own studio as a starting point. He insists that corrections be done by his hand on the actual painting rather than having a designer make changes in Photoshop; no short-cuts for Jerry. And then there is, of course, the delivery of the always-dazzling final art, with careful packaging and matting fit for museum pieces.

Even after illustrating more than one hundred children's books, Jerry still continually raises his own bar. Projects that don't present some sort of problem-solving challenge for him seem to attract him less. He once turned down a project because he felt he would deliver something too predictable: "It's a great story, but we'd all know exactly what we were going to get."

According to Jerry, "Almost every book project seems to present one spread in particular that is a tremendous challenge." Jerry never panics during that struggle, because he knows "it forces me to think differently, and as a result it often ends up being the best spread in the book." A true artist is never afraid to work outside his comfort zone.

That, I believe, was the reason he relished the challenge of creating a (nearly) wordless book with *The Lion and the Mouse*. The absence of a text forced him to grapple with questions like *What should the lion's expression be when he is debating whether or not to spare the mouse's life?* or *Is there enough indication of how much work it takes for the mouse to gnaw through that rope?* Jerry genuinely enjoyed engaging in the conversation—even when it required creating entirely new pieces of art.

There were many moments during the creation of this book when I got that shiver of excitement that comes when you're watching something magical bloom, including my first glimpse of Jerry's jacket sketch, which eventually became the art for the case cover. The cover's striking pictographic conceit, as well as the paneled art pages in his thumbnail sketches, sent a strong signal that Jerry was breaking away from his norm.

And, of course, there was the day Jerry delivered the art. I was overwhelmed, seeing those majestic, tender images for the first time. The relevance and timeliness of the book suddenly struck me. I was particularly moved by the depictions of animals living together in peace on the endpapers, the tragic expression on the lion's face in his netted prison, and the mouse's carrying of the rope fragment back to her family. "Oh!" I exclaimed, choking up. "It's as if the knot represents a lesson she's learned from this experience, which she's passing on to her children!" Perhaps that was the first of many instances to come of one reader creating his or her own narrative for the book.

I'll venture to say that the book is profoundly resonant to so many because the compassion brilliantly embodied in the pictures reflects Jerry's own compassionate nature. Their warmth is his warmth. Their wisdom and sensitivity are his own, enhanced by a rich life experience. And that work ethic, so beautifully represented by the mouse gnawing through that rope to free the lion, is Jerry's, too.

It would be remiss not to mention how many others outside the children's book arena have recognized Jerry's exceptional talents. He is frequently commissioned for nationally significant works and has created art for the NASA Art Collection, the White House, and the U.S. National Park Service, as well as extraordinary life-size figure paintings for the African Burial Ground

Interpretive Center in Manhattan. He designed stamps for the U.S. Postal Service's Black Heritage series in addition to serving on the Postal Service's Citizens' Stamp Advisory Committee for nine years. From 2003 to 2009 he sat on the NEA's National Council of the Arts, for a grand total of sixteen years of public service—so far. "I wanted to show that an African American artist could make it on a national level in the graphic arts," he says. "I wanted to be a strong role model for my family and other African Americans."

A stronger role model would be difficult to find. Illustrator James Ransome is one of many artists who have been inspired by Jerry. Beyond the mentoring and many generous critiques Jerry has offered to James, he also has taught him "how to be a true professional. How to strike a balance between being completely committed to your art and to your family." James also notes that "there's a steadiness to Jerry's work that has transcended time. Everyone in this business admires the longevity of his career and his art."

Jerry's art has been displayed in dozens of one-man exhibits in museums across the nation, and a major exhibition at the Norman Rockwell Museum is in the works. In 1997, Jerry was a United States nominee for the Hans Christian Andersen Illustrator Award. He has been the recipient of the Coretta Scott King Illustrator Award five times and of the Coretta Scott King Illustrator Honor five times. Then, of course, there are his five Caldecott Honor Books, and now his Caldecott Medal.

At long last, that gold medal. At age seventy. Which brings me back to the theme of patience. And the airports.

Jerry would be the first to say that he's been blessed in many ways, but luck is not always in his favor when it comes to traveling. Every time I speak to him after a trip, there is a story of wretched flight delays or other mishaps. And yet he always relays these tales with a bemused chuckle, in the spirit of "Such is life! Why complain?" Jerry's even keel is one of many admirable qualities his colleagues cherish. For it's not just the art that is a national treasure; it's the artist himself.

Even after all his success, Jerry remains a humble and passionate artist. "It still amazes me how much the projects have given back to me in terms of personal and artistic satisfaction. They have given me the opportunity to use my imagination, to draw, to paint, to travel through the voices of the characters, and, above all else, to connect with children."

CREDITS

TEXT CREDIT

ALSC and *The Horn Book* sincerely thank the Newberry- and Caldecott-winning authors and illustrators herein for permission to print their speeches.

Good Masters! Sweet Ladies!	Text © 2007 by Laura Amy Schlitz. Illustrations © 2007 by Robert Byrd
The Graveyard Book	Used with permission of HarperCollins. Text copyright © Neil Gaiman. Illustration copyright © 2008 Dave McKean
The Hello, Goodbye Window	Disney Publishing Worldwide
The Higher Power of Lucky	*The Higher Power of Lucky* by Susan Patron. Illustrated by Matt Phelan © 2006. Used with permission of Atheneum Books for Young Readers, an imprint of Simon and Schuster Children's Publishing.
The House in the Night	Houghton Mifflin Harcourt
The Invention of Hugo Cabret	From *The Invention of Hugo Cabret* by Brian Selznick. Scholastic, Inc. / Scholastic Press. Copyright © 2007 by Scholastic, Inc. Used by permission.
Kira-Kira	*Kira-Kira* by Cynthia Kadohata. © copyright 2004. Used with permission of Atheneum Books for Young Readers, an imprint of Simon and Schuster Children's Publishing.
Kitten's First Full Moon	Jacket illustration © 2004 by Kevin Henkes. Reprinted by permission of Greenwillow Books, an imprint of HarperCollins Publishers.
The Lion and the Mouse	Art © Jerry Pinkney
The Man Who Walked between the Towers	Permission granted by Mordicai Gerstein and his agents Raines & Raines
My Friend Rabbit	Eric Rohmann
A Single Shard	Jacket and case cover illustration © 2001 by Jean and Mou-sien Tseng
So You Want to Be President?	David Small
The Tale of Despereaux	Text © 2003 Kate DiCamillo. Illustrations © 2003 Timothy Basil Ering
The Three Pigs	Jacket cover illustration © 2001 by David Wiesner
When You Reach Me	*When You Reach Me* by Rebecca Stead, published by Wendy Lamb Books, an imprint of Random House Children's Books
A Year Down Yonder	Dial Books for Young Readers/Penguin

INDEX

You may also be interested in

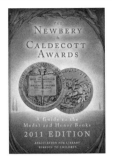

THE NEWBERY AND CALDECOTT AWARDS: A GUIDE TO THE MEDAL AND HONOR BOOKS
Association for Library Service to Children

This annual guide covers awards for the most distinguished American children's literature and illustration. Librarians and teachers everywhere rely on this up-to-date resource for quick reference, collection and curriculum development, and readers' advisory.

ISBN: 978-0-8389-8569-4 / 184 PGS / 6" × 9"

NEWBERY MEDAL SEALS (GOLD):
Association for Library Service to Children

The Newbery Medal recognizes the most distinguished contribution to American literature for children. Use these gold seals highlight the medal books in your collection. Newbery Honor Seals (Silver), Caldecott Medal Seals (Gold), and Caldecott Honor Seals (Silver) are also available. 24 per pack.

ITEM #: 5301-0101 / 24 PACK

THE CORETTA SCOTT KING AWARDS, 1970–2009, FOURTH EDITION
Edited by Henrietta M. Smith

Coinciding with the fortieth anniversary of the Coretta Scott King Award, this one-of-a-kind volume gathers together the best of the best in African American children's literature with comprehensive coverage of the award winning books, biographical profiles that introduce the creative artists and illustrators, color plates that give a vital sense of the story and art, and a new subject index ideal for curriculum planning.

ISBN: 978-0-8389-3584-2 / 152 PGS / 8.5" × 11"

EL DÍA DE LOS NIÑOS/EL DÍA DE LOS LIBROS: BUILDING A CULTURE OF LITERACY IN YOUR COMMUNITY THROUGH DÍA
Association for Library Service to Children

A celebration of children, families, and reading held annually since 1996, Children's Day/Book Day, known as Día, emphasizes the importance of literacy for children of all linguistic and cultural backgrounds. In anticipation of Día's fifteenth anniversary, the Association for Library Service to Children (ALSC) presents a collection of the best of its Día programming ideas.

ISBN: 978-0-8389-3599-6 / 120 PGS / 8.5" × 11"

Order today at www.alastore.ala.org or 866-746-7252!
ALA Store purchases fund advocacy, awareness, and accreditation programs for library professionals worldwide.